CW01249345

MULTICULTURAL EDUCATION SERIES
James A. Banks, Series Editor

Speculative Pedagogies:
Designing Equitable Educational Futures
Antero Garcia & Nicole Mirra, Eds.

Seeing Whiteness:
The Essential Essays of Robin DiAngelo
Robin DiAngelo

Educating for Equity and Excellence:
Enacting Culturally Responsive Teaching
Geneva Gay

Becoming an Antiracist School Leader:
Dare to Be Real
Patrick A. Duffy

The Hip-Hop Mindset: Success Strategies for
Educators and Other Professionals
Toby S. Jenkins

Education for Liberal Democracy: Using Classroom
Discussion to Build Knowledge and Voice
Walter C. Parker

Critical Race Theory and Its Critics:
Implications for Research and Teaching
Francesca López & Christine E. Sleeter

Anti-Blackness at School: Creating Affirming
Educational Spaces for African American Students
Joi A. Spencer & Kerri Ullucci

Sustaining Disabled Youth:
Centering Disability in Asset Pedagogies
Federico R. Waitoller &
Kathleen A. King Thorius, Eds.

The Civil Rights Road to Deeper Learning:
Five Essentials for Equity
Kia Darling-Hammond &
Linda Darling-Hammond

Reckoning With Racism in Family–School
Partnerships: Centering Black Parents' School
Engagement
Jennifer L. McCarthy Foubert

Teaching Anti-Fascism: A Critical Multicultural
Pedagogy for Civic Engagement
Michael Vavrus

Unsettling Settler-Colonial Education: The
Transformational Indigenous Praxis Model
Cornel Pewewardy, Anna Lees, &
Robin Zape-tah-hol-ah Minthorn, Eds.

Culturally and Socially Responsible Assessment:
Theory, Research, and Practice
Catherine S. Taylor, with Susan B. Nolen

LGBTQ Youth and Education:
Policies and Practices, 2nd Ed.
Cris Mayo

Transforming Multicultural Education Policy and
Practice: Expanding Educational Opportunity
James A. Banks, Ed.

Critical Race Theory in Education: A Scholar's Journey
Gloria Ladson-Billings

Civic Education in the Age of Mass Migration:
Implications for Theory and Practice
Angela M. Banks

Creating a Home in Schools: Sustaining Identities for
Black, Indigenous, and Teachers of Color
Francisco Rios & A Longoria

Generation Mixed Goes to School:
Radically Listening to Multiracial Kids
Ralina L. Joseph & Allison Briscoe-Smith

Race, Culture, and Politics in Education:
A Global Journey from South Africa
Kogila Moodley

Indian Education for All:
Decolonizing Indigenous Education in Public Schools
John P. Hopkins

Racial Microaggressions: Using Critical Race Theory
to Respond to Everyday Racism
Daniel G. Solórzano & Lindsay Pérez Huber

City Schools and the American Dream 2:
The Enduring Promise of Public Education
Pedro A. Noguera & Esa Syeed

Measuring Race: Why Disaggregating Data Matters
for Addressing Educational Inequality
Robert T. Teranishi, Bach Mai Dolly Nguyen,
Cynthia Maribel Alcantar,
& Edward R. Curammeng

Campus Uprisings: How Student Activists and
Collegiate Leaders Resist Racism and Create Hope
Ty-Ron M.O. Douglas, Kmt G. Shockley,
& Ivory Toldson

Transformative Ethnic Studies in Schools:
Curriculum, Pedagogy, and Research
Christine E. Sleeter & Miguel Zavala

Why Race and Culture Matter in Schools: Closing the
Achievement Gap in America's Classrooms, 2nd Ed.
Tyrone C. Howard

Just Schools: Building Equitable Collaborations
with Families and Communities
Ann M. Ishimaru

Immigrant-Origin Students in Community College:
Navigating Risk and Reward in Higher Education
Carola Suárez-Orozco & Olivia Osei-Twumasi,
Eds.

For a complete list of series titles, please visit www.tcpress.com/MCE   *(continued)*

MULTICULTURAL EDUCATION SERIES, *continued*

"We Dare Say Love"
NA'ILAH SUAD NASIR ET AL., EDS.

Teaching What *Really* Happened, 2nd Ed.
JAMES W. LOEWEN

Culturally Responsive Teaching, 3rd Ed.
GENEVA GAY

Music, Education, and Diversity
PATRICIA SHEHAN CAMPBELL

Reaching and Teaching Students in Poverty, 2nd Ed.
PAUL C. GORSKI

Deconstructing Race
JABARI MAHIRI

Is Everyone Really Equal? 2nd Ed.
ÖZLEM SENSOY & ROBIN DIANGELO

Transforming Educational Pathways for Chicana/o Students
DOLORES DELGADO BERNAL & ENRIQUE ALEMÁN JR.

Un-Standardizing Curriculum, 2nd Ed.
CHRISTINE E. SLEETER & JUDITH FLORES CARMONA

Global Migration, Diversity, and Civic Education
JAMES A. BANKS ET AL., EDS.

Reclaiming the Multicultural Roots of U.S. Curriculum
WAYNE AU ET AL.

Human Rights and Schooling
AUDREY OSLER

We Can't Teach What We Don't Know, 3rd Ed.
GARY R. HOWARD

Diversity and Education
MICHAEL VAVRUS

Mathematics for Equity
NA'ILAH SUAD NASIR ET AL., EDS.

Race, Empire, and English Language Teaching
SUHANTHIE MOTHA

Black Male(d)
TYRONE C. HOWARD

Race Frameworks
ZEUS LEONARDO

Class Rules
PETER W. COOKSON JR.

Streetsmart Schoolsmart
GILBERTO Q. CONCHAS & JAMES DIEGO VIGIL

Achieving Equity for Latino Students
FRANCES CONTRERAS

Literacy Achievement and Diversity
KATHRYN H. AU

Understanding English Language Variation in U.S. Schools
ANNE H. CHARITY HUDLEY & CHRISTINE MALLINSON

Latino Children Learning English
GUADALUPE VALDÉS ET AL.

Asians in the Ivory Tower
ROBERT T. TERANISHI

Diversity and Equity in Science Education
OKHEE LEE & CORY A. BUXTON

Forbidden Language
PATRICIA GÁNDARA & MEGAN HOPKINS, EDS.

The Light in Their Eyes, 10th Anniversary Ed.
SONIA NIETO

The Flat World and Education
LINDA DARLING-HAMMOND

Educating Citizens in a Multicultural Society, 2nd Ed.
JAMES A. BANKS

Culture, Literacy, and Learning
CAROL D. LEE

Facing Accountability in Education
CHRISTINE E. SLEETER, ED.

Talkin Black Talk
H. SAMY ALIM & JOHN BAUGH, EDS.

Improving Access to Mathematics
NA'ILAH SUAD NASIR & PAUL COBB, EDS.

"To Remain an Indian"
K. TSIANINA LOMAWAIMA & TERESA L. MCCARTY

Beyond the Big House
GLORIA LADSON-BILLINGS

Teaching and Learning in Two Languages
EUGENE E. GARCÍA

Improving Multicultural Education
CHERRY A. MCGEE BANKS

Transforming the Multicultural Education of Teachers
MICHAEL VAVRUS

Learning to Teach for Social Justice
LINDA DARLING-HAMMOND ET AL., EDS.

Learning and Not Learning English
GUADALUPE VALDÉS

The Children Are Watching
CARLOS E. CORTÉS

Multicultural Education, Transformative Knowledge, and Action
JAMES A. BANKS, ED.

Speculative Pedagogies

Designing Equitable Educational Futures

Edited by Antero Garcia
and Nicole Mirra

TEACHERS COLLEGE PRESS
TEACHERS COLLEGE | COLUMBIA UNIVERSITY
NEW YORK AND LONDON

Published by Teachers College Press,® 1234 Amsterdam Avenue, New York, NY 10027

Copyright © 2023 by Teachers College, Columbia University

Front cover photo by Jongsun Lee via Unsplash.

All rights reserved. No part of this publication may be reproduced or transmitted in any form or by any means, electronic or mechanical, including photocopy, or any information storage and retrieval system, without permission from the publisher. For reprint permission and other subsidiary rights requests, please contact Teachers College Press, Rights Dept.: tcpressrights@tc.columbia.edu

Library of Congress Cataloging-in-Publication Data is available at loc.gov

ISBN 978-0-8077-6886-0 (paper)
ISBN 978-0-8077-6887-7 (hardcover)
ISBN 978-0-8077-8198-2 (ebook)

Printed on acid-free paper
Manufactured in the United States of America

Contents

Series Foreword   *James A. Banks*   vii

Introduction: "Always a War Story": Speculative Pedagogies and Breaking the Narrative of Multicultural Education Possibilities   *Antero Garcia and Nicole Mirra*   1

PART I: DESIGNING LEARNING FUTURES

1. Critical Constructionist Design: A Design Framework and Analytic Tool for Developing and Documenting Speculative Learning Experiences   11
   Nathan Holbert, Michael B. Dando, and Isabel Correa

2. "A Deep Reckoning": Re/Mixing Literacies and Imaginative Rupture in "Let's Talk About Election 2020"   35
   Emma P. Bene, Emma C. Gargroetzi, Lynne M. Zummo, and Alexandra R. Aguilar

3. Speculative Pedagogies in Video Gameplay: Designing for New Social Futures in Collaborative Worldmaking   51
   Arturo Cortez and José Ramón Lizárraga

4. Abolitionist and Afrofuturist Game Design Pedagogies   67
   Matthew W. Coopilton, Brendesha M. Tynes, Olivia Peace, and De'Andra Johnson

PART II: KINDLING COMMUNITY

5. Dreaming Together: Exploring Youth–Adult Partnerships in Speculative Educational Design   87
   Lauren Leigh Kelly

6. Community-Engaged Culturally Sustaining Social and Emotional Learning as an Approach to Speculative Education — 105
Jingjing Sun, Ronda Howlett, Debbie Hogenson, Lindsey M. Nichols, Anisa N. Goforth, Sisilia Kusumaningsih, Niki Graham, and Emily Brooke

7. "I Think a Song Would Be Good": Grounding Youth Speculative Practices in Theories of Relationality and Desire — 121
Lee Melvin M. Peralta and Joanne E. Marciano

8. Participatory Methodologies to Transform the Project of Schooling: Student Voices Leading — 139
Leyda W. Garcia, Edwin Cruz, Jaune Reyez, Aliza Manalo, Eduardo Galindo, Adriana Rios-Cruz, Alex Alejo, Nareli J. Lopez, Le'kie Hatfield-Whitlock, Claire Matias, and Walter Hernandez Mejia

9. "Is This How It's Always Going to Be?": Speculative Teacher Education With(in) Community Toward Liberatory Praxis — 155
Kristen Jackson and Rubén A. González

10. Education as a Fundamental Right: A Speculative Narrative About Educational Dignity — 169
Raquel Isaac, Maria Karina Sanchez, Duy Tran, Tania Soto Valenzuela, and mandy wong, with Remi Kalir, on behalf of the Right2Learn Dignity Lab

About the Editors and Contributors — 183

Index — 190

Series Foreword

This visionary, timely, and informative book describes innovative and creative pedagogical strategies that can be used to engage students from diverse racial, ethnic, identity, and cultural groups in robust and absorbing teaching and learning. "Speculative pedagogies," which imagine potential futures for teaching and learning, is the conceptual framework for this book. Speculative pedagogies require transforming educational systems rather than fixing or mending those that are institutionalized. The 10 chapters in this book describe vivid and ingenious examples of speculative pedagogy in formal and informal learning environments. The digitally mediated and video-game lessons depicted in this book are practical and highly motivating. They will inspire readers to create speculative pedagogies for their own students and classrooms. This edited volume builds from "traditions of speculative theory that have shaped popular imagination through an increased engagement with Afrofuturism and Latinx-futurism . . . and takes seriously the act of imagining new forms of engagement for multicultural learners and classrooms" (p. 1, this volume).

Garcia and Mirra and the other contributors to this volume argue compellingly that speculative visions of pedagogy, which incorporate the past, present, and future experiences of diverse groups, can guide radical school reform. Speculative notions of instruction can also help teachers implement emancipatory pedagogy, as envisioned by Paulo Freire (2000), that affirms student identities as human, helping them regain their lost humanity, a result of inequality and marginalization, and attain full humanization. According to the volume editors, speculative pedagogies "(1) decenter the state as the primary locus of education in favor of informal, local affiliative relationships; (2) take an iterative, practice-based approach to learning; and (3) engage in joyful social dreaming to confront injustice" (p. 5). Powerful teaching strategies that exemplify speculative pedagogies that are joyful and deeply engaging are woven throughout this volume.

This book includes the insights and perspectives of a new generation of scholars working in diversity and education, making an original and significant contribution to the Multicultural Education Series. The major purpose of the Multicultural Education Series is to provide preservice educators, practicing educators, graduate students, scholars, and policymakers with an interrelated and comprehensive set of books that summarizes and analyzes important research, theory, and practice related to the education of ethnic, racial, cultural, and linguistic groups in the United States and the education of mainstream students about diversity. The dimensions of multicultural education, developed by Banks and described in the *Handbook of Research on Multicultural Education* (J. A. Banks, 2004), *The Routledge International Companion to Multicultural Education* (J. A. Banks, 2009), and in the *Encyclopedia of Diversity in Education* (J. A. Banks, 2012), provide the conceptual framework for the development of the publications in the series. The dimensions are content integration, the knowledge construction process, prejudice reduction, equity pedagogy, and an empowering institutional culture and social structure. The books in the Multicultural Education Series provide research, theoretical, and practical knowledge about the behaviors and learning characteristics of students of color (Conchas & Vigil, 2012; Lee, 2007), language minority students (Gándara & Hopkins, 2010; Valdés, 2001; Valdés et al., 2011), low-income students (Cookson, 2013; Gorski, 2018), multiracial youth (Joseph & Briscoe-Smith, 2021; Mahiri, 2017); and other minoritized population groups, such as students who speak different varieties of English (Charity Hudley & Mallinson, 2011) and LGBTQ youth (Mayo, 2022).

The speculative pedagogies described in this book illustrate how students who have been marginalized by structural and institutional racism can construct possible futures in which they attain equity, social justice, and agency. Other books in the Multicultural Education Series that focus on *institutional and structural racism* and ways in which students can be empowered to take action to reduce it are Özlem Sensoy and Robin DiAngelo (2017), *Is Everyone Really Equal? An Introduction to Key Concepts in Social Justice Education* (Second Edition); Gary Howard (2016), *We Can't Teach What We Don't Know: White Teachers, Multiracial Schools* (Third Edition); Zeus Leonardo (2013), *Race Frameworks: A Multidimensional Theory of Racism and Education*; Daniel Solórzano and Lindsay Pérez Huber (2020), *Racial Microaggressions: Using Critical Race Theory to Respond to Everyday Racism*; and Gloria Ladson-Billings (2021), *Critical Race Theory in Education: A Scholar's Journey*.

Speculative pedagogies enable students from diverse racial, ethnic, and cultural groups to attain self-acceptance and identity affirmation. Self-acceptance and identify affirmation are prerequisites to valuing outside racial, ethnic, and linguistic groups and for developing cosmopolitan attitudes and values. Students from marginalized groups who have historically experienced institutionalized discrimination, racism, or other forms of marginalization—such as being refugees (Dryden-Peterson, 2020) or undocumented (A. M. Banks, 2021)—often have a difficult time accepting and valuing their own cultures, languages, and experiences because of the ways in which their languages and cultures are marginalized within the schools and the larger society. The chapters in this helpful book describe how the culture of schools can be re-envisioned and transformed in ways that will enable students from diverse groups to attain reflective understandings and acceptance of their families and communities, affirmation of their community and family cultures and identities, and comprehension of the institutionalized structures that have victimized and dehumanized them (Baldwin, 1985; Freire, 2000).

I am especially pleased to welcome this volume by Professors Garcia and Mirra and their colleagues to the Multicultural Education Series. As multicultural education and equity scholars of the next generation, they bring to this book and their other publications unique insights, perspectives, theories, and concepts that enrich and deepen the work that has been done in the field during the last 6 decades (Banks, 2004; 2009; Ladson-Billings, 2014). I hope this enlightening and edifying book will attain the wide influence it deserves.

—James A. Banks

REFERENCES

Baldwin, J. (1985). A talk to teachers. In *The price of the ticket: Collected nonfiction 1948–1985* (pp. 330–337). Beacon Press.

Banks, A. M. (2021). *Civic education in the age of mass migration: Theory and practice.* Teachers College Press.

Banks, J. A. (2004). Multicultural education: Historical development, dimensions, and practice. In J. A. Banks & C. A. McGee Banks (Eds.), *Handbook of research on multicultural education* (pp. 3–29). Jossey-Bass.

Banks, J. A. (Ed.). (2009). *The Routledge international companion to multicultural education.* Routledge.

Banks, J. A. (2012). Multicultural education: Dimensions of. In J. A. Banks (Ed.), *Encyclopedia of diversity in education* (vol. 3, pp. 1538–1547). Sage Publications.

Charity Hudley, A. H., & Mallinson, C. (2011). *Understanding language variation in U.S. schools.* Teachers College Press.

Conchas, G. Q., & Vigil, J. D. (2012). *Streetsmart schoolsmart: Urban poverty and the education of adolescent boys.* Teachers College Press.

Cookson, P. W., Jr. (2013). *Class rules: Exposing inequality in American high schools.* Teachers College Press.

Dryden-Peterson, S. (2020). Civic education and the education of refugees. *Intercultural Education, 31*(5), 592–606. https://doi.org/10.1080/14675986.2020.1794203

Freire, P. (2000). *Pedagogy of the oppressed* (30th anniversary ed., M. B. Ramos, Trans.). Continuum.

Gándara, P., & Hopkins, M. (Eds.). (2010). *Forbidden language: English language learners and restrictive language policies.* Teachers College Press.

Gorski, P. C. (2018). *Reaching and teaching students in poverty: Strategies for erasing the opportunity gap* (2nd ed.). Teachers College Press.

Howard, G. (2016). *We can't teach what we don't know: White teachers, multiracial schools* (3rd ed.). Teachers College Press.

Joseph, R. L., & Briscoe-Smith, A. (2021). *Generation mixed goes to school: Radically listening to multiracial kids.* Teachers College Press.

Ladson-Billings, G. (2014). Culturally relevant pedagogy 2.0. a.k.a. the remix. *Harvard Educational Review, 84*(1), 74–84. https://www.hepg.org/her-home/issues/harvard-educational-review-volume-84-number-1/herarticle/culturally-relevant-pedagogy-2-0

Ladson-Billings, G. (2021). *Critical race theory in education: A Scholar's journey.* Teachers College Press.

Lee, C. D. (2007). *Culture, literacy, and learning: Taking bloom in the midst of the whirlwind.* Teachers College Press.

Leonardo, Z. (2013). *Race frameworks: A multicultural theory of racism and education.* Teachers College Press.

Mahiri, J. (2017). *Deconstructing race: Multicultural education beyond the color-bind.* Teachers College Press.

Mayo, C. (2022). *LGBTQ youth and education: Policies and practices* (2nd ed.). Teachers College Press.

Sensoy, Ö., & DiAngelo, R. (2017). *Is everyone really equal? An introduction to key concepts in social justice education* (2nd ed.). Teachers College Press.

Solórzano, D. G., & Pérez Huber, L. (2020). *Racial microaggressions: Using critical race theory to respond to everyday racism.* Teachers College Press.

Valdés, G. (2001). *Learning and not learning English: Latino students in American schools.* Teachers College Press.

Valdés, G., Capitelli, S., & Alvarez, L. (2011). *Latino children learning English: Steps in the journey.* Teachers College Press.

INTRODUCTION

"Always a War Story"
Speculative Pedagogies and Breaking the Narrative of Multicultural Education Possibilities

Antero Garcia and Nicole Mirra

A PRELUDE

This edited volume imagines. It imagines future learning environments devoid of the systemic inequities that mire student learning opportunities and teacher decision-making in most U.S. classrooms today. It imagines the necessary steps—playful, participatory, historically informed—that will be required to broker the pathway from the present U.S. educational landscape to an unpromised yet freer tomorrow. Building from traditions of speculative theory that have shaped popular imagination through an increased engagement with Afrofuturism and Latinx-futurism, this edited volume takes seriously the act of imagining new forms of engagement for multicultural learners and classrooms. It works pragmatically and snips into the seams of what is taken for granted and offers contemporary exemplars of how new social fabrics can be sewn from the scraps of today's schools.

In keeping with this ethos of imagination, we begin with a story. Well, we actually begin with the *ending* of a story. The history of this present moment hangs in the balance of what we—you, us, our kin—decide to do *now*. Each moment is a cliffhanger, followed by another cliffhanger. We are not seeking a preordained resolution. We are seeking to persist and quell the harm of normative, standardized living.

So let's talk about Animorphs.

CLIFFHANGER ENDINGS

The *Animorphs* series by K. A. Applegate was a speculative fiction publishing behemoth that was ubiquitous in classrooms, libraries, and major bookstores across the globe. During its 5-year publishing run and in the 2 decades since, millions of readers encountered the strange stories of adventure and human-to-animal (and back again) transformation. The books pre-dated the Hollywood rush for adapting dystopian children's literature into films in the mid-2000s, but they have continued to make a lasting impression on how and what kinds of stories are marketed to and consumed by young people (e.g., Garcia, 2013). Spanning more than 50 novels and additional spin-off titles during the time it was published between 1996 and 2001, the series centers on several characters that can transform into animals and their attempts to protect the Earth from an alien invasion.

Even if you haven't read any of the *Animorphs* books, you are likely familiar with the iconic covers. Featuring rudimentary computer graphics, each book features a character transforming from a human to some other animal species. Cheetahs, birds, crocodiles, cats: If it is a nonhuman animal, it is likely something a character *morphed* into over the course of the series.

Like *Harry Potter*, *Goosebumps*, and *A Series of Unfortunate Events*, the *Animorphs* series was a collection of engaging books about kids leading in difficult circumstances. These were fun books and—in our own classrooms—they helped students build their interests as readers. Which is why the conclusion of the *Animorphs* series is striking. Rather than a hopeful ending as the wrap-up to a series-long conflict, the books end on a bleak note of loss. Best captured in an open letter that Applegate wrote after a mixed response to her series' conclusion, the author does not mince words about the mixed feedback to the conclusion of *Animorphs*:

> Dear Animorphs Readers:
> Quite a number of people seem to be annoyed by the final chapter in the Animorphs story. There are a lot of complaints that I let Rachel die. That I let Visser Three/One live. That Cassie and Jake broke up. That Tobias seems to have been reduced to unexpressed grief. That there was no grand, final fight-to-end-all-fights. That there was no happy celebration. And everyone is mad about the cliffhanger ending.

Applegate's letter makes clear that she is not remorseful for the tone that readers took from the book. She states, later, that "Animorphs was always a war story. Wars don't end happily. Not ever." Emphasizing the events that "always" occur in wars, Applegate explains that death is a part of war and that "always people are left shattered by the loss of loved ones. That's what happens, so that's what I wrote." The middle of her letter, then, challenges the kind of Hollywood victory that readers expected from her books:

> Here's what doesn't happen in war: there are no wondrous, climactic battles that leave the good guys standing tall and the bad guys lying in

the dirt. Life isn't a World Wrestling Federation Smackdown. Even the people who win a war, who survive and come out the other side with the conviction that they have done something brave and necessary, don't do a lot of celebrating.

Received frustratingly by fans seeking closure, Applegate's letter reads, today, with a sense of clinical dismissal. This is the hard-earned lesson that young readers receive after toiling through dozens of novels and finding their progenitor lacking in a bedside manner. For fans of the series, the letter can be read as patronizing, bitter, and angry. It might be, perhaps, sober and pragmatic instead. What's most striking, as we reflect on this letter and the relationship between fans, authors, and the "real" world, is the two very different worldviews described in the tone between Applegate and her frustrated reading audience. While readers might have been hoping for resolution and hope—perhaps one optimistic purpose of speculative fiction—the author instead chose to offer a lesson of unresolved tension and loss. This is not simply a difference in opinions but a pedagogical moment spelled out in clarity. The lack of fulfillment that readers experienced *is* the aim of a series that otherwise appeared to adhere to traditional story tropes. That bitter emptiness that filled readers? That's the moral lesson Applegate's series deliberately worked toward.

MULTICULTURAL, MULTIVERSAL, AND PLURIVERSAL LEARNING OPPORTUNITIES

As we write this, our world, as Applegate described, is also "shattered by the loss of loved ones" from myriad forms of systemic harm. This is the cold reality of a world that is recovering from the COVID-19 pandemic, from state-sanctioned violence and mass shootings, and from climate devastation that will upend familiar forms of living within the next generation. And while we might learn from the more-than-human life around us, there are no metamorphosing creatures to save us from this future.

We note this pragmatically but also hopefully; while this may seem to be as bleak a world as the truths passed along by Applegate, we believe that a more hopeful speculative future—via scholarship grounded in seeking critical possibilities beyond the familiar horizons of the present moment (e.g., Garcia & Mirra, 2023)—is possible.

From the ideologies that shape our daily organization of school structures to the inhumane logics that construct literal and metaphorical borders on colonized land, ours is a world mediated by forms of speculative imagination. Just as Applegate might have offered one set of lessons about the inevitability of loss in times of war, we offer here the recognition that radical transformation can be seeded in speculative imaginaries.

We write this introduction with the conviction that stories can function as pedagogical stars for us to navigate this vessel of education. Throughout this volume, we offer a description of speculative education to differentiate it from education that is bound by the here and now. Building from our ongoing learning with other researchers, we define speculative pedagogies in this volume as intentionally building beyond existing inequalities. As we have written elsewhere, speculative pedagogies incorporate "an expansive set of ideas related to visionary and future-oriented approaches to teaching and learning that operate beyond the bounds of current social, economic, and cultural arrangements that perpetuate white supremacy, capitalism, patriarchy, heteronormativity, and related forms of oppression" (Garcia & Mirra, 2023, p. 4).

For generations, U.S. educational systems have served up interventions meant to fix or repair an educational ship that's been taking on water for too long. This vessel—for many of our historically marginalized students—has never been seaworthy. Pipelines tied to prison and to poverty-related servitude have maintained the kinds of academic disparities that Gloria Ladson-Billings describes as an "educational debt" (2006). Research methodologies for educational scholarship haven't fared much better in these seas. Our positivist traditions and ongoing search for a universal empiricism suggest that this present scientific paradigm (e.g., Kuhn, 1996) has plateaued.

As we've argued in preliminary, speculative scholarship, we are seeking work that emphasizes reconstituting educational systems entirely over trying to simply repair them (Mirra & Garcia, 2022). As proponents of a speculative approach to teaching, learning, and educational research, our work is heavily influenced by Afro-, Latinx-, and Indigenous-futurisms in literature and other multimedia. We have sought hope and possibility in the imaginations of authors and creators and have found solutions waiting for us in their works. This is not to say that the stalwart nature of Applegate's stance is a *wrong* one, per se. Rather, alongside texts that employ dystopian tropes to critique social ills such as war, we might also seek texts that do not have to center the conflict of alien colonial pillage or that must culminate in transglobal annihilation. Violence might be a selling point, but we might imagine new tropes in our work and our stories.

And stories abound. One narrative and one system of schooling cannot choke off the dreams and tales told in other minds. Building from Zapatista-driven theories, Arturo Escobar (2018) describes the pluriversal possibilities of a "a world where many worlds fit" (p. xvi). In this speculative dreaming of the infinite worldmaking possibilities in all of our classrooms, Escobar reminds us that an embrace of the "multi" in our multicultural teaching and research cannot be bound by singular practices or curriculums. Heartened by the abundance of multicultural approaches to education today (as represented by the longstanding series of books we are humbled to contribute to with this volume), we must demand that a "multi" can never be fully acknowledged in standardized and "universal" designs for education and learning.

CURATING ACCOUNTS OF THE SPECULATIVE IN EDUCATIONAL DREAMSPACES

The majority of research and practitioner-facing resources about equity in today's U.S. classrooms work to address the present conditions that might produce a fair learning opportunity for young people who have been historically disadvantaged. This is obviously necessary and important work and must persist. At the same time, the gradualistic inch-by-inch efforts of this research only yields small gains in the lives of learners in any given year. This volume takes a different approach. Recognizing the pragmatism of needing to work within present conditions, the contributors in this volume seek *speculative* approaches to teaching and learning that might disrupt and transcend the anxieties and tensions that bind up young people in classrooms today. Based on several years of ongoing research (Mirra & Garcia, 2020, 2022), in this volume we understand speculative approaches to education as practices that (1) decenter the state as the primary locus of education in favor of informal, local affiliative relationships; (2) take an iterative, practice-based approach to learning; and (3) engage in joyful social dreaming to confront injustice. Each chapter in this volume illuminates these principles of speculative education as enacted within current learning environments.

Over the past several years, our research on youth civic development, classroom learning, and digitally mediated teaching practices have focused on imagining *what if* we were working within radically new spaces of possible learning and teaching. How might classroom cultures and student learning opportunities shift if educators were able to set aside the taken-for-granteds of neoliberal educational settings and work toward more justice-driven ends. Though this speculative approach may seem like an unrealistic and lofty approach to schooling, what we have found is that simply in imagining new possibilities, the pragmatics of enacting them are often within reach. As a result, this volume offers nearly a dozen examples of speculative approaches to supporting multicultural education in K–12 classrooms today.

As editors, we have garnered enthusiasm and success in these efforts. Initially announced 3 weeks before and held during the days of the cancelled 2020 American Educational Research Association meeting, we convened annual online Speculative Education Colloquia to sustain our personal and collective interests in the topic at hand. Each of these convenings grows and have had hundreds of registrants. This work, too, has sparked journal issues, speculative scholarship, and practitioner designs that push beyond the boundaries of traditional schooling (as described in the chapters that follow). The desire for clearly voiced examples of what speculative education can look like in practice is being voiced loud and clear. We—Nicole, Antero, and our esteemed contributors—answer this request with this volume. We've curated 10 powerful examples of what speculative approaches to multicultural education *can* look like today. These are not prescriptive and, as you'll see, respond to the specific conditions and demands of the learning environments and communities in which they are situated. Instead of asking you to read this scholarship as a template for curricula, we hope you excavate inspiration and kindle your own imaginations with the sparks of insight in the chapters to come.

The polyphonic voices in this volume speak across content areas, grade levels, and ethnic, cultural, and socioeconomic backgrounds. Too, while the authors of these chapters include members of the professoriate, as expected, they are often coauthored by students, community members, and teachers; the speculative is a realm explored and enacted alongside a wide range of participants.

And while we recognize the diversity in voices in this volume, there are two themes within speculative education that are closely linked throughout this volume. First, much of the work we curate here extends where and how scholarship is taken up and used within K–12 contexts. Building off of more than a decade of work we have done as leading researchers in the areas of youth participatory action research (YPAR) and social design–based experiments (SDBE) (e.g., Mirra & Garcia, 2020; Mirra et al., 2015), this work expands on how scholarship is taken up in formal learning environments and who is at the table in this process. Second, as approaches that are built on imagination and design, an ethos of play imbues much of these chapters. This, too, informs our approach to speculative research as much of our research agenda has been built around utilizing existing classroom technologies to *play into new realities*.

STRUCTURE OF THE BOOK

Organized into two parts, this volume speaks to the theoretical foundations that expand our field's understanding of speculative education, offers critical current examples in classrooms, and pushes toward the boundaries of what can transpire today. The first part of this volume, Designing Learning Futures, offers lessons in design for speculative pedagogy. These chapters illuminate formal and informal contexts of engagement and settings that go from the seemingly traditionally academic to the digitally mediated worlds of videogame play. These chapters, in the words of Bene et al. (this volume), "rupture" the present moment and ask us to design beyond the assumed resolution of traditional schooling enclosure.

The second part of this book, Kindling Community, emphasizes the relationships that are sustained and brokered in speculative learning contexts.

Beyond merely developing trusting camaraderie, these chapters dare readers to consider where the locus of relationality shades unseen possibilities. These authors ask us to consider the historical contexts that have partitioned learning structures into hierarchies of power. The final chapter of this book, "Education as a Fundamental Right: A Speculative Narrative about Educational Dignity," is written by a large team of the Right2Learn Dignity Lab. As a speculative act that operates beyond traditional scales of schooling, this team edits the Colorado Constitution, imagining and changing the structures of power and knowledge. This work acts as a speculative testament to a world yet to come. Taken as a whole, this book imagines new worlds and, alongside our contributors and readers, seeks to step into these alternate futures in the name of educational equity.

A CODA

Not all lessons from the opening narrative about fan reception to the *Animorphs* series speak to a speculatively aligned world. Applegate's letter to disappointed *Animorphs* fans offered some useful and hard truths. However, as we seek to pave a new set of trails for where schooling might venture, we must recognize that Applegate concludes her letter with a sneering call to action:

> So, you don't like the way our little fictional war came out? You don't like Rachel dead and Tobias shattered and Jake guilt-ridden? You don't like that one war simply led to another? Fine. Pretty soon you'll all be of voting age, and of draft age. So when someone proposes a war, remember that even the most necessary wars, even the rare wars where the lines of good and evil are clear and clean, end with a lot of people dead, a lot of people crippled, and a lot of orphans, widows and grieving parents.

Applegate pairs her finger-wagging tirade with a normative reminder that young people will "be of voting age." Though the lessons of youth organizing can help mobilize social change one ballot at a time, we break with Applegate's admonition. Leigh Patel (2021) reminds us that alongside justice-driven struggle, deep forms of study and knowledge development are always present.

We do not endorse speculative pedagogies that remind young people to wait until they are old enough to participate in the tenuous systems of electoral democracy awaiting them. Rather, building on the designs in Part I of this volume and the communities kindled in Part II, young people are *already* of an age for transformation and multiversal world-building. Let us write, build, and traverse toward new worlds burgeoning with shared freedom.

REFERENCES

Escobar, A. (2018). *Designs for the pluriverse: Radical interdependence, autonomy, and the making of worlds*. Duke University Press.

Garcia, A. (2013). *Critical foundations in young adult literature: Challenging genres*. Sense.

Garcia, A., & Mirra, N. (2023). Other suns: Designing for racial equity through speculative education. *Journal of the Learning Sciences, 32*(1), 1–20. https://doi.org/10.1080/10508406.2023.2166764

Kuhn, T. S. (1996). *The structure of scientific revolutions* (3rd ed). University of Chicago Press.

Ladson-Billings, G. (2006). From the achievement gap to the education debt: Understanding achievement in U.S. schools. *Educational Researcher, 35*(7), 3–12. https://doi.org/10.3102/0013189X035007003

Mirra, N., & Garcia, A. (2020). "I hesitate but I do have hope": Youth speculative civic literacies for troubled times. *Harvard Educational Review, 9*(2), 295–321. https://www.hepg.org/her-home/issues/harvard-educational-review-volume-90,-issue-2/her-article/i-hesitate-but-i-do-have-hope%e2%80%9d

Mirra, N., & Garcia, A. (2022). Guns, schools, and democracy: Adolescents imagining social futures through speculative civic literacies. *American Educational Research Journal, 59*(2), 345–380. https://doi.org/10.3102/00028312221074400

Mirra, N., Garcia, A., & Morrell, E. (2015). *Doing youth participatory action research: Transforming inquiry with researchers, educators, and students*. Routledge.

Patel, L. (2021). *No study without struggle: Confronting settler colonialism in higher education*. Beacon Press.

Part I

DESIGNING LEARNING FUTURES

CHAPTER 1

Critical Constructionist Design
A Design Framework and Analytic Tool for Developing and Documenting Speculative Learning Experiences

Nathan Holbert, Michael B. Dando, and Isabel Correa

INTRODUCTION

The many challenges of the 21st century range from problems that seem particularly science-oriented, such as climate change, to systemic social issues such as white supremacy. Though scientific and technological innovations may be necessary to address each of these global challenges, the persistence and evolution of these problems over decades of growth in STEM fields (Science, Technology, Engineering, and Mathematics) suggest that simply doubling down on teaching "21st century skills" won't be enough.

In our work we have proposed that education should be about inviting learners to imagine possible or probable futures that might disrupt persistent systems of destruction and oppression. To engage young people in critiquing inequalities that pervade our current social and political systems we have proposed the Critical Constructionist Design framework (CCD). This framework invites learners to leverage speculative design to construct future-thinking counter-stories and critical artifacts that center their histories, perspectives, and values (Dando et al., 2019; Holbert, Dando, & Correa, 2020). CCD adds to a growing collection of educational frameworks for enacting speculative design with young learners. However, a challenge for the research community has been systematically documenting the relationship between the designed components of speculative educational experiences and learners' exploration of target topics with diverse media in complex and dynamic construction environments. Put another way, we need tools to assist us in both the creation of educational speculative design experiences, and in empirically validating the impact of these experiences on learners.

We believe the CCD framework can help address both needs. In prior writing we have shown that CCD offers a powerful structure for designing future-thinking yet critically reflective constructionist experiences (Holbert, Berland, & Kafai, 2020). In this chapter, we highlight the methodological contribution of the CCD framework and show how this tool can illuminate the thinking, learning, and storying (Thomas & Stornaiuolo, 2016) that happens when learners adapt, repurpose, and remix their personal and communal histories in the construction of speculative artifacts (Jennings, 2017). We illustrate the methodological affordances of the CCD framework by describing two different implementations of maker workshops aimed at engaging Black teens in speculative design.

The CCD framework supports the design of speculative pieces that bring together past, present, and future possibilities. In the first implementation, called Remixing Wakanda, Black teen girls in New York City worked in a university makerspace to brainstorm, design, and construct a speculative artifact that represented their vision of the future. In Lion Man, the second implementation, middle school art students in Minnesota explored iterative graphic narrative and comic book design processes as they constructed comics characters and stories. In both implementations, participants were invited to look back into family and cultural histories, connect those memories with present-day experiences, and then project forward to imagine possible future societies and technologies according to their personal and communal values, aesthetics, and passions. In describing each of these two implementations, we explicitly describe how the CCD framework guided the design of the physical learning environment; the selection of construction tools, technologies, and materials; and the experiences and activities that participants engaged in.

Turning to the data produced from these experiences (including in-process and complete physical and digital artifacts, participant interviews, design journals, field notes, video/audio of construction activities, etc.), we document how the CCD framework also can be used to empirically trace how participants' past history and present personal experiences are projected into speculative artifacts, and which key features of the experience—practices, materials, people, technologies—mediate participants' (re)construction of their social, cultural, and political identities. In illustrating how this framework can be used to highlight important moments of learning, and connecting these moments to educational design, we hope CCD will offer a valuable tool for educators to enact and chronicle speculative and critically oriented design that will disrupt dominant ideologies of race, gender, and class.

THE THEORETICAL FOUNDATIONS OF CRITICAL CONSTRUCTIONIST DESIGN

We see speculative and critical design practices as key to educating a population that will be prepared to take on and solve the world's most pressing challenges. Speculative, for our purposes, entails the imagining of science, technologies, cultural practices, and societies that do not yet exist in the present universe. The speculative is intentionally provocative in that by drawing our attention to what might come to pass, we are better positioned to critically reflect on our present condition and to consider ways we might change our present to create new futures.

Of particular significance to the way in which we conceptualize speculative design in this study is the notion of critical pedagogy and forms of re-storying and counternarrative. Critical pedagogy is an approach to instruction that invites participants to critique power structures and oppressive systems thoroughly and vigorously (Kincheloe, 2008, p. 59). This framework is vital here because of the sometimes tacit and often explicit social narratives of dominance in STEM, making, and other educational spaces. In many of these spaces there is an underlying, sociopolitical understanding—a hidden curriculum (Apple, 1971; Giroux & Penna, 1979)—of who should or should not exist in a particular space, such as a science lab or classroom space, and whose knowledge and lifeways are valorized as legitimate forms of knowledge. Critical pedagogy takes seriously the deliberately constructed social and political realities of the personal, communal, and (inter)national positions of both educators and learners.

Speculative practices also enable us to engage in what Mentor and Sealey-Ruiz (2021) call "self excavation" (p. 19); that is, the ways that understandings of race, gender, class, ability, and other subjectivities live within us as educators and learners and impacts how we navigate learning opportunities and possibilities. This process of articulating a critical sense of self requires the tools and capacity to engage in *counter-storying*, a central tenet of Critical Race Theory that emphasizes centering and highlighting often erased or othered perspectives in order to interrupt or disrupt racist, hegemonic systems and structures reinscribed through dominant discourses (Giroux & Simon, 1989; Mirra & Garcia, 2020; Solórzano & Yosso, 2002). Popular culture is a powerful avenue through which this might be achieved. As Giroux and Simon (1988) remind us, popular culture is a contested social and political terrain and site of struggle, tension, and contradiction whose function is "not an insignificant force in shaping how students view themselves and their relations to various forms of pedagogy" (p. 11).

The formulation of the CCD framework came about from collaborations with professional comic book artists and work with Black teens from neighborhoods and communities deeply connected to the broader African diaspora. These relationships led us to the speculative subgenre of Afrofuturism (Dery, 1994). Afrofuturism addresses various sociopolitical and cultural themes and concerns of Black communities in America through technoculture and speculative fiction that envisions Black futures stemming from Afro-diasporic experiences, cultures, and backgrounds. The intersectional subject positions of the Black community in America broaden and enrich our collective imagination of social utopias and reveal "how the past and present shape what we imagine as a positive future" (Nelson, 2002, p. 11). The Afrofuturistic perspective takes up the speculative, as Nelson notes, because it imagines "backward and forward in seeking to provide insights about identity, one that asks what was and what if" (Nelson, 2002, p. 19).

Afrofuturism's longstanding ideological and philosophical perspectives have been central to our development of the CCD framework in our work with Black youth. For example, the Ghanaian concept of *Sankofa*, roughly meaning "it is not wrong to go back for that which you have forgotten," lies at the heart of the practice of reflecting on history, communal lifeways, family resources, and creative practices in order to reckon with present challenges and design speculative futures that CCD offers. However, we note here that other speculative genres or aesthetic movements may be more appropriate for learners from different backgrounds, histories, and communities. Science fiction through its capacity for no-holds-barred creative generativity invites participants to create and make well beyond the restrictive notions offered up by the status quo. Story creation can be an act of resistance during sociopolitical periods actively set against those from nondominant communities. Similarly, "restorying" (Thomas & Stornaiuolo, 2016) invites us to reshape existing and create new narratives that better reflect past and present experiences. For young people excluded from popular discourses, this speculative narrative acts as a kind of "testimony" (Toliver, 2020, p. 509) and serves as a way for students to declare or reaffirm their humanity under sociocultural conditions of erasure and epistemic violence. Speculative storying invites students to critically take up and construct intersectional understandings of issues of race, gender, class, and a host of others (Low, 2017).

The CCD framework builds upon these concepts to illuminate the critical and constructionist design elements at work as students create new visions of self and future.

CRITICAL CONSTRUCTIONIST DESIGN AS A FRAMEWORK FOR IMPLEMENTATION

The CCD framework invites learners to design and construct speculative technologies, artifacts, and stories that critique the current state of our society. Synthesizing critical and speculative design practices (Dunne & Raby, 2013, 2014) with the constructionist design paradigm (Holbert, Berland, & Kafai, 2020; Papert, 1980), this student-centered framework includes three core practices: Learners connect to their past, reflect on the present, and project forward possible futures that might emerge from the current state of society, science, and technology (Figure 1.1). In connecting to the past, learners unearth their personal and family histories and consider how values,

Critical Constructionist Design

Figure 1.1. In the Critical Constructionist Design framework, learners engage in a cycle of connecting to their past and reflecting back on the present to imagine possible and probable future societies, science, and technology.

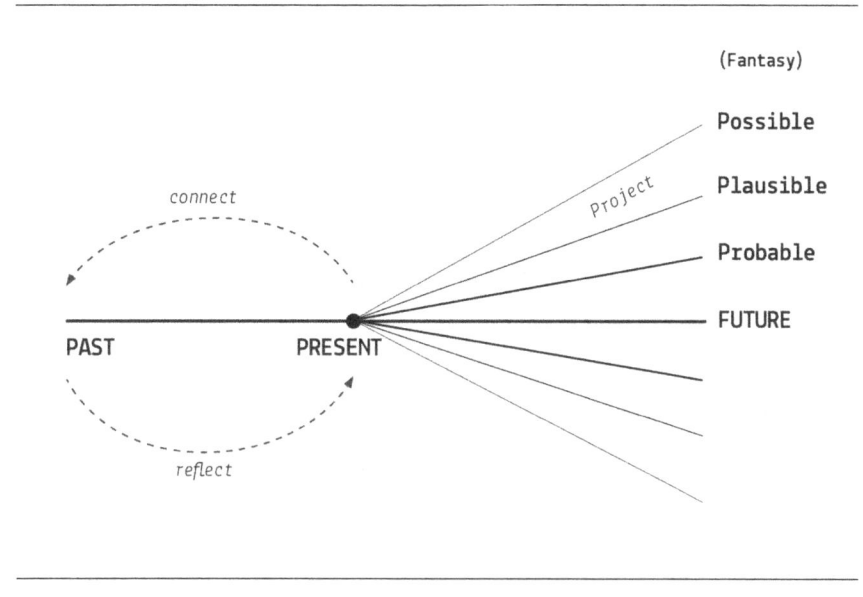

traditions, geography, and shared practices have shaped their physical and social environment. In reflecting on the present, CCD asks learners to notice and critique the current state of their society—to consider the strengths and victories of their community as well as structural injustices, challenges, and barriers. Finally, CCD asks learners to project forward and imagine possible and probable futures that might emerge from the current state of our society, science, and technology. To imagine technological innovations, political systems, or civic designs that might come about in a future that centers their values, aesthetics, and needs.

CCD takes a systems approach to the design of speculative learning environments. Thoughtful consideration of the technologies and materials made available to students during such an experience is vital. Furthermore, CCD also elevates the importance of the makeup of the physical and social environment, the design of the activities students encounter, the instructional support available, and the cultivated culture of the construction space. As a design framework, CCD is not meant to dictate every detail of all maker experiences, but rather to provide a theoretical stance for the design and implementation of learning-focused speculative design experiences.

Beyond serving as a design framework, in this chapter we show how CCD can support the documentation and analysis of explorations and activities that emerge in speculative design experiences. Through a series of tapestry representations, we leverage a weaving metaphor to examine the entangled relationship between design and learning. Weaving a tapestry consists of passing a thread under and over another set of threads that was previously placed. Likewise, the CCD analysis tapestry emerges from the threads representing the design choices we make when creating a speculative learning experience and the threads participants bring in when exploring personal concerns and goals.

At its heart, the CCD analysis tapestry involves three steps: (1) articulate design choices made in the formulation of the speculative design experience; (2) analytically code the topics and values represented in conversations and artifacts produced by learners; and (3) identify how our design choices and learner's experiences interact. The analysis tapestry in Figure 1.2 offers an example. The horizontal threads are the intentional design choices we made in the creation of our speculative design workshop. In the creation of the workshop, we intend for these "designed mediators," which include activities, tools and materials, and the physical space to connect learners with their past, present, and future. The vertical threads code the past, present, and future topics that students engaged with in response to encountered mediators. As a whole, the analysis tapestry reveals how designed mediators support the student in meaningful speculative constructions that leverage their experiences with the past and present. A webpage to view the CCD design and analysis tapestries described here and a tool to create your own tapestry can be found at https://www.snowdaylearninglab.org/ccd-tapestry.

In the remainder of this chapter, we illustrate the construction and use of this analysis tapestry by describing two educational maker experiences where

Figure 1.2. A small example of the CCD analysis tapestry. The horizontal threads are a list of the design choices meant to support speculative design practices ("design mediators") across past, present, and future considerations. We break up these design choices into activities, tools and materials, and physical space and culture. Vertical threads represent topics that students explore throughout the designed experience, and are organized by how these topics engage past, present, and future speculation.

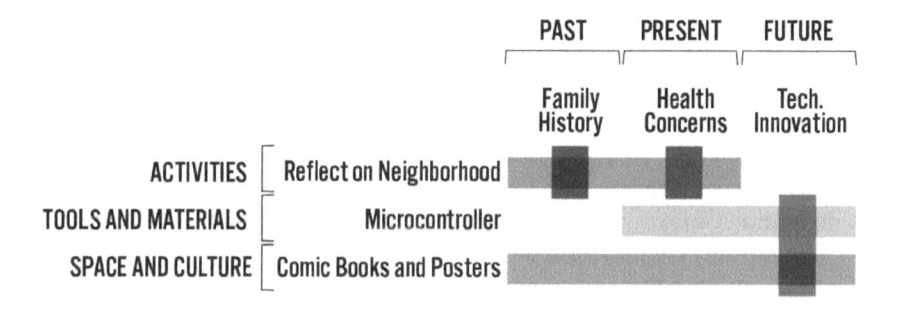

	PAST	PRESENT	FUTURE
	Family History	Health Concerns	Tech. Innovation
ACTIVITIES — Reflect on Neighborhood	■	■	
TOOLS AND MATERIALS — Microcontroller			■
SPACE AND CULTURE — Comic Books and Posters			■

Critical Constructionist Design 17

we have deployed the CCD framework. We first describe how the framework was instantiated in each setting, outlining how our design choices were both informed by the framework and modified to fit the unique needs of each context. For each, we also show how the CCD framework can be used to make sense of the diverse data collected in these complex and dynamic spaces and how the framework can assist the researcher as they look for connections between the design of the implementation and the goals and experiences of participants. In doing so, we hope these examples suggest ways to adapt critical constructionist design for a host of topics and activities as well as for a diverse range of communities, and point to CCD as an analytic tool for drawing empirical conclusions from speculative design work.

REMIXING WAKANDA: THE DEVELOPMENT AND IMPLEMENTATION OF CCD

The Remixing Wakanda workshop was a series of maker sessions taking place in 2018. "Making" here refers to educational design and construction activities that engage young people in using high-tech prototyping equipment such as laser cutters, 3D printers, programmable sewing machines, and microcontrollers to build working robots, wearable electronic fashion, interactive art, etc. (Halverson & Sheridan, 2014). In Remixing Wakanda, five Black teen girls, ages 14–16, from a public high school in Harlem, New York, were recruited by their art teacher to engage in speculative design practices to imagine and create Afrofuturist artifacts, technologies, and systems. These girls attended maker sessions at the Snow Day Learning Lab, a small makerspace located on the campus of Teachers College, Columbia University, not far from their school, for about 4 hours once a week for 8 weeks (for an extensive description of the implementation and each session of the workshop see Holbert, Dando, & Correa, 2020).

For the Remixing Wakanda implementation, participating girls were encouraged to create Afrofuturistic artifacts that addressed a personally meaningful local or global challenge. The CCD framework guided decisions about key designed mediators in terms of activities, tools and materials made available to participants, and the ways in which we organized the physical makerspace and encouraged a culture of critical design during the Remixing Wakanda experience.

To show how these designed mediators enact the CCD framework we developed a representation we call a *design tapestry* (Figure 1.3). The design tapestry displays in the form of horizontal threads how the designed mediators might support learners in connecting to the past, present, and future throughout the workshop. Others creating a speculative design experience using the CCD framework might create a similar design tapestry to plan for how the chosen activities, tools and materials, and physical space and culture will each invite learners to consider the past, present, and future in their design process.

The design tapestry for the Remixing Wakanda implementation can be seen in Figure 1.3. It is important to note that as a planning tool, this design tapestry does not represent the actual experience of the learners, but rather the intention and assumptions of the designers. For example, while all participants in our Remixing Wakanda implementation encountered the *activities* listed in Figure 1.3 (*activities* designate the top collection of rows or threads in the tapestry), we expect each individual may come away with a different experience. In this implementation, some participants engaged more deeply in reflections on their local neighborhood, while others thought more broadly about the needs of the African diaspora. Likewise, while the listed *tools and materials* (the middle collection of threads in the tapestry) were made available to all participants, most projects took advantage of just a few. Finally, the project team aimed to create an inviting and inspiring *physical space and culture* (the bottom collection of threads) for the

Figure 1.3. The CCD design tapestry is a representation created by the designer to articulate how each designed mediator (rows) of an implementation *might* invite learners to connect to their past, reflect on the present, and to project possible and probable futures (columns). This tapestry represents the design assumptions of the Remixing Wakanda implementation. The rows are grouped to designate the activities, tools and materials, and physical space and culture groups of designed mediators.

Afrofuturist work. In Remixing Wakanda, we filled the space with comics and example design projects, as well as books on Black artists, art from the *Black Panther* movie (an extremely popular example of Afrofuturism when the workshop was held in 2018), and posters of Adinkra symbols. Likewise, we also invited Black artists, scholars, and activists to join each session to share how they enact Afrofuturism in their own work.

Figure 1.3 highlights a core feature of the CCD framework, that the threads of the past, present, and future are pulled together by a wide range of designed mediators. In the Remixing Wakanda implementation it should be noted that all designed mediators involve participants reflecting on the present (middle column). Certainly, it is not uncommon for a maker workshop to involve learners in building futuristic technologies or examining historical materials and practices. But as a framework for critical design, CCD is primarily concerned with using the past and future to invite learners to consider and challenge the current state of our society, science, and technology (Darder et al., 2004). For example, posters of Adinkra symbols were added to the walls of the physical makerspace where the project took place. Though they have their origin in an African past, these symbols were mobilized in a passport activity to represent students' present-day identities, needs, and goals. This tying together of the past, present, and future is a key feature of CCD that is made evident through the design tapestry.

USING CCD TO ANALYZE JALISE'S FUTURISTIC CITY

CCD offers a framework for planning construction activities, choosing materials and tools, and configuring the context and culture of a space to invite learners to bring the past, present, and future into their speculative design work. We believe CCD is also a useful tool for empirically documenting the relationship between the design of a speculative educational experience and learner's actual experiences. In this section we connect the design tapestry—a planning document for creating a CCD implementation—with data generated from a particular participant's activities during a speculative design experience to create an *analysis tapestry*.

To illustrate this analytic utility of CCD, we turn to the work of Jalise, a participant in the Remixing Wakanda project. Jalise is a talented and motivated high school student with diverse interests in science, medicine, and art. She attended every meeting and she spent hours building a complex and detailed model of a fictional city for her final design (Figure 1.4).

During the 8-week implementation, we collected a diverse range of multimodal data of all participants that included pictures of in-process and complete artifacts, images of design journals, video recordings of the working makerspace, transcripts of interviews and focus groups, and field notes. For this analysis, we first gathered all data that involved Jalise directly (e.g.,

Figure 1.4. Jalise's futuristic city was made from found and craft materials, and represented a range of future scientific, technological, and social innovations.

a mid-implementation interview with her, pictures of her working, etc.) or indirectly (e.g., a video of the laser cutter engraving her design). Then, the first and third authors went through each piece of data attempting to code it along two dimensions. First, what topics or design goals explored by Jalise are represented by this piece of data, and second, what designed mediators are involved.

Because this process is specific to each learner, the codes we generated with Jalise's data will *not* represent the entire Remixing Wakanda dataset. Data from other participants of this same implementation might reveal additional topics and entirely different codes would emerge when analyzing data from a different CCD implementation (as we will show in the Lion Man sections later in this chapter). Furthermore, if a piece of data could not be coded for both a topic as well as a designed mediator, it was not included in this analysis. For example, a picture of Jalise talking with a guest speaker was not included in this analysis because while we could identify the relevant design mediators (*guest scholars*), we could not be certain what topics were being discussed. Finally, it's important to note that data collection was not necessarily uniform—some activities or moments may have been more documented than others. For example, more pictures were taken of Jalise's design notebook than of her sitting at the computer working with design software. Consequently, in the data presented below, the presence of any co-occurrences between topics and designed mediators is more relevant to this analysis than the frequency of these co-occurrences.

The ways in which a participant leveraged different designed mediators through the exploration of personally meaningful topics or goals is illustrated through an analysis tapestry (Figure 1.5). In the analysis tapestry, the original design tapestry is preserved as a base of horizontal threads that represent the

Critical Constructionist Design

Figure 1.5. The analysis tapestry of Jalise's experience in the Remixing Wakanda workshop. The horizontal threads are replicated from the design tapestry shown in Figure 1.3. The past, present, and future columns have been broken down to specific topics explored by Jalise. The vertical threads and cell counts indicate co-occurrences of topics explored by Jalise and the relevant designed mediator.

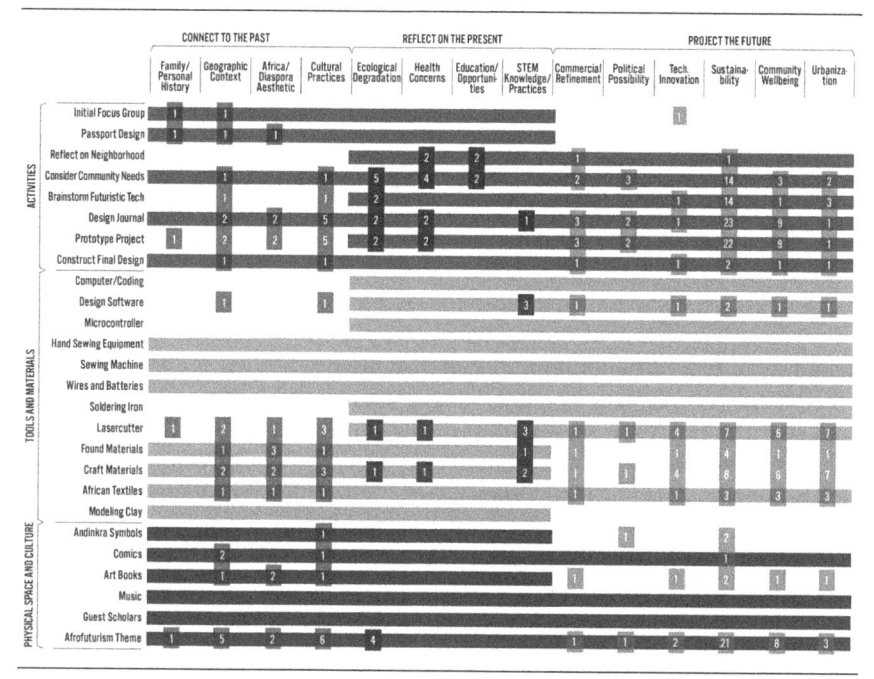

designed mediators we assumed would encourage participants to connect to the past, present, and future. The *actual* ways in which participants make those connections is now illustrated in vertical threads that weave through the horizontal threads to complete the tapestry.

To document the specific ways Jalise explored the past, present, and future, each vertical thread identifies the emergent topics she brought into her design experience. Yet, these vertical threads only occasionally intersect with horizontal threads. These intersections indicate a co-occurrence between a designed mediator and a particular topic explored by Jalise, with the numbers in each cell indicating the frequency of this co-occurrence. For example, nine pieces of data were coded as being related to Jalise's design journal, *and* her concern for the Community Well-being.

The analysis tapestry (Figure 1.5) makes visible the relationship between the designed mediators of the Remixing Wakanda workshop and Jalise's particular experience using speculative design to make connections to her past, present, and possible futures. In other words, this interlacing allows us to validate empirically the alignment between our design assumptions and one participant's' actual experience. In Figure 1.5 we can see designed mediators that primarily support Jalise's exploration across the full connect/reflect/project cycle were: *consider community needs, the design journal, prototyping,* the use of the *laser cutter* and *craft materials,* and the *Afrofuturist theme.*

The analysis tapestry also allows us to focus on the role particular designed mediators play in the CCD process. For example, when engaging in the prepared activity to *consider community needs* (a designed mediator), Jalise described the lack of available fresh foods in her neighborhood, saying, "If it is affordable, it is not healthy!" and suggests future cities and farms should be brought together. This piece of data was coded as corresponding to the topics (vertical threads) *Reflect on the Present: Health Concerns; Project the Future: Nature Conservation, Commercial Refinement* (Figure 1.6). Later, describing her *prototype,* Jalise again explained that her futuristic city would include a farm community but also acknowledged the need to "find a better way to farm without having problems with runoff or problems with like the pollution of water, and everything like that" (corresponding to the topics *Reflect on the Present: Ecological Degradation; Project the Future: Sustainability, Tech Innovation*). While describing her final project, Jalise reminds us that these farms are "including the African culture as well, because we are known for harvesting and agriculture" (*Connect to the Past: Cultural Practices*). She also references her Caribbean heritage, telling us the farm buildings would be constructed using Creole cloth to "bring some color to the farm community" (*Connect to the Past: African/Diaspora Aesthetics*). By looking at how designed mediator threads are brought together by the threads of topics and goals explored by Jalise, we can better document how the CCD framework supports Jalise's critical and speculative practice.

The CCD analysis tapestry also illuminates aspects of the Remixing Wakanda design assumptions that were relevant to Jalise's design work as well as those that weren't. Visually this can be seen in Figure 1.5 where vertical threads (Jalise's explored topics and design goals) do and do not align with the horizontal threads (the expected role played by the designed mediators).

Figure 1.6. A close-up look into Jalise's analysis tapestry focusing on one particular designed mediator thread as it relates to topics explored by Jalise across the past, present, and future.

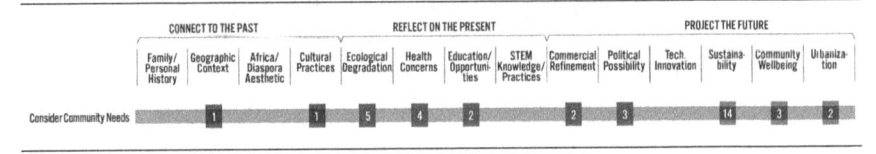

	CONNECT TO THE PAST			REFLECT ON THE PRESENT			PROJECT THE FUTURE					
	Family/ Personal History	Geographic Context	Africa/ Diaspora Aesthetic	Cultural Practices	Ecological Degradation	Health Concerns	Education/ Opportunities	STEM Knowledge/ Practices	Commercial Refinement	Political Possibility	Tech Innovation	Sustainability	Community Wellbeing	Urbanization
Consider Community Needs		1		1	5	4	2		2	3		14	3	2

For example, rather than occur across all aspects of the designed experience, Jalise's critical examination of the present state of society and technology (the middle collection of columns labeled *Reflect on the Present*) occurred primarily through her reflection on her *community's needs* and the *design journal*. However, as expected, the *Afrofuturism theme* was key in supporting Jalise in considering important project topics across time. Furthermore, the diverse range of materials, instructional support, and experience that were part of Jalise's process highlight the systemic nature of CCD.

Finally, Jalise's exploration of STEM ideas and practices primarily occurred in connection with the use of materials and tools. For example, to make the many different buildings of her fictional city, Jalise used a tablet, computer, and the Illustrator design software. She spent many hours considering how to make the complex 3D buildings out of 2D cardstock, working this out through sketches in her notebook, on the computer, and using sample cuts from the laser cutter. Though it is not surprising that the workshop's materials and tools were important in the exploration of STEM ideas and practices, seeing the absence of these explorations in other aspects of the Jalise's Remixing Wakanda experience suggests opportunities for future implementations.

LION MAN PROJECT: WAKANDA 2.0

A second iteration of this Critical Constructionist Design (CCD) project involved similar curricular and aesthetic moves, but implemented a more explicitly comics-centric approach. That is, rather than use computers, 3D printers, and laser cutters for design and fabrication, participants used professional-grade comics equipment, including paper called bristol board, copic markers, and inkpots to engage in critical speculative design. Connecting with Eisner-award–nominated comics creators John Jennings and David Brame, this iteration engaged a critical Afrofuturist anchor text as a foundation for inquiry.

Lion Man was created by Orrin C. Evans in 1947 and is considered to be the first Black Superhero character in U.S. comics, first appearing in *All Negro Comics #1*. Allegedly, when Evans attempted to publish a second issue, racist paper suppliers prevented him from securing the necessary newsprint, and the character went out of print and eventually passed into the public domain.

As a way to provide a common set of resources, vocabulary, and aesthetic principles for this project, Jennings, Brame, and Dando created a completely new Lion Man story (Figure 1.7) titled *Lion Man: The Tower*. This new comic intentionally drew from Afrofuturist aesthetics and speculative storytelling elements to invite students to think about the challenges their communities have encountered and consider ways they might be equipped to engage with change-making. They were also invited to think

Figure 1.7. Copies of the Lion Man comic book were distributed to each participant. This text modeled Afrofuturist aesthetics and storytelling and served as a creative jumping-off point for project participants.

about multimodal forms of storytelling that would support them in doing so. During our discussions of the *Lion Man* comics, the group took up similar design processes to the initial iteration, but this time also focused on how the medium of comics both told the story and how design played a particular role in the aesthetics and functionality of the comics page itself. The group also discussed narrative and critical literacy issues such as theme, character, Afrofuturist aesthetic, narrative choice, and color palette selection (Figure 1.8).

This implementation took place at a local public middle school in central Minnesota. Sixty 7th-grade art students participated in this design process over the course of 4 weeks, three times a week for 90 minutes each session. Students predominantly self-identified as female and as Black. During this iteration, we employed several of the same pedagogic and aesthetic moves used in Remixing Wakanda, such as the questions for critical inquiry including "What are your/communities' superpowers?" and envisioning the future in 25 years. However, while the initial brainstorming process was

Critical Constructionist Design   25

Figure 1.8. The CCD framework design tapestry applied to the Lion Man implementation. Of particular note are the different activities and tools and materials (horizontal threads) used in this implementation. Likewise, the assumptions about how these designed mediators will connect across the past, present, and future are different from those of Remixing Wakanda as seen in Figure 1.3.

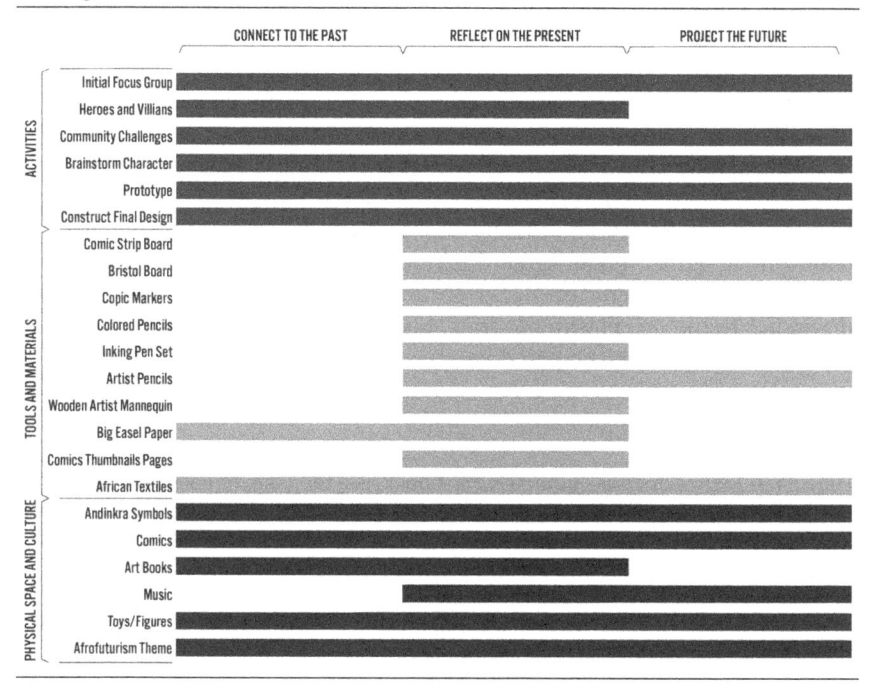

similar, the creative material engagement differed significantly, as did the final artifact prototypes. In Lion Man, the focus was on the design of a singular character, world/cityscape, or diegetic artifact that aided in telling a particular story. Participants were also encouraged to explore and experiment with analog materiality in particular ways, including differing graphite pencil types, brush tips and usage, and various marker tips. Additionally, students took up aesthetic principles of design such as shading technique, figure drawing, perspectives, and vanishing points, among others not explored in previous iterations.

There were several emergent themes and concerns students expressed throughout the process (some shared with the Remixing Wakanda implementation and some new), the most salient being "peace," issues of environment/climate/sustainability, and increased representation of marginalized communities in the public square.

USING CCD TO ANALYZE TASHI'S ORIGINAL COMIC CHARACTER *FLASHBACK*

Tashi created a character named Flashback (Figure 1.9), a teenage girl who could travel 5 seconds forward or backward through time drawing on the strength, knowledge, and stories of her ancestors. Flashback had an elaborate backstory that involved mythic quests, parental stressors, generational traumas, castles, and political intrigue. Tashi also intentionally added the *Adinkra* symbol for time, "Mary Dane," to her character's design, locating it on the right sleeve.

Through the construction of this character, Tashi engages in critical counternarrative construction. Tashi was a self-identifying female, Muslim, first-generation middle school student who was interested in pursuing a future career in design of some kind. Tashi wore a traditional Muslim Khimar and, because this iteration occurred during COVID, a KN-95 mask, not dissimilar to the one Flashback dons. Like Jalise, Tashi appeared highly motivated and eagerly participated in every class session.

Figure 1.9. Tashi's original character, Flashback, is a teenage, female, Muslim superhero. This final version was created with bristol artboards, copic markers, micron ink markers, and artist pencils.

Through the Lion Man workshop, Tashi designed a character whose very premise is reliant on the interconnection of past, present, and future and explicitly reflected her understanding of a needed subjectivity. In reflective writing, Tashi noted that she created a Muslim superhero because "there weren't that many and the world needs to see more." Tashi quite literally wrote a narrative she needed to see. Ultimately Tashi's character (Figure 1.9) embodies a synthesis of past, present, and future. Not only can Flashback travel to the future, but her present and her past are directly connected through the costume she wears and the powers she manifests. Tashi chose the name "Mary Dane" for her character as an explicit reference to *Sankofa* and its Adinkra symbol linking the past tradition with the contemporary character in a way, going back to bring the past into the present. Moreover, Flashback's costume design was intended to invoke the hourglass shape of the symbol as well.

We employed the same coding technique described earlier to illuminate similarities and differences across the implementations (Figure 1.10). Again, it is important to note that changes in outcomes, in this case, the creation of a character through sequential art, resulted in a focus on past and present as an engine for future thinking. Participants here were implementing different sets of materials (pens, papers, etc.) and outcomes (artistic renderings) rather than more technical fabrications, which provided different avenues for attention and focus. It is important to note that materiality matters, especially with regard to the speculative.

With Tashi, we can see that through the creation of this character, she engages connections across past, present, and future but intentionally situates her character firmly in the past through family, cultural practice, and tradition. To that end, significant designed mediators included the activities: *consider community needs* and *prototyping* and the tools and materials: *big easel papers, copic markers, art books*. While we expected the professional comic artist tools and materials would be central in participants' design work, Tashi's use of these tools to connect to the past was surprising. Though we may not have intended the markers and pencils to be used to link to the past (as can be seen by the absence of horizontal threads extending to the left-side of the tapestry), participants nonetheless engaged these materials for the purposes they needed—that is, these were emergent practices rather than intentionally designed ones.

When reflecting on how her character represented ways youth might engage the topic of *community well-being*, Tashi noted the significance of situating choices, decisions, and practices in the past while not being bound to or limited by them. Particularly she noted that it was important to "learn from our mistakes and make a powerful impact on learning" and that intentionality rather than reactivity was an important part of making decisions, remarking that "the process I went through was questioning, and I had to choose what I like and don't like." This decision-making process, especially

Figure 1.10. An analysis tapestry of Tashi's experience in the Lion Man project. Once again cells indicate co-occurrence counts of topics (vertical threads) explored in Tashi's work and the relevant designed mediators (horizontal threads).

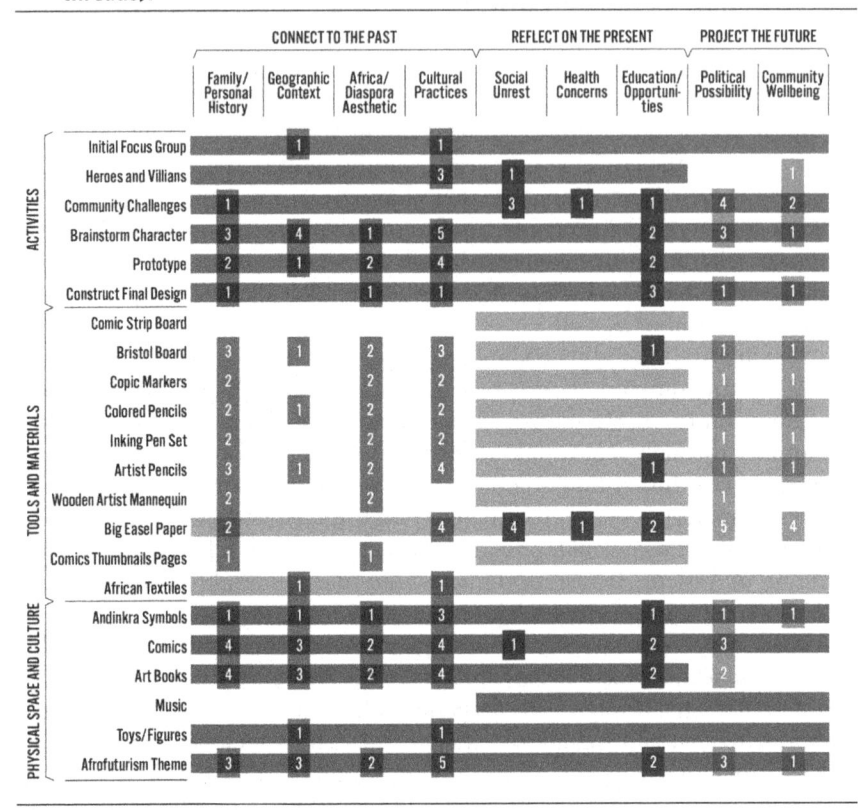

		CONNECT TO THE PAST				REFLECT ON THE PRESENT			PROJECT THE FUTURE	
		Family/ Personal History	Geographic Context	Africa/ Diaspora Aesthetic	Cultural Practices	Social Unrest	Health Concerns	Education/ Opportunities	Political Possibility	Community Wellbeing
ACTIVITIES	Initial Focus Group			1		1				
	Heroes and Villians				3	1				1
	Community Challenges	1				3	1	1	4	2
	Brainstorm Character	3	4	1	5			2	3	1
	Prototype	2	1	2	4			2		
	Construct Final Design	1		1	1			3	1	1
TOOLS AND MATERIALS	Comic Strip Board									
	Bristol Board	3	1	2	3			1	1	1
	Copic Markers	2		2	2				1	1
	Colored Pencils	2	1	2	2				1	1
	Inking Pen Set	2		2	2				1	1
	Artist Pencils	3	1	2	4			1	1	1
	Wooden Artist Mannequin	2		2				1		
	Big Easel Paper	2		4	4	4	1	2	5	4
	Comics Thumbnails Pages	1			1					
PHYSICAL SPACE AND CULTURE	African Textiles			1	1					
	Andinkra Symbols	1	1	1	3			1	1	1
	Comics	4	3	2	4	1		2	3	
	Art Books	4	3	2	4			2	2	
	Music									
	Toys/Figures		1		1					
	Afrofuturism Theme	3	3	2	5			2	3	1

with regard to community uplift, bears itself out in Flashback's set of powers, which allows her to literally commune with and draw upon the knowledge of her ancestors in order to make a decision or to chart a path forward, which was ultimately her responsibility—a none-too-subtle metaphor for caretaking of family and community. This was directly connected to the designed mediators encountered during the character creation process as Tashi utilized the *art books* and *comic books* in the initial design phase with particular attention paid to *The Art of Assassin's Creed*, *Black Comix Returns*, and *The Art of Into the Spider-Verse*. Tashi also experimented with various color palettes using a variety of *copic markers* and *ink pens*, and explored penciling techniques as she delved into *Afrofuturist themes* and *Adinkra symbols* using a wide array of graphites during prototyping.

Finally, *Afrofuturism* played a significant part in the speculative design of the character Flashback. As noted earlier, the entirety of Tashi's character draws from a non-Western conception of time. For many African cultures, such as the Yoruba, "time is a two-dimensional phenomenon, with a long past, a present and virtually no future" (Mbiti, 1976). This is contrary to the more linear conception of time present in Western thought that espouses an indefinite and more sequential past, present, and future. Further, in looking through *art books*, Tashi noted a character whose design incorporated the Somali flag and another whose aesthetic scheme and color palette was directly linked to the Puerto Rican flag. These aesthetic influences, while still solidly incorporating the visual rhetoric of superheroes—bright, often primary colors—were also chosen specifically to demonstrate and incorporate a particular sense of identity, culture, and belonging. Additionally, the character of Ms. Marvel (Kamala Khan), the first Muslim, female superhero, served as inspiration for Tashi to construct and situate her character intentionally, both ideologically (what motivates the character) and aesthetically (what the character looks like).

DISCUSSION

Looking across the data presented above for both the Remixing Wakanda and Lion Man implementation of the CCD framework highlights that effective speculative design experiences require a systems approach. Speculative design doesn't come for free with 3D printers or laser cutters. In fact, the Lion Man implementation makes it clear that sometimes well-crafted markers are more important than expensive design software or prototyping tools. More than that, the tools and technologies must be supplemented with carefully designed activities that put learners in contact with their personal and family histories, that challenge them to reflect on the needs of their community and neighborhood, and that invite them to imagine a world where these needs have been met.

For Jalise, in the Remixing Wakanda implementation, the design and analysis tapestry reveal that this bridge between the past, present, and future was mediated primarily through designed activities that asked her to consider the needs of her community and to brainstorm design solutions to those needs in her design journal. Jalise also found inspiration and concrete construction techniques that would be useful in her Afrofuturist artifact in the art books and comics available in the physical makerspace. Tashi's work was facilitated by the professional tools of the artist (pencils, markers, and Bristol boards) but given shape by the comic superheroes she was introduced to in the Lion Man workshop who shared her own experiences as a young woman from a marginalized community.

Analyzing the data from each implementation using the CCD framework also reveals potential gaps and opportunities for speculative design. As noted above, the lack of opportunities for Jalise to encounter STEM ideas and practices in materials and activities other than the use of design software and the laser cutter is unfortunate. Future implementations with STEM aspirations may look for ways to make more explicit the engineering found in the work of related artists (e.g., the engineering of the buildings and cities made by Kingelez) or could examine mathematical algorithms used in African textiles (Eglash et al., 2006).

We also note that attempting to predict how participants might utilize materials and tools to engage in different aspects of the connect, reflect, and project cycle is challenging! While the design team made many assumptions about how certain tools or activities might encourage learners to make connections to the past or future imaginings, and documented those assumptions in the design tapestry, our analysis of Jalise and Tashi's practice as shown in the analysis tapestry indicates these assumptions only occasionally went as planned or expected. Instead, we found that they were using these resources in revelatory, remarkable, and revolutionary ways. The CCD framework provides a much-needed empirical validation of our work in the design of speculative educational experiences.

Furthermore, we hope the CCD framework offers immediate utility and potential implications for classroom teachers and other educational professionals interested in enacting speculative design. By creating a design tapestry, either explicitly or mentally, we can see that there are many possible ways young people might explore the past, present, and future. Consider, for example, a speculative experience similar to Lion Man described above. What if a student does not want to draw, or is reluctant to write? Here a teacher might choose to invite students to collaborate with each other on a speculative project or artifact as is customary within the comics industry. Likewise, we might imagine students designing equipment, costumes, headquarters, home cities, etc., using fabrication tools such as 3D printers and laser cutters rather than writing or drawing. Even still, students may form collectives where they distribute these various design tasks among themselves to create rich characters, contexts, histories, etc. Collaborative efforts engaging this framework may well create spaces for generative and agentic knowledge production while simultaneously promoting intellectual and interpersonal competencies. Finally, by imagining critical futures and their spaces in it, learners can potentially bring these multiliterate perspectives (The New London Group, 1996) to bear in other curricular spaces both within a particular content area such as mathematics, or interdisciplinarily in finding meaningful interplay between concepts in social studies and chemistry, for example.

Lastly, we encourage readers and educators to think of these speculative artifacts and creations not simply as creative, high-interest activities that engage the imagination, but to reckon with the deeply critical and personal connections these artifacts hold for both the creator and the community in terms of thinking about civic engagement and their literate lives. The CCD framework is an opportunity for educators and designers to reflect meaningfully and thoroughly in a manner that recognizes the interwoven nature of knowledge creation and production. Rather than an assessment that sorts, selects, and quantifies expertise or skills, this framework invites us to document the interconnected ways that students create, play, and learn.

We believe this documentation process is vital for both educators interested in enacting speculative design practices, as well as researchers aiming to understand how these experiences can support meaningful learning and critical reflection on the relationship between our past, present, and possible futures.

CONCLUSION

We opened this chapter highlighting the importance of providing young people with opportunities to engage in speculative design practices. We agree with our colleagues in the learning sciences that these practices have the potential to open up new questions in science, mathematics, and computing (Eglash et al., 2013) and invite the imagination of new social and civic institutions necessary for overcoming the white supremacy that is persistent and systemic in existing institutions (Mirra & Garcia, 2020). Speculative practices also invite learners to develop critical, multimodal literacy skills necessary to create stories by, for, and about themselves (Kelly, 2018).

As this work matures beyond small-scale prototypes and aspirational proposals, there is a real need to create analytic tools that can empirically document the affordances and constraints of this speculative design work. Such tools should allow us to build educational experiences that provide the necessary materials, instructional support, and community culture that invite students to go beyond imagining futuristic technologies devoid of critical reflection on their present-day implications. Rather, we need models that help us build learning experiences where learners critically reflect on the past and present as they imagine those speculative futures. This chapter offers the CCD framework as a tool for both thoughtfully designing educationally minded speculative experience and for documenting how those design decisions are taken up (or not) by participants. A webpage to view the CCD design and analysis tapestries described here and a tool to create your own tapestry can be found at https://www.snowdaylearninglab.org/ccd-tapestry.

REFERENCES

Apple, M. W. (1971). The hidden curriculum and the nature of conflict. *Interchange*, 2(4), 27–40. https://doi.org/10.1007/BF02287080

Dando, M. B., Holbert, N., & Correa, I. (2019). Remixing Wakanda: Envisioning critical Afrofuturist design pedagogies. *Proceedings of FabLearn 2019*, 156–159. https://doi.org/10.1145/3311890.3311915

Darder, A., Baltodano, M., & Torres, R. D. (2004). Critical pedagogy: An introduction. In A. Darder, M. Baltodano, & R. D. Torres (Eds.), *The Critical Pedagogy Reader* (pp. 1–21). Routledge.

Dery, M. (Ed.). (1994). *Flame wars: The discourse of cyberculture*. Duke University Press.

Dunne, A., & Raby, F. (2013). *Speculative everything: Design, fiction, and social dreaming*. MIT Press.

Dunne, A., & Raby, F. (2014). *Dunne & Raby: Critical design FAQ*. http://dunneandraby.co.uk/content/bydandr/13/0

Eglash, R., Bennett, A., O'Donnell, C., Jennings, S., & Cintorino, M. (2006). Culturally situated design tools: Ethnocomputing from field site to classroom. *American Anthropologist*, *108*(2), 347–362. https://doi.org/10.1525/aa.2006.108.2.347

Eglash, R., Gilbert, J. E., & Foster, E. (2013). Toward culturally responsive computing education. *Communications of the ACM*, *56*(7), 33–36. https://doi.org/10.1145/2483852.2483864

Giroux, H. A., & Penna, A. N. (1979). Social education in the classroom: The dynamics of the hidden curriculum. *Theory & Research in Social Education*, *7*(1), 21–42. https://doi.org/10.1080/00933104.1979.10506048

Giroux, H. A., & Simon, R. I. (1988). Schooling, popular culture, and a pedagogy of possibility. *Journal of Education*, *170*(1), 9–26. https://doi.org/10.1177/002205748817000103

Giroux, H. A., & Simon, R. (1989). Popular culture and critical pedagogy: Everyday life as for curriculum knowledge. In H. A. Giroux & P. McLaren (Eds.), *Critical pedagogy, the state, and cultural struggle* (pp. 236–252). SUNY Press.

Halverson, E. R., & Sheridan, K. (2014). The maker movement in education. *Harvard Educational Review*, *84*(4), 495–504. https://doi.org/10.17763/haer.84.4.34j1g68140382063

Holbert, N., Berland, M., & Kafai, Y. (2020). 50 years of constructionism. In N. Holbert, M. Berland, & Y. Kafai (Eds.), *Designing constructionist futures: The art, theory, and practice of learning designs*. MIT Press.

Holbert, N., Dando, M., & Correa, I. (2020). Afrofuturism as critical constructionist design: Building futures from the past and present. *Learning, Media and Technology*, *45*(4), 1–17. https://doi.org/10.1080/17439884.2020.1754237

Jennings, J. (2017, February 15). *Remixing the trap: Race, space, and the speculative South*. Hutchins Center for African & African American Research, Harvard.

Kelly, L. L. (2018). A snapchat story: How black girls develop strategies for critical resistance in school. *Learning, Media and Technology*, *43*(4), 374–389. https://doi.org/10.1080/17439884.2018.1498352

Kincheloe, J. L. (2008). *Critical pedagogy primer*. Peter Lang.

Low, D. E. (2017). Students contesting "colormuteness" through critical inquiries into comics. *The English Journal*, *106*(4), 19–28.

Mbiti, J. S. (1976). *African religions and philosophy*. Heinemann Educational Books Ltd.

Mentor, M., & Sealey-Ruiz, Y. (2021). Doing the deep work of antiracist pedagogy: Toward self-excavation for equitable classroom teaching. *Language Arts*, *99*(1), 19–24.

Mirra, N., & Garcia, A. (2020). "I hesitate but I do have hope": Youth speculative civic literacies for troubled times. *Harvard Educational Review*, *90*(2), 295–321. https://doi.org/10.17763/1943-5045-90.2.295

Nelson, A. (2002). Introduction: Future texts. *Social Text*, *20*(2), 1–15. https://doi.org/10.1215/01642472-20-2_71-1

The New London Group. (1996). A pedagogy of multiliteracies: Designing social futures. *Harvard Educational Review*, *66*(1), 60–92.

Papert, S. (1980). *Mindstorms: Children, computers and powerful ideas*. Basic Books.

Solórzano, D. G., & Yosso, T. J. (2002). Critical race methodology: Counter-storytelling as an analytical framework for education research. *Qualitative Inquiry*, *8*(1), 23–44. https://doi.org/10.1177/107780040200800103

Thomas, E. E., & Stornaiuolo, A. (2016). Restorying the self: Bending toward textual justice. *Harvard Educational Review*, *86*(3), 313–338. https://doi.org/10.17763/1943-5045-86.3.313

Toliver, S. R. (2020). Can I get a witness? Speculative fiction as testimony and counterstory. *Journal of Literacy Research*, *52*(4), 507–529. https://doi.org/10.1177/1086296X20966362

CHAPTER 2

"A Deep Reckoning"
Re/Mixing Literacies and Imaginative Rupture in "Let's Talk About Election 2020"

Emma P. Bene, Emma C. Gargroetzi, Lynne M. Zummo, and Alexandra R. Aguilar

> People of color know what it's like to experience racism in society and that's why we stand with our Black community in these difficult times. That's why I have contributed to my community in any way I can. I have contributed by protesting, donating, signing petitions, giving food to those in need and more. George Floyd is just one of many innocent lives lost all due to racism or police brutality. And according to *The Washington Post*, these killings have exposed long-standing racial inequalities in every aspect of American life enforcing a deep reckoning across society.
>
> —Jazmin from California, Excerpted from "KQED Video: Black Lives Matter," 2020

In the final months of 2020—a season scarred by pandemic, racial violence, and the most polarizing election in modern U.S. history—Jazmin from California, along with youth across the nation, engaged civically to contend with what Jazmin names "a deep reckoning across society" and to reimagine their turbulent, unjust worlds. Unprecedented numbers of youth created and published media surrounding this election to make their voices heard on issues meaningful to them (Center for Research on Civic Learning and Engagement, 2021). Many did so on popular public platforms such as TikTok and Instagram. Others engaged with civic media-making supported by a teacher or class at school.

A widely viewed website run by National Public Radio affiliate KQED, *Let's Talk about Election 2020*, provided one such educational platform for youth civic media. The platform hosted over 1,200 pieces of youth media, including audio and video segments, produced during the months leading up to the 2020 U.S. presidential election. Youth addressed their messages to each other, to a future president, and to the broader public, calling for action on issues such as Black Lives Matter and climate change and proposing new visions of our collective future. Teachers facilitated these media composing projects in diverse classrooms across the United States with educational expectations as varied as the classrooms themselves. One constant across these classrooms was that students themselves selected the issue of concern they explored.

The collection of media published via *Let's Talk About Election 2020* (E2020) provides a rich set of examples of *youth civic composing*—the multimodal production activities surrounding issues deeply meaningful to young people as members of multiple communities and society at large. Reflecting converging global crises, nearly one-third of media segments addressed either Black Lives Matter, like Jazmin's, or climate change. The summer of 2020 saw the country reckoning with the murder of George Floyd by a police officer and California enduring red, smoke-filled skies from wildfires. With the backdrop of the COVID-19 pandemic bringing racial and environmental crises into stark relief, youth civic composing on these particular topics illuminate humanity's need for a radical reimagining.

Speaking to this need, we begin this chapter by theorizing *rupture* as any reimagining of our world that challenges the status quo; rupture is, as such, a speculative act. Specifically, in the context of the E2020 youth civic media, we found that rupture occurred as youth mixed multiple literacies and genres that often go unmixed (Bakhtin, 1980) to write themselves into their civic media as historical actors (Gutiérrez et al., 2019). We illuminate this phenomenon through analysis of two media pieces by California youth that evidenced rupture—one from Jazmin on Black Lives Matter and one from Luke on climate change. In doing so we contribute one lens for noticing the powerfully imaginative activity of youth and learning to nourish such youth worldmaking as youth allies (educators) ourselves.

CIVIC COMPOSING AND THE SPECULATIVE IMAGINATION

The notion of youth speculative civic composing (Garcia & Mirra, 2020) brings together expansive orientations to youth civic composing with the joint potential and urgency of speculative imagination to compose a world that is joyful and just, remaking and replacing current structures of racial and economic oppression. Garcia and Mirra (2020) draw on the work of Afrofuturist artist, organizer, and 2016 Detroit mayoral candidate Ingrid LaFleur, explaining that she sees youth "acting upon the future through sensemaking of the present and critical reinterpretation of the past. She orients these as imaginative acts that work toward achieving healing and justice in an inequitable world" (p. 2). Youth speculative civic composing is here posed as both an aspiration and a current reality, an activity in which youth are always already engaged, if at times in fleeting or subtle ways. When young people create media speaking to issues of concern to them and their communities, they produce words and images, but also worlds and futures. They necessarily build from the tools available, but do so in new ways, mixing civic, historical, quantitative, and literary forms to "read" the social-political world and "inscribe" their own participation (Freire & Macedo, 2005).

Rupture as a Speculative Activity

A fundamental tension of the speculative is that it necessarily finds its ingredients in existing tools and narratives. E2020, hosted by a national public radio affiliate, positioned youth as legitimate, potentially transformative civic composers with a national public audience. Still, youth worked with tools laden in dominant discourses (Gee, 2001) such as normative civic conceptions of history, time, identity, and electoral politics and did so in the context of a school-based project hosted by an educational platform committed to youth creating media acceptable for public radio. Even under these conditions, we observed that youth diverged from or challenged normative binaries of past/present and us/them, rupturing the presumed structures and fabrics of normative public discourse in their own civic media compositions to remake them anew. Whereas rupture can connote destruction, a tear in a fabric, or a break in relations, we instead propose rupture as an imaginative act with creative possibility. Like a redwood cone that must be heated by fire to open and release its seeds, rupture here speaks to the breaking open of the constraints of existing norms making possible new dreams for today and tomorrow.

Multiliteracies and Heteroglossia

We see speculative civic literacies as resonant with Bakhtin's idea of heteroglossia, or the capacity of a text to contain a multitude of different voices, and the necessity of this very mixing for storying a world different from that already known. In rupture, we recognize vast heteroglossia—genre busting at multiple points and scales. We further draw on Bakhtin's theories of language, in particular the idea that words and images have histories and come laden with meaning (Bakhtin, 2010). While Bakhtin presumes heteroglossia as ever present, in youth speculative civic compotesing we take these heteroglossic acts as potentially agentic acts of rupture, the remixing and repurposing of multiple literacies for imagining new possibilities.

Youth as Historical Actors

We do not presume that every act of heteroglossic composing is a reimagining; many largely entail reproductions of techno-capitalism as panacea.

Rather, rupture occurred when youth remixed literacies to position themselves as historical actors—people who "rehearse emergent visions of the social world and their place in them" and connect their own story to "a larger stream of historical events" (Gutiérrez et al., 2019, p. 294).

In this context, we sought to explore how youth enact imaginative rupture to articulate a vision of the future yet to be realized. We wondered, *what is the texture of rupture in youth civic media composing? In what ways and with what tools do youth imagine a liberatory future through rupture?* In this chapter, we examine two examples of speculative civic composing, in which two youths—Jazmin and Luke—remix with the tools of today to imagine a more just tomorrow.

METHODOLOGY AND HISTORICIZING AUTHORSHIP (POSITIONALITY)

We, the authors, are four emerging scholars; we identify as educators, activists, and mothers with personal and political commitments to Black joy, climate action, and dreaming a more just and inclusive world for future generations. As former K–12 teachers and current teacher educators focused on the disciplines currently named as mathematics, science, social studies, and language arts, we are driven to seek the power and potential for multiliteracies that transgress disciplinary boundaries for civic imagination. In this chapter and beyond, we seek to learn from youth about how another future might be possible, even (and especially) beyond the imagination of today's adults, including us. We continue to watch, listen, and wonder at youth-created civic media with a lens of fascination and admiration, attending to what insights we may glean, while assuming youth ingenuity and imagination will always overflow the capacities of scholarly analysis.

We came together through a related analysis of the E2020 media (Gargroetzi et al., under review). As we engaged that process, a new line of analytic attention emerged related to the notion of rupture. Through ongoing collective viewing and consensus process, we identified media segments that suggested rupture—*moments or segments in which youth reimagined the world and challenged the status quo*. We noticed in these segments that youth *mixed literacies and modalities as they articulated their role as historical actors within their communities, simultaneously looking to the past and present to imagine a more just future*. From the media segments tagged as suggesting rupture, we selected two segments from students in California, the location of KQED and where two-thirds of youth composers were located. The two segments by Jazmin and Luke on Black Lives Matter and climate change, respectively, represent two cases of rupture. We engaged in a textual analysis, using fine-grained video analysis techniques to further explore the texture and tools of rupture.

FINDING/LOCATING RUPTURE IN THE YOUTH CIVIC MEDIA OF JAZMIN AND LUKE

> Black lives matter and they will always matter. America needs to end racism and educate everyone about the racism that still exists in the world.
>
> —Jazmin

> We are on a path to having unhealthy and extreme climate changes that could affect our entire ecosystem. Not only are we setting ourselves up for detrimental conditions but also helpless animals who have done nothing to hurt this planet. Since you care about posterity and the future of our world, not just country or state, the entire world is depending on our actions now.
>
> —Luke

In two videos, each less than 3 minutes long, two California youth from different high schools and communities each positioned themself as a powerful historical actor, explicitly reflected on their place in history, and creatively (re)mixed civic, historical, experiential, and quantitative literacies to (re)imagine a different future for themselves and their communities.

Within each media, youth remixed literacies to create compositions that move across time and space in scope and forge connections across communities for expanded notions of solidarity. By rupturing traditional timelines, geographies, and identity categories, they became historical actors, storying the world they wished to inhabit. Our analysis hopes to explicate the diverse tools that Luke and Jazmin used to accomplish rupture as they (1) challenged status quo conceptions of time and space; (2) connected their own stories to the larger stream of historical events; and (3) envisioned a more just future.

1. Reimagining Time and Space

One form of rupture that emerged in both media segments was a breach of normative conceptions of time and space. Normative Western views of time, such as those taught in history class, treat time as linear, with past and present disjointed, distinct time periods. Connections, when made, are often articulated as causal—as in, what were the causes of World War I—or cyclical—as in history is repeating itself. Similarly, geographical space, in the post- and settler-colonial world, is treated as having clear boundaries such as those thick dark lines drawn on maps, that require "crossing" to navigate. Both Jazmin and Luke employed heteroglossia and multiliteracies to rupture these normative constructs, challenging the status quo by creating compositions that moved fluidly across time and space. They communicated the texture of this rupture through re/mix and heteroglossia: interweaving literacies of past and present, connecting the historical and personal, and the global to the local, each in distinct ways.

Jazmin on Black Lives Matter: Experiencing History Now

Jazmin's composition mixed historical protest literacies with present-day experiential literacies, using both visuals and narration to create a textured composition that ruptured divisions between the past and present (see Figure 2.1). Over a period of less than 1 minute, Jazmin incorporated multiple images of Black Lives Matter protests, a portrait of Breonna Taylor, and images from the Civil Rights Movement of the 1960s. All four images in Figure 2.1 are heteroglossic—they come laden with histories of their own, and viewers of Jazmin's media composition would recognize these images and have their own associations with them. By stitching together these commonly recognized images, Jazmin took the viewer on a journey from present to past and back again.

Minute 1:23 displays a split-screen composition of the March on Washington and a Black Lives Matter protest. In both images, protestors stretch as far as the eye can see, holding up signs demanding justice and equal rights. The parallel composition of these images, taken more than 5 decades apart, effectively challenges the division between past and present, a message underlined by Jazmin's words: "These killings have exposed long-standing racial inequalities." The composition then displays an iconic image of past oppression: a "colored waiting room," as Jazmin's voice declares

Figure 2.1. An excerpt from the transcription and images from Jazmin's video about Black Lives Matter, coded by timescale.

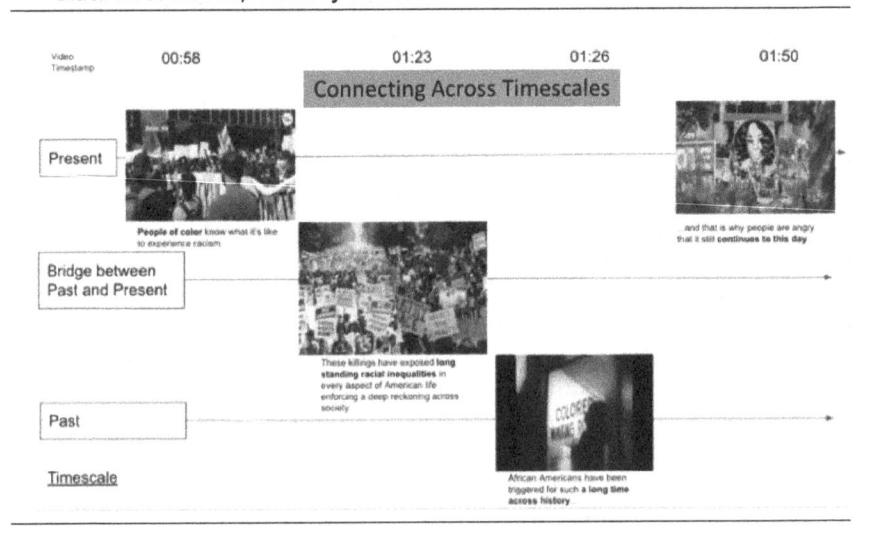

that African Americans have suffered for "such a long time across history." The viewer is then transported to the present through the image of Breonna Taylor as we hear her say, "and that is why people are so angry that it still continues today." By interweaving images from history and current events, Jazmin's composition created a portal between past and present, rupturing assumed linearity of time and emphasizing Black American's unending and ongoing fight against oppression and systemic racism. This remix challenges the status quo idea of "progress" in American history and uplifts the way people of color continue to fight back against systemic oppression.

Not only does her media segment move fluidly across timescales, but the story it tells also spans geographical space. Again, through a series of images, Jazmin takes the viewer across the world: from protests in New York to Arizona, then to Mexico and England, before arriving at the BLM protest that she documented in her own community. By mixing visual, historical, and civic literacies, this media composition ruptured taken-for-granted divisions between past and present and united often-separated geographies.

Luke on Climate Change: Zooming out/Zooming in

Like Jazmin did with racial justice, Luke used multiliteracies to rupture status-quo conceptions of how time and place relate to climate change. His video opens with an animated heat map that shows how the world's temperature has changed since 1969. While the viewer watches the map change from blue and yellow to orange and red as the years accelerate to the present, we hear Luke's voice declaring "climate change is plaguing the entire world." The composition then flashes to two images: first, a smokestack billowing pollution, followed by an image of a barren landscape, the remains of a house and a few tree trunks smoldering under a smoke-filled sky. The heat map is a form of quantitative literacy that effectively communicates abstract ideas about change over time and the global consequences of climate change. The visual, place-based literacies of the smokestack and barren landscape root the abstractions in specificity. By layering these diverse literacies, his composition expresses the global scale of climate change and then immediately provides the viewer with a specific example of how that problem manifests in a particular time and place. Linking the abstract to the specific allows the viewer to conceptualize the scientific, far-reaching scale of the climate crisis without losing sight of how it manifests in the individual lives of people.

Luke's composition repeatedly moves between representations of the planet Earth—for instance, a satellite image of Earth in space where half of Earth looks normal, the other half is edited to look like it is burning up into small particles, and visuals of particular places—the Amazon on fire, the ice caps melting. He remixed these literacies of scale and place with visual representations of time passing—a countdown clock, and years flashing as they speed by over images of a changing landscape.

This movement from global to local, from broad-reaching timescales to specific moments, articulates connections between past and present, between local and worldwide, that rupture our status quo understanding of these concepts. A layering of quantitative literacies with place-based literacies, Luke's remix occurred on multiple scales: the global intertwined with the local, the past fused with the present and future. The fluidity through which his composition moves across these scales creates a space of rupture that allows him to articulate both the scope and immediacy of the climate crisis.

2. Connecting One's Story to History

Youth become historical actors when they connect their own stories to the broader stream of history. When they are able to articulate the way their story connects to a broader movement, they open up the possibility of becoming transformative members of that movement. Both Jazmin and Luke used remixing and heteroglossia to connect their own stories to the broader Black Lives Matter and climate change movements, respectively. In doing so, they considered their own identities and experiences with racism and climate change, placing themselves inside these charged historical narratives.

Jazmin on Black Lives Matter: "That's me!" in the Ongoing Story of Protest Movements

> As a person of color myself, racism has existed all 17 years of my life. I have witnessed it and experienced it as well and it is truly horrifying. I am a Latina even though I was born in the U.S. I still have experienced racist jokes, getting stared at differently, or being alienated because I'm Brown. People of color know what it's like to experience racism in this society and that's why we stand with our Black community in these difficult times.
>
> —Jazmin

Returning to the quote that opened this chapter, we draw attention to the ways Jazmin mixed literacies to traverse identity categories and connect her own experience to the broader BLM movement in a way that bespoke rupture. Her composition fluidly moves from the broad "a person of color"—to more specific, "Latina," before returning to a broad conception of identity, calling all people united by their experience of oppression to "stand with the Black community" (see Figure 2.2).

In her composition, quantitative literacies communicate the pervasiveness of racism both in her own life and the lives of other people of color and civic literacies articulate her own identity and connection to community. Challenging the use of ethnic or racial labels as boundaries between people, Jazmin, who self-identifies as Latina, used a shared experience of oppression

"A Deep Reckoning"   43

Figure 2.2. An excerpt from Jazmin's transcript with concurrent images from Jazmin's video about Black Lives Matter. Coded for literacies evidenced: quantitative literacies around timescales and pervasiveness (magnitude) and civic literacies around identity and solidarity.

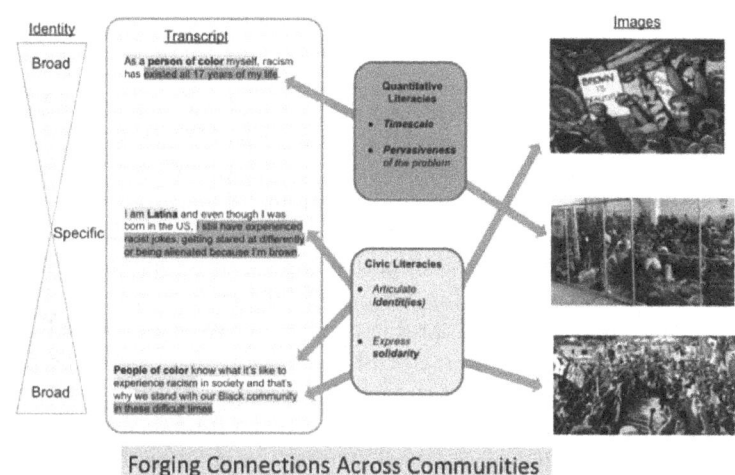

---

to forge connections with other historically oppressed groups, particularly Black Americans and the BLM movement.

Here, as with her work with time and space, rupture functions as a creative act. Just as crossing the boundaries of time and space allowed for creative remixing of literacies in the service of worldmaking, redrawing the boundaries of identity helped Jazmin forge allegiances across minoritized groups, united in the fight against injustice, and imagine a new future in which people of color achieve lasting change.

Not only did Jazmin map her own Latina identity in an expression of solidarity with the Black community, but she also explicitly articulated her place in a lineage fighting injustice. Her composition interweaves her own footage of BLM protests she attended with other BLM protests and Civil Rights protests of the 1960s. At one point, the screen shows an arrow, saying "that's me" while narrating how she had "contributed to my community by protesting, donating, signing petitions, giving food to those in need." In integrating her own protest footage with iconic images from BLM protests across the country, the Chicanx protest movement, and the Civil Rights Movement, Jazmin storied herself as a historical actor within a deep lineage of protest movements, past and present. Remixing quantitative and civic literacies and historical images with personal, experiential visuals created a textured composition in which Jazmin could articulate her own place as a change agent in history and asserted her vision for racial justice and change.

Luke on Climate Change: Gen Zers and Californians in a Global Crisis

> Being a part of Gen Z, we will have to deal with the ramifications and repercussions of the unhealthy living conditions of today.
>
> —Luke

Luke interwove quantitative literacies with personal and place-based literacies to articulate his connection to the climate crisis. He began by acknowledging that he and his fellow youth will need to "deal with the ramifications and repercussions of unhealthy living conditions." He asserted his identity as a member of Gen Z who has inherited the problem of climate change from previous generations and is experiencing its consequences firsthand. He then pivoted to talk about his place-based experience with the climate crisis, through footage of the wildfires in California, where he lives. His composition interweaves visual literacies of place and quantitative literacies, narrating how climate change is "putting the majority of Californians in miserable conditions." Here, he moved from a generational, age-based identity to a multigenerational place-based identity. By claiming his identity on multiple dimensions, Luke called for people to work together to combat climate change and opened a path for rupturing identity boundaries that might prevent collaboration.

Like Jazmin's assertion of her own place in the Black Lives Matter movement, Luke connected his own lived experience of climate change, through California fires, to the global climate crisis. He made this connection by pairing quantitative visual literacy, through multiple time-lapse videos showing changing temperatures over the planet and melting ice caps, with personal literacies of place through footage of destruction from wildfires in his local community. Moving from the global to the local, Luke's composition displayed images of the California 2020 wildfires. As he reported, "Having grown up in California, dangerously close to the numerous wildfires, I have experience and a first-hand look at the dangers climate change is producing." By inserting local footage into his composition, he interwove the transformation of our planet through time and space with the particularity of his own location, thereby claiming his place in the larger phenomenon of climate change. Through this integration of multiple literacies, Luke ruptured identity categories and showed signs of becoming a historical actor.

3. Rehearsing A Vision for the Future: Tensions Between Rupture and Stasis

> These murders have gotten way out of hand and some cities are even considering defunding the police. So many more actions are being demanded to fight for our Black community and for the future of people in color in

general. Black lives matter and they will always matter. America needs to end racism and educate everyone about the racism that still exists in the world. And educate people about how it affects minorities because of the color of their skin. Police brutality needs to come to an end as well and protect the people instead of continuously killing innocent people. There should be justice and equality for all and until there's justice, there will be no peace.

—Jazmin

Since you care about posterity and the future of our world, not just country or state, the entire world is depending on our actions now. There is no time to waste, the climate and fate of our world is riding on the decisions made by our representative. Wouldn't it be nice to have a representative that not only believes in climate change, but also has solutions and ideas on how to mitigate this crisis? So now, I ask you, vote for someone who will work to significantly muffle the non-stop growth of our climate extremities and save our world from future downfall.

—Luke

While both Jazmin's and Luke's videos evidence rupture, the imaginative possibilities of their solutions varied. As we described above, throughout her video, Jazmin articulated the ways in which she stood in solidarity with her community to fight racial injustice. Throughout her video, she also argued for specific changes that she believed could improve America, for example defunding the police. She concluded her media segment with her footage of a local Black Lives Matter protest that she participated in, and with a call to action: "There should be justice and equality for all and until there's justice, there will be no peace." This expression contains echoes of many different protest movements in the fight for racial equality. In it, we can hear her commitment to continuing to fight the injustice that she has experienced and borne witness to, and her tribute to the ancestors who have fought before her. By layering a video of her participation in change with this open-ended statement, she did not only offer prescribed "solutions" to the deeply rooted systemic inequities in American society. Rather, she contextualized her demands as the starting point, not the end, inviting the viewer to join her in making a commitment to the fight for justice and equality, through whatever means necessary.

Luke's media segment ends with a plea for the viewer to "care about posterity and the future of our world, not just country or state," because "there is no time to waste." In a critique of capitalism and the narrative of American superiority, he called out America for being "second highest in global emissions," while simultaneously calling *in* American citizens to transform American practices for the "future of our world." This powerful critique, coupled with his reimagination of temporal and spatial scales, opened the possibility for imaginative rupture.

Yet even in moments of rupture, stasis—the reproduction of normative expectations—remains a powerful force to contend with. The solution Luke proposes is a normative one for election media: vote! Vote for a representative who "has solutions and ideas on how to mitigate this crisis." In the face of a phenomenally multidimensional and unimaginable problem, his video offers the viewer a simple and concrete solution. A reliance on the vote suggests the encroaching limits to a reimagined fight against climate change. By saying "the fate of our world is riding on the decisions made by our representative," Luke's composition allows his audience to punt responsibilities for climate change onto government officials, potentially absolving corporations, consumer culture, and capitalism. This straightforward suggestion for how to solve the problem of climate change, while normative for the election media genre, offers a quite limited path toward change. Whereas Jazmin's call to action promised commitment and a lasting fight, a viewer who narrowly attended to Luke's call to vote might feel their job was finished after exiting the voting booth. The contrast is telling. Luke's media segment is a reminder that stasis and rupture may exist simultaneously within the same composition. Stasis is pernicious and pervasive, barging into even the most creative moments of rupture. But rupture too is sneaky, finding cracks and pushing them open, even when the inertia of stasis threatens to overwhelm.

AN INVITATION FOR EDUCATORS: NOTICING AND NURTURING IMAGINATIVE RUPTURE IN YOUTH SPECULATIVE CIVIC ACTIVITY

Seeing Youth as Speculative Actors

We invite educators into our fine-grained analyses of images and text in youth media to provide examples of rupture and radical imagination. Our hope is that as we highlighted two phenomena that challenge or break dominant narratives, educators might likewise attune to these possibilities in their own classrooms: namely an orientation to time and space that is textured and multidimensional rather than linear, and an orientation to identity and community memberships as a way to build solidarity. Through the erasure of taken-for-granted boundaries around time, space, and identity, Jazmin and Luke were able to call, write, and draw multiple others *into* imagining a different future and write themselves as historical actors. Your own learners are likely always and already doing some of the same.

Certainly, Jazmin and Luke's speculative civic compositions are artfully crafted, imaginative, and deeply moving. Yet, while unique in the individual products, their brilliance and creativity is not. Young people are too often treated as lacking—lacking in education, in political awareness, in motivation, or in skills. We chose the work of Jazmin and Luke not because it was singular, but because their work adds to the vast evidence of what youth are capable of—evidence that is too often ignored. Before we can discuss what pedagogical or instructional moves might nurture rupture in organized learning spaces, we have to invest faith in the ability of rupture in youth. Here we provide evidence that it is happening, in small and big ways, all around us. We invite and implore educators to look and see, listen, and be curious about youth composing, even when it is not connected to a school project or a national public media platform.

Making Space for Rupture Inside the Classroom

While rupture may be less likely in the work of adults given our extended training in normative practices, we are optimistic that we as educators may have the capacity to feed, support, and nurture the possibilities of rupture for youth. How can we as educators nurture rupture in our learning spaces? What pedagogical choices can we make to support youth speculative civic composing?

Creativity and Platforms for Public Voice

We invite educators to consider how Jazmin's and Luke's teachers offered "choice and voice" to their students and how we might be able to create similarly nurturing environments in our own classrooms (Gargroetzi & Garcia, 2022). The teachers sought out and provided access to a platform for public voice. In doing so, they offered legitimacy to the civic composing and creativity that young people are already engaged in but are not usually invited to participate in within schools. They provided both structure and open space for students to create rupture. Students chose not only the topic—one of immediate concern to them—but also the multiple elements necessary to any multimedia composition. We can create similarly nurturing spaces by offering our students options, not prescriptions. We must recognize when a student's drawing outside the lines reflects a brilliant dream that could not have been captured in the rubric or graphic organizer provided. We can also seek out opportunities for the public to hear our students' voices, whether by presenting at a town hall meeting, performing at an open mic, or writing to a local nonprofit.

Multimodal Composing

The vast majority of composing that youth do within classrooms is still writing papers. With E2020, Jazmin, Luke, and their peers had the option of creating audio or video. In either case, the medium demanded more than a single-dimensional text on a page. We see the possibilities for rupture increase multifold when youth are given the freedom to experiment with other mediums, and therefore we encourage educators to incorporate multimedia projects into their classroom. In some of the most powerful moments from Jazmin and Luke, they layered their own voices with known musical clips, juxtaposed black-and-white with color images, used movement to speed up or slow down, flashed images, words, and numbers, all to create multisensory experiences for viewers that insisted on new perspectives and possibilities for taking on familiar issues. At the most basic, imaginative rupture likely grows in spaces where multimodality is on offer, whether in the form of audio and visuals, or mixing across genres of audio or visual modalities. We as educators must embrace the possibilities of multimodality, breaking free of the tyranny of the five-paragraph essay to nurture students' imaginative potential.

Multiple Literacies

We invite teachers to reflect on how Jazmin, Luke, and their peers integrated multiple literacies, bringing literacies from across their lives into their compositions. Inviting students' experiences and ways of knowing into the classroom is essential for powerful learning (Moll et al., 1992). Consider how youth employed historical, quantitative, civic, narrative, musical, visual, and arts literacies in ways that refused the traditional boundaries drawn between disciplines. We believe imaginative rupture likely depends upon a transdisciplinarity that is uncommon in schools, but that all humans as sociopolitical and historical beings participate in every day. As teachers, we must break free of the disciplinary silos that school creates so our students can, too. We know learning is most powerful when it is connected across multiple spaces (Barron, 2006; Ito et al., 2012). We invite teachers to look across the hall to colleagues in other disciplines and consider what new avenues might open if we support youth in crossing disciplinary divides. How can we create multidisciplinary projects, interdisciplinary experiences, and transdisciplinary learning?

Youth as Part of Multiple Timescales: Historical and Speculative Actors

We as educators know that learning happens when the learner can see themselves in their own learning, and see their learning as connected to something more than themselves (Bishop, 1990). Consider how Jazmin's and Luke's composition situated their own stories as part of our collective histories, positioning themselves as historic actors (Gutiérrez et al., 2019). They located themselves in our collective future, proposing a vision of themselves as *speculative* actors—those who participate in visioning and bringing into being a more just and joyful future. With the possibility of youth as speculative actors in mind, we encourage educators not only to support students in locating their own story in the history, numbers, or a novel being taught, but also to offer opportunities for writing themselves into a more desirable future.

Limitations

Our choice to explore youth-made media posted to KQED's E2020 platform limited aspects of our analysis. Students reported limited information about their identities for their own safety. We did not have insight into student creation processes or the pedagogical structures that supported them. Therefore, the pedagogical possibilities we propose come from insights provided through media created by Jazmin, Luke, and their peers, as interpreted through our lenses as educators and scholars. We hope others will likewise be moved to imagine their own pedagogical innovations to nurture rupture.

Concluding Thoughts

While these media compositions re/mixed genres in ways that created rupture, media topics in these civic media segments remained largely single-issue in design. Like the boundaries around disciplinary genres, dominant forms of civic argumentation suggest that one must *choose* one major issue to tackle, or tackle first. Drawing on the ways that youth supported notions of solidarity by forging connections across communities, educators who support speculative civic imagination may do well to challenge the siloing of issues. Rather, support for systemic understandings that illuminate connections between issues as well as communities likely will be necessary. The future of our climate and humanity remains powerfully connected to the mattering of Black life. Any sustainable and just "house" of our future will depend on this very recognition, centered on interconnectedness and solidarity amongst not only people and the planet but the issues that drive us as well.

NOTE

The research reported in this chapter was made possible by a grant from the Spencer Foundation (#202100262). The views expressed are those of the authors and do not necessarily reflect the views of the Spencer Foundation.

REFERENCES

Bakhtin, M. M. (2010). *The dialogic imagination: Four essays* (Vol. 1). University of Texas Press.

Barron, B. (2006). Interest and self-sustained learning as catalysts of development: A learning ecology perspective. *Human Development*, 49(4), 193–224. https://doi.org/10.1159/000094368

Bishop, R. S. (1990). Windows and mirrors: Children's books and parallel cultures. *California State University reading conference: 14th annual conference proceedings* (pp. 3–12).

Center for Research on Civic Learning and Engagement (2021). Young people created media to uplift their voices in 2020. https://circle.tufts.edu/latest-research/young-people-created-media-uplift-their-voices-2020

Freire, P., & Macedo, D. (2005). *Literacy: Reading the word and the world*. Routledge.

Garcia, A., & Mirra, N. (2020). Writing toward justice: Youth speculative civic literacies in online policy discourse. *Urban Education, 56*(4), 640–669. https://doi.org/10.1177/0042085920953881

Gargroetzi, E., & Garcia, A. (2022). "I don't think kids nowadays feel like they have a lot of power": Exploring teacher civic commitments in a national online letter writing project. *Journal of Teacher Education, 73*(5), 479–493. https://doi.org/10.1177/00224871221105791

Gargroetzi, E., Zummo, L. M., Aguilar, A., & Bene, E. (under review). Quantitative civic literacies: "Let's talk about election 2020" and youth use of numbers in digital civic media.

Gee, J. P. (2001). Discourse and sociocultural studies in reading. In M L. Kamil, P. B. Mosenthal, P. D. Pearson, and R. Barr (Eds.), *Methods of literacy research* (Vol. III) (pp. 129–142). Routledge.

Gutiérrez, K. D., Becker, B. L. C., Espinoza, M.L., Cortes, K. L., Cortez, A., Lizárraga, J. R., Rivero, E., Villegas, K., & Yin, P. (2019). Youth as historical actors in the production of possible futures. *Mind, Culture, and Activity, 26*(4), 291–308. https://doi.org/10.1080/10749039.2019.1652327.

Ito, M., Gutiérrez, K., Livingstone, S., Penuel, B., Rhodes, J., Salen, K., Schor, J., Sefton-Green, J., & Watkins, S. C. (2012). Connected learning: An agenda for research and design. Digital Media and Learning Research Hub.

Moll, L. C., Amanti, C., Neff, D., & Gonzalez, N. (1992). Funds of knowledge for teaching: Using a qualitative approach to connect homes and classrooms. *Issues In Educational Research*, *31*(2), 132–141. https://doi.org/10.1080/00405849209543534

CHAPTER 3

Speculative Pedagogies in Video Gameplay
Designing for New Social Futures in Collaborative Worldmaking

Arturo Cortez and José Ramón Lizárraga

INTRODUCTION

The enduring COVID-19 pandemic has taught the educational research and practitioner community that there will be no "return to normal." In fact, we might consider our current context as an opportunity to engage in an educational "hard reset," following Gloria Ladson-Billings's (2021) invocation to mobilize our collective energy toward justice. We stand at the precipice of a new world transformed by the speculative imagination, where collectives can reimagine a new world that is not steeped in inequity, violence, and coloniality. Here, we point to the importance and consequential meaning-making that emerges as people theorize from their everyday experiences, developing new resistance practices (hooks, 2003) and just futures.

As learning scientists and social design–based researchers (Gutiérrez, 2016, 2018), we are attuned especially to the everyday theorizing and praxis of youth, specifically youth from nondominant, Black, Brown, and Queer communities (cf. Gutierrez, Becker, et al., 2019; Gutiérrez et al., 2017). During the COVID-19 pandemic, we observed that many of these youth turned to multiplayer video games to overcome the ensuing isolation, but also to connect, build solidarity, and world-build (Cortez et al., 2022). In our work, we take heed of the practices we observed and used this knowledge in codesigning a learning ecology that centered the generative power of play (Gutierrez, Higgs, et al., 2019) and intergenerational learning (Gee et al., 2017).

Through our work, we have found that play, learning, and the speculative can be interwoven to support expansive meaning-making and consequential learning (Hall & Jurow, 2015). This stands in stark contrast to what we commonly see in the design of traditional learning environments, particularly those that use digital technologies in service of maintaining control over young people's learning. This is to say that classroom teaching and learning are rarely designed such that the everyday practices of young people are valued and used. During the pandemic we broadly observed how emergent technologies were used to enact practices of surveillance and control in remote education (Williamson et al., 2020), failing to take advantage fully of the collaborative and transformative learning possibilities that these tools can afford. Thus, we seek to continue efforts by equity-oriented educational scholars who center imagination and ingenuity in everyday practices (Gutiérrez et al., 2017) in the use of digital tools in learning design. Specifically, we look at how the socio and technical affordances of networked video gameplay can be employed in potent collaboration and imaginings of new social futures.

In the following, we will begin by reviewing scholarship that highlights the important role of play and the playful imagination in learning processes, specifically as a *leading activity*. We will then use this framing to define *speculative pedagogies*, as informed by theories of generative collaboration and relationships that can lead to future learning. We will continue with the presentation of three vignettes from our social design–based project where teachers and youth engaged in collaborative video gameplay. We conclude with implications of our work in the design of learning ecologies that make thoughtful and robust use of video games.

PLAY AND LEARNING

Spaces of play are increasingly being recognized as sites for robust meaning making (Cortez et al., 2022; Gutierrez, Becker, et al., 2019), literacy development (Gee, 2007), and complex negotiations over historically produced power structures (Gray, 2014; Leonard, 2003; Shaw, 2012). Linking learning and play has been a project emerging across the traditions of history and culture (Huizinga, 1938) and sociocultural psychology (Vygotsky, 1967). We are aligned with the positions proposed by these and other scholars, arguing that play and the playful imagination opens up possibilities, new horizons, and readily creates opportunities for what could be in our immediate and far future, as we draw on our experiences in the past and present. Herein lies the connection between play and temporality, more precisely the *speculative*. We take a concerted sociopolitical take on the role of play in the design of consequential learning that is future-oriented, specifically for learners from nondominant (racialized, gendered, dispossessed) communities.

Our take on play and the playful imagination is aligned with expansive notions of how one socially organizes for learning. In this regard, we design for robust participation frameworks that rupture hierarchical teaching/learning arrangements and facilitate the intergenerational distribution of expertise (DiGiacomo & Gutiérrez, 2016). In other words, we trouble notions that adults are the primary holders of knowledge in any given learning interaction and look at how youth also can be experts. Here, we further highlight how educational research has sought to trouble ideas that meaningful learning only happens in formal schooling (Engeström, 1991) and to design for possibilities of play to facilitate *syncretic* forms of learning that blends academic and everyday knowledges and practices (Gutiérrez, 2008).

As we engage with the *speculative* to design for consequential and meaningful learning, we leverage the notion of *prolepsis*, or organizing for futures within a given socially organized activity (e.g., teachers teaching toward a future world and life they are coenvisioning with learners). Cole (1995) explores how mediated activity—activity that involves specific participation arrangements and tools—can be less adult-defined and more collective by default. This latter consideration is important in our efforts to organize for learning where all learners are active participants in the design of their own present and future social circumstances (see Gutierrez, Becker, et al., 2019). Toward this end, we seek to uncover and identify forms of mediation, or pedagogical practices, that we have seen emerge in the context of worldmaking learning activities of gameplay. In other words, we want to highlight teaching and learning that is deeply collaborative, transformative, and agentic (Sannino et al., 2016), and that we have seen emerge in intergenerational game-mediated environments.

SPECULATIVE PEDAGOGIES

In our study, *speculative pedagogies are seen* in the activities between adults and young people as they work together toward the construction of fantastical new worlds, in the here and now, as well as in more distant futures. Here, we note that our futures are increasingly undefined, and that a *speculative* approach to learning requires that we engage in proleptic, future-oriented work where young people and adults envision social futures together. In this regard, speculative pedagogies emerge as adult learners use pedagogical practices that trouble familiar roles of novice and expert, jointly define complex social issues with young people, and rehearse embodied practices that center equity and justice in fantastical imaginings of new worlds. In our studies of gaming ecologies, we observe activities that are speculative as they are imbued with hope for a new social world that is just beyond our individual and collective grasp, where adults and young people grapple with, interrogate, and design for a future world that is not yet here (Muñoz, 2009) and at the limits of what is currently possible. We propose the following speculative pedagogical practices that emerge within microinteractional moments as young people and adults dream together:

- *Speculative Relationality*: This involves practices that build relationships between individuals and collectives, with the intention of moving toward future interactions within gaming activity. This relationality is strategic and *speculative* in that it is simultaneously marked by playfulness, irreverence, and an intention to engage in future gaming, but with undefined and malleable roles.
- *Speculative Complexity*: This describes observed multiplicity and complexity in how dilemmas and contradictions are explored in gaming activity. This is speculative in that the goal of learning activity is not predefined, perpetually dynamic, and often fantastical.
- *Speculative Transdisciplinary Worldmaking*: This form of activity is one where an individual or collective engages in the creation of a new digital world within the gaming ecology by leveraging expertise across disciplines. Specifically, we looked at instances where the geography and/or social organization of said world move beyond models present "in real life" (IRL), thus making it speculative.

To clarify, these forms of mediation and activity emerged within the context of online gaming that was part of the design of this project. Further, these speculative practices were enacted by youth and adults alike.

OUR GAMING LEARNING ECOLOGY

The vignettes and analysis presented in this chapter draw from data collected from The Learning to Transform (LiTT) Video Gaming Lab research project. Data included 195 hours of video data recordings during gaming sessions between high school youth and instructors/coordinators who were part of our project. Our intergenerational group of youth and adult participants engaged in Role Play (RP) on a customized online server environment of *Grand Theft Auto V* (GTA5) or approximately 5 hours a week, for 13 weeks during the summer of 2022.[1]

Young people and adults crafted digital identities in this gaming ecology called LiTT City and were expected to engage with each other while "in character," as they collectively organized, designed, and planned for new modifications to the GTA5 sandbox environment. Team meetings were held in the game, with synchronous Discord channel communication. Furthermore, activities were organized to serve as scaffolds toward the creation of a virtual learning environment that was codesigned by all involved.

Role-Playing (RP) as a Cultural Practice. In the following vignettes we will describe RP activities that are part of broader cultural practice in online gaming. Role players are expected to immerse themselves fully in the digital corporeality/embodiment of the game without any reference to IRL, or their in-person physical embodiment/environment. Failure to adhere to these guidelines of engagement are commonly described as "fail RP" and can result in expulsion from other gaming communities. While our customized gaming environment did not enact such punitive responses, we did encourage all participants to fully participate in the experience of shedding their IRL identities in order to craft a new one in LiTT City.

To maintain RP, any references to IRL technical practices are referred to as "flexing a muscle." For instance, if a fellow gamer asks how to launch a certain function in the game, someone might tell them to "flex the F1 muscle" indicating that they should press the F1 key on their keyboard. In addition, instead of indicating that the game is lagging, a player might say that their head is popping or that they are having a headache. Strict attention is made to use metaphors that reference what is happening IRL, while not indicating as such. To reiterate, it is our belief that the RP practices, as mediated by our designed learning ecology, are marked by the *speculative* because of the conditions that orient our youth toward participating in fantastical worlds that free them from the constraints of the physical world. In doing so, they imagine, create, and participate in prototypes of new possible futures that are just and of their own design.

Our Core Participants. For the purposes of this chapter we will focus on the participation of 15 individuals: 3 high school youth, 3 collaborating artists who are well-known public gamers and streamers, 3 undergraduate project coordinators and research assistants, 3 community educators from our collaboration with the Youth Empowerment Broadcasting Organization (YEBO), 2 PhD students, and the principal investigator (PI) of the project (first author). Participant names, gaming character, and role within the project are listed in Table 3.1.

SPECULATIVE PEDAGOGIES IN GAMEPLAY

The vignettes described here draw from a 2-hour-and-45-minute gaming session between our youth and educators that occurred in the early summer of 2022. At this point, our group had been working together for 5 weeks and had several synchronous meetings both in the game and via video conferencing (Zoom). The purpose of this particular session was to

Table 3.1. Study Participants

Name*	In-City Character	Role
Cristian	Karma	High School Freshman
Linda	LindaLuna	High School Junior
Azel	Vex McNamara	High School Junior
Tee	Bethany	Streamer/Collaborating Artist
Vanessa	Sunset Sanchez	Streamer/Collaborating Artist
Carlos	Nelson Campos	Streamer/Collaborating Artist
Matthew	Shandy Greene	Computer Science Undergraduate
Steve	Nomi Sunrider	Ethnic Studies Undergraduate
Nate	Shaba Down	Chemistry Undergraduate
Monica, Gerald, John	Gaidyn	YEBO Educators
Manuel	Beall Feelall	PhD Student
Annette	Carson Henderson	PhD Student
Arturo	Professor	Principal Investigator

*Pseudonyms are used for those who are not authors.

begin planning for the building of LiTT city, with some demonstrations of possible modifications.

The following excerpt from a recording of our session occurs as members of our team began to gather at LiTT City Hall, at the start of our session. At this moment we see a male-presenting character (who we discover to be Christian as Karma) walk toward a group that has already gathered at the steps of LiTT City Hall. Suddenly, he is punched by a fellow character named LindaLuna, played by Linda.

EXCERPT 1: KARMA ARRIVES

1. [LindaLuna punches Karma]
2. *Professor:* Oh nooo! Who is that?
3. *LindaLuna:* You know I had to start. You know I had to start.
4. *Professor:* Hey, Christian.
5. *LindaLuna:* Hi, Christian.
6. *Professor:* Wait, is that your truck over there, Christian?!
7. *Karma:* Yeah.
8. *Professor:* Daaaang. He's ready for the apocalypse [laughing].
9. *Karma:* Actually, I have a better car that's literally a [inaudible] car.

10. *Professor:* Oh you got a whole arsenal. I'm coming to your house for the apocalypse.
11. [laughs]
12. *Bethany:* No 'cause Christian has been working hard.
13. *LindaLuna:* He's ready.

In this, one of the first virtual interactions in the game, we observe what can ostensibly be described as a violent act (line 1). On the surface this can be seen as a manifestation of an activity that is commonly inscribed in games like *GTA5*: unbridled aggression. What we find significant about this initial interaction is how rhetorical moves center the emerging relationality of the gaming environment. First, LindaLuna (played by Linda) appears to consider her punching of Karma as a playful greeting, noting "You know I had to start" (line 3). In our view, this connotes Linda's prior expertise in the game, illustrating that she has an understanding of the predesigned functionality of the game—namely, one that centers violence. However, she does not pursue this aspect of the game further and others in the interaction quickly shift to enthusiastically greeting Karma (played by Christian). We see this shift as a profoundly relational move that privileges a desire to continue the game with a peer over continuing normative practices that we often see in these violent games.

Of importance, the players begin to center Karma's expertise in the game. Namely, we see how Professor (played by Arturo) expresses how impressed he is with Karma's truck, noting that he is "ready for the apocalypse" (line 8). A speculative orientation, building relationally, begins to emerge such that Professor projects into the future by imagining a moment when he would go "to [Karma's] house for the apocalypse" (line 10). Others chime in agreeing that Karma has used his adeptness in the game to become a valuable future collaborator (lines 12–13). The nature of that future gaming relationship is undefined and, indeed, leaves open multiple possible future storylines, including an apocalypse.

From a cooperative action perspective (Goodwin, 2017), this interaction illustrates *an instrumental stance* where attention is drawn to joint meaning-making (line 6), an *epistemic stance* where knowledge is enacted in generative and productive ways (lines 1 and 9), and a *cooperative stance* shows a willingness and desire to sustain activities in progress and in the future (lines 10–12). We propose that this microinteraction illustrates a proleptic arrangement for future engagement and learning within the game (Figure 3.1). Importantly, this is done through playful relationship building for an undefined future activity: a *speculative relationality*. This is to say that our participants strategically privilege continued in-game friendships to set the stage for future collaboration in a virtual world that is still in development.

Figure 3.1. Professor (foreground) and Karma discuss the latter's vehicle.

It is important to note how this moment of speculative relationality quickly became a collective accomplishment for the whole group. On the surface, one may suggest that Professor engages in a correction of LindaLuna's initial greeting of Karma. However, we claim that rather than a correction, it was an illustration of a natural and typical fluid engagement that occurs in a gaming environment such as *GTA5*. Here, in the context of gameplay, we highlight how relationality necessarily depends on meaning-making as a process of mutual engagement, interpreting actions, and shaping of the gaming experience. Jenkins (2004) posits "A focus on meaning [. . .] would emphasize the knowledge and competencies possessed by game players starting with their mastery of the aesthetic conventions that distinguish games from real world experience" (p. 2). In this regard, speculative relationality highlights the aesthetics of collaboration that facilitate opportunities for players to move beyond the intentions of designers, creating openings for fantastical world-building. In the context of this interaction, we point to how the players moved beyond the familiar conventions of competitive gameplay, as traditionally observed in *GTA5*, to the emergence of a storyline that was collaboratively constructed (i.e., surviving an apocalypse).

Speculative Complexity. Across the gaming ecology, we designed opportunities for young and adult participants to build relationships through play that facilitated a proleptic, future-oriented engagement with collective problem-solving. In this subsection, we illustrate an interaction that began roughly at the 1-hour, 42-minute mark of the gaming session. At this point

Speculative Pedagogies in Video Gameplay

the 15 participants had gathered at LiTT City Hall to have an opening introduction activity as well as to begin ideating in-game projects for the building of their virtual world. As a reminder, prior to this session, our group of youth and educators already had met on a weekly basis for approximately 5 weeks, making this the sixth week they were meeting. The following excerpt features our young participant Azel.

EXCERPT 2

1. *Azel:* Uhm. I have a question.
2. *Professor:* Go ahead.
3. *Azel:* 'Cause the more I listen, like. Do we have a position [inaudible] city that has
4. separated from society? Is it something that's entirely its own entity? Like we've had
5. multiple, uhm, cities in America that have separated from the capital state and are fully
6. functional. So I'm wondering if we're taking that route with LiTT city.
7. *Professor:* That's a big hell yeah Azel, right. So. I think so, right? I mean, right. Shouldn't
8. we do that?
9. *Azel:* Uhm, like, the thing is, like it's clearly set, in like an American, like, structure, but I
10. can definitely see it being seen as its own individual separate from the rest of the state.
11. *Professor:* Yes, you know I think Caleb [YEBO partner not present] had this idea as
12. well in respect to the Island. Azel, have you been to the island yet?
13. *Azel:* I have not.
14. *Professor:* We got to get you there because I think that will give you some ideas about
15. how to create a new space that is separate from the city. If that's how I'm understanding
16. what you're saying. Is that right?
17. *Azel:* Yeah, and also like, uhm. Because, I feel Caleb might know more about this,
18. because like in America, there's been historical Black cities that separated and were
19. thriving in all their neighborhoods, but instead of having uhm, lead to the role of
20. segregation. It defeats the purpose of healing one city at a time. Because the concept of
21. trying to heal everything at once without having a proper, uhm, structure and proposition

22. to change. How you guys were talking about LiTT City is solutionist.
23. *Professor:* I love that. I even think Vanessa was trying to lift off some Indigenous
24. communities as well, if I'm not mistaken. Is that right, Vanessa [playing Sunset
25. Sanchez]?
26. *Sunset:* Yeah, definitely.

This interaction within the game illustrates a pivotal moment in the designing of a new city and new world from scratch; or what we initially perceived as being from scratch. Our young participant asks what our collective position is in trying to design a society, albeit virtual, that breaks away from the "American structure"(lines 3–4; 9). Notably, Azel challenges the group to consider how the Westernized aesthetics and infrastructure of the game should be considered in the creation of an environment that truly centers Blackness, Brownness, and Indigeneity (lines 17–20). We see Azel's provocative and generative question as a pivot toward *speculative complexity*, or a pedagogical move toward multiplicity and complexity in how dilemmas are explored in gaming activity. This is speculative in that the goal of learning activity is not predefined but still full of possibility. In this regard, we lean on scholars like Paavola et al. (2012) who urge us to consider "the complexity of modern society which means that people must combine their expertise to solve often unforeseen complex problems because individuals cannot solve problems alone" (p. 1). The complexity described herein relates to the substrates or foundations on top of which one laminates and builds a new world, substrates that are problematic, indeed, but can be transformed and repurposed.

An important contribution is made by Professor (played by Arturo) in his uplifting of Azel's line of questioning as a legitimate and necessary framing for our work within the game (lines 7–8). Professor further offers a pathway for Azel, and others, to pursue alternative ontologies and epistemologies—ways of viewing and acting in the world—to create a world of their choice in the game; centering indigeneity and exploring parts of the gaming geography that are not as "urban" (lines 14–16). Here, we are reminded of the ways in which video gameplay is at its core a complex and dynamic interplay between what is and what can be. Juel Larson and Kampmann Walther (2020) posit that "Games can, like play, be viewed as a dyad divided between a here constituted by the experience when engaging or interacting with the game and a there understood as a future desired state" (p. 622). This is to say that in our work, *speculative complexity* is not solely about moving toward a fantastical future, but a constant oscillating between the past and the future; what our colleagues have called historicity and the leverage of our histories to design toward the future (Bang et al., 2016).

Transdisciplinary Worldmaking. Finally, we explore an instance where our participants engage in transdisciplinary—moving back and forth between disciplines—worldmaking as part of a speculative pedagogical move. Here, at around 1 hour and 20 minutes into the gaming session, we observe a moment where our young participants are ideating potential stories to tell in our city, using the *GTA5* gaming environment as a backdrop for digital storytelling.

EXCERPT 3

Planning for a Digital Story

1. *Professor:* I remember that before we had also talked about RPing a scenario if
2. Columbus were, you know, coming to our spot. What would it look like if Columbus
3. never had a chance to land? What kind of . . .
4. *Karma:* We shoot 'em down.
5. *Professor:* Yes.
6. *Karma:* Couldn't we do something like that like in Caleb's island. Earlier I accidentally
7. flew over there, by accident, and there was like a naval ship next to it.
8. *Professor:* Yeah.
9. *Karma:* I think we can do something like that. Like a bunch of people just spawning their
10. ships or something, and they're coming to the island and maybe we just don't give them
11. that chance. Maybe we just blow them up with new artillery.
12. *Professor:* Yaaass.
13. *Nomi:* I love it.
14. *Azel:* Maybe we can put a Kraken in the water, Matthew. That's [inaudible] my
15. mythology brain.
16. *Professor:* What's a Kraken?
17. *Azel:* It's basically a giant squid. It's a mythological squid that, uhm, crashes pirate ships,
18. uhm. In seventeenth . . .
19. *Professor:* I love that so much.
20. *Karma:* It's an ancient, I believe, Greek.
21. *Azel:* OMG, I think it stemmed from Greek.
22. *Karma:* Yeah, it's from Greek because it was like Poseidon's pet or something. Like that.
23. *Professor:* This is next level. Not that.
24. *Karma:* I know a lot about the mafia, I know a lot about Greek history. I know a lot about
25. just history in general.

26. *Bethany:* I love this [inaudible]
27. *Karma:* It's what I like spending the rest of my day doing if I'm not playing video games.

As our participants explored potential stories to tell in our virtual environment, these quickly moved toward those narrating an alternate history that interrupts colonial violence from the onset (Figure 3.2). Notably, while Professor reintroduces the story idea of reimagining Columbus's arrival (lines 1–3), it was initially conceived of by our young participants in prior conversations. It is for this reason that high schoolers Azel and Karma readily take up the idea in this planning session.

We draw attention to how Azel and Karma begin enacting their expertise in the planning process, namely expertise from inside and outside the game, and from other academic and nonacademic disciplines. Karma, for instance, mentions how the game players could "spawn" ships mimicking those that arrived in the Americas 5 centuries ago (lines 9–11), communicating an adeptness with the gaming environment and in the potential of creating compelling imagery for their film. Secondly, Azel proposes introducing a Kraken in the story, leveraging an understanding of maritime mythology to similarly bring an element of fantastical drama into their creation (lines 14–15; 17). Karma offers support for this idea by contributing his own academic knowledge on the creature, bolstering the transdisciplinary nature of the world-building in the game.

Figure 3.2. "Spawned" of La Niña in the LiTT City Gaming Environment.

In effect, the possibilities of storytelling and worldmaking within LiTT city are pushed to the boundaries by the enactment of knowledges and literacies outside of those inscribed by *GTA5*. Specifically, the assumed default of unmitigated violence (Excerpt 3, line 11) is complemented, and in some ways overwritten, by a more fantastical and unexpected solution to the problem of Columbus's invasion. It is our claim that this collaborative interdisciplinarity was mediated by a project design that centered on relationality and the sociopolitical. Indeed, as we have seen throughout the three vignettes, intentional speculative pedagogical moves have facilitated a repurposing of a tool for networked gaming beyond its designed purpose, amplifying the agency of our participants within and beyond our designed learning environment.

WHAT THE FUTURE HOLDS

This chapter highlighted examples of speculative pedagogical practices as observed in networked video game play that we believe have important implications for how educators can use video games and other play-based practices in their classrooms. We believe that by using video games, educators can strategically lean into and center the expertise of youth, creating new types of relationships that trouble hierarchies in classrooms. By integrating video gaming practices and/or ecologies, educators can design for new possibilities in worldmaking that build across academic disciplinary domains, foster equitable relationships, and support young people and adults in learning how to wrestle with enduring questions that our society faces. In the LiTT Lab, we have noticed that video games have vast storylines, reflecting complex social issues (e.g., racism, misogyny, homophobia, etc.) that we face in our everyday lives, serving as fertile ground for educators and young people to use their respective life experience and expertise in complex discussions about the world they want to build, as a collective. By positioning video games as objects of inquiry, educators signal that these everyday artifacts are worthy of attention, but more importantly, that they also can be interrogated and transformed using skills and tools from multiple disciplines in meaningful ways. For example, as we discussed above, we drew upon the tools of computer science, history, theater, and the language arts to develop an alternative mythology around Columbus's colonization of the Americas through our in-game role play. Lastly, educators in our project have stated simply that by playing video games with young people and on their own, they have been able to learn new ways for integrating them into their classrooms; in other words, educators should be open to the possibilities that these tools and texts can provide!

In our work we have observed activity across three areas: *speculative relationality*, *speculative complexity*, and *transdisciplinary worldmaking*. Our claim is that the tools and participation frameworks of our designed gaming ecology mediated these proleptic practices—organizing learning toward an undefined future and the crafting of a world that centers the hopes and desires of Black, Brown, Queer and other nondominant communities. In our analysis, we see a movement from individual endeavors to collective formations as youth and educators enact their expertise beyond the gaming environment and into visions of what society could be. By engaging in this speculative work, our learning community expanded beyond the limits of our physical world, conjuring social dreams that summon new futures as part of their everyday technological ingenuity.

NOTE

1. GTA5 can be played locally on gaming consoles as well as online using a personal computer. The open-source (sandbox) capabilities of the game allow for enclosed "cities" to be created where, by invitation, communities of gamers can play together.

REFERENCES

Bang, M., Faber, L., Gurneau, J., Marin, A., & Soto, C. (2016). Community-based design research: Learning across generations and strategic transformations of institutional relations toward axiological innovations. *Mind, Culture, and Activity, 23*(1), 28–41. https://doi.org/10.1080/10749039.2015.1087572

Cole, M. (1995). Culture and cognitive development: From cross-cultural research to creating systems of cultural mediation. *Culture & Psychology, 1*(1), 25–54. https://doi.org/10.1177/1354067X9511003

Cortez, A., McKoy, A., & Lizárraga, J. R. (2022). The future of young Blacktivism: Aesthetics and practices of speculative activism in video game play. *Journal of Futures Studies, 26*(3), 53–70. doi: 10.6531/JFS.202203_26(3).0005

DiGiacomo, D. K., & Gutiérrez, K. D. (2016). Relational equity as a design tool within making and tinkering activities. *Mind, Culture, and activity, 23*(2), 141–153.

Engeström, Y. (1991). Non scolae sed vitae discimus: Toward overcoming the encapsulation of school learning. *Learning and Instruction, 1*(3), 243–259.

Gee, J. P. (2007). *Good video games+ good learning: Collected essays on video games, learning, and literacy*. Peter Lang.

Gee, E., Takeuchi, L., & Wartella, E. (Eds.). (2017). *Children and families in the digital age: Learning together in a media saturated culture*. Routledge.

Goodwin, C. (2017). *Co-operative action*. Cambridge University Press.

Gray, K. (2014). *Race, gender, and deviance in Xbox live: Theoretical perspectives from the virtual margins*. Routledge.

Gutiérrez, K. D. (2008). Developing a sociocritical literacy in the third space. *Reading Research Quarterly, 43*(2), 148–164. https://doi.org/10.1598/RRQ.43.2.3

Gutiérrez, K. D. (2016). 2011 AERA presidential address: Designing resilient ecologies: Social design experiments and a new social imagination. *Educational Researcher, 45*(3), 187–196. https://doi.org/10.3102/0013189X16645430

Gutiérrez, K. D. (2018). Social design–based experiments: A proleptic approach to literacy. *Literacy Research: Theory, Method, and Practice, 67*(1), 86–108. https://doi.org/10.1177/2381336918787823

Gutiérrez, K. D., Becker, B. L. C., Espinoza, M. L., Cortes, K. L., Cortez, A., Lizárraga, J. R., Rivero, E., Villegas, K., & Yin, P. (2019). Youth as historical actors in the production of possible futures. *Mind, culture, and activity, 26*(4), 291–308. https://doi.org/10.1080/10749039.2019.1652327

Gutiérrez, K. D., Cortes, K., Cortez, A., DiGiacomo, D., Higgs, J., Johnson, P., Lizárraga, J. R., Mendoza, E., Tien, J., & Vakil, S. (2017). Replacing representation with imagination: Finding ingenuity in everyday practices. *Review of Research in Education, 41*(1), 30–60. https://www.jstor.org/stable/44668686

Gutierrez, K. D., Higgs, J., Lizárraga, J. R., & Rivero, E. (2019). Learning as movement in social design-based experiments: Play as a leading activity. *Human Development, 62*(1–2), 66–82. https://doi.org/10.1159/000496239

Hall, R., & Jurow, A. S. (2015). Changing concepts in activity: Descriptive and design studies of consequential learning in conceptual practices. *Educational Psychologist, 50*(3), 173–189. https://doi.org/10.1080/00461520.2015.1075403

Hooks, B. (2003). *Teaching community: A pedagogy of hope* (Vol. 36). Psychology Press.

Huizinga, J. (1938). *Homo ludens: proeve fleener bepaling van het spel-element der cultuur*. Tjeenk Willink.

Jenkins, H. (2004). The cultural logic of media convergence. *International Journal of Cultural Studies, 7*(1), 33–43.

Juel Larsen, L., & Kampmann Walther, B. (2020). The ontology of gameplay: Toward a new theory. *Games and Culture, 15*(6), 609–631. https://doi.org/10.1177/1555412019825929

Ladson-Billings, G. (2021). I'm here for the hard re-set: Post pandemic pedagogy to preserve our culture. *Equity & Excellence in Education, 54*(1), 68–78. https://doi.org/10.1080/10665684.2020.1863883

Leonard, D. (2003). Live in your world, play in ours: Race, video games, and consuming the other. *Studies in media & information literacy education, 3*(4), 1–9. doi:10.3138/sim.3.4.002

Muñoz, J. E. (2009). *Cruising utopia*. New York University Press.

Paavola, S., Engeström, R., & Hakkarainen, K. (2012). The trialogical approach as a new form of mediation. In A. Moen, A. I. Mørch, & S. Paavola (Eds.), *Collaborative knowledge creation: Practices, tools, concepts* (pp. 1–14). Brill. https://doi.org/10.1007/978-94-6209-004-0_1

Sannino, A., Engeström, Y., & Lemos, M. (2016). Formative interventions for expansive learning and transformative agency. *Journal of the Learning Sciences, 25*(4), 599–633. https://doi.org/10.1080/10508406.2016.1204547

Shaw, A. (2012). Do you identify as a gamer? Gender, race, sexuality, and gamer identity. *New Media & Society, 14*(1), 28–44. https://doi.org/10.1177/1461444811410394

Vygotsky, L. S. (1967). Play and its role in the mental development of the child. *Soviet Psychology*, *5*(3), 6–18.
Williamson, B., Eynon, R., & Potter, J. (2020). Pandemic politics, pedagogies and practices: digital technologies and distance education during the coronavirus emergency. *Learning, Media and Technology*, *45*(2), 107–114. https://doi.org/10.1080/17439884.2020.17616

CHAPTER 4

Abolitionist and Afrofuturist Game Design Pedagogies

Matthew W. Coopilton, Brendesha M. Tynes, Olivia Peace, and De'Andra Johnson

This is a story that could be told by the descendants of today's students, when they become elders. Sitting in the reclaimed ruins of a youth jail, they might say, "Back in the day it seemed like Earth might not have a future, so people made games imagining one. As they played these games together, they kept redesigning them. Doing this helped them get through the hard times and the joyful ones, together. It motivated them to participate in the revolution, and as they did, their games became ceremonies, where we remember our ancestors and what they experienced. We honor how they abolished police and prisons, and we celebrate how they formed symbioses with more-than-human relatives to heal the toxicity of the harm they left behind. So now, we play for our ancestors who were not allowed to." Pausing, the elders would look around them at an unpoliced world, where Black people are thriving, where money no longer exists and love is valued, where there is no gender binary, heteropatriarchy, ableism, or colonialism. They would smile at a group of young people whose needs are met, and would prepare them to play well so they can learn to tend the wildness of a regrowing planet.

    This chapter tells the story of how we are prototyping such worlds and playful learning experiences—not as perfect utopias, but as potentials in how we study, play, design, and organize together. Our goal is to equip young people and those who teach/nurture them to prototype their own unpoliced futures together through critical speculative game design practices. We narrate an ongoing collaborative design process we have been doing with our friends and colleagues, from (1) abolitionist organizing and high school teaching, through (2) the design of one of the first abolitionist video games, called *Kai UnEarthed*, toward (3) the creation of a Critical Game Jam (CGJ) where young people are making their own games about liberated worlds. This is a story of teachers and students becoming game designers, creating our own games for learning in this time of pandemics, uprisings, and climate change. We analyze a key theme in this design process: scaffolding Afrofuturist world-building. This theme is informed by Afrofuturist development (Tynes et al., 2023), a theory and design lens that Dr. Tynes, Matthew, and colleagues have generated to support Black people in using technology to prototype their own liberation.

SUMMARY OF AFROFUTURIST DEVELOPMENT THEORY AND GAME LITERACY CONCEPTS

Afrofuturist development (AD) is a "praxis for Black child, adolescent, and emerging adult thrival" (Tynes et al., 2023). It combines frameworks from Black studies, education, and developmental psychology with insights from Afrofuturism, a pan-African cultural movement focused on race and technology that involves challenging anti-Black notions of the future and imagining pro-Black ones. AD is rooted in Black feminism and emphasizes support for Black LGBTQIA+ people. This makes it relevant to *Kai UnEarthed*, a game featuring Black characters who exist outside the gender binary. It also informed the CGJ, a pro-Black and pro-Queer space. This synergy between Afrofuturism and Queer liberation builds on educators' attempts to develop intersectional Queer futurities within critical literacies learning (Storm & Jones, 2021).

Here are definitions of key concepts that are woven throughout this story; they are distinct but related. This chapter narrates how educators can apply AD in critical speculative pedagogies that nurture *critical game literacies*. These are the skills required to play, analyze, modify, and design games in ways that challenge systemic oppression. They are developed through *metagaming*: everything that surrounds and relates to games, including activities like modding and streaming (Boluk & LeMieux, 2017). They also involve *critical speculative imagination*: "The capacity to conjure, enact, and rehearse future worlds free from oppression" (Tynes et al., 2023). This imagination is an important part of *abolitionism*, the movement to abolish police, prisons, and related carceral infrastructure, including prison-like discipline practices in schools. The abolitionist movement has grown in the wake of uprisings against police over the past decade. Educators such as Bettina Love (2019) are developing abolitionist pedagogies, and scholars have argued that abolitionism must be a part of critical digital literacy learning (Garcia & de Roock, 2021). Abolitionism also involves building futures where police and prisons are not needed or wanted. For that reason, abolitionist pedagogies often include *critical world-building*, the process of imagining a liberated world, including its ecology, modes of production, cultures, technologies, spiritualities, and so forth. Educators have imagined the creation of learning environments as world-building, which they sometimes call worldmaking; Shirin Vossoughi described worldmaking as, "The creative process of imagining, embodying, and midwifing possible futures in the here-and-now" (personal communication, 2022).

ABOUT THE AUTHORS

Dr. Brendesha M. Tynes and De'Andra Johnson are researchers focused on race and technology, and Olivia Peace is an Academy Award–winning interdisciplinary artist and film director. All three are Black intellectuals who engage with Afrofuturism. Matthew Coopilton is an abolitionist teacher, researcher, and designer who embodies Queer futurities in collaboration with Afrofuturists; they are not Black, so they do not claim to be an Afrofuturist.

SUMMARY OF OUR PARTICIPATORY DESIGN RESEARCH PROCESS

We designed the CGJ to embody and study aspects of Afrofuturist development, drawing on what we learned while designing *Kai UnEarthed* and previous abolitionist pedagogies. In that sense, this chapter describes a decade-long participatory design research process (Bang & Vossoughi, 2016). In collaboration with participants, we codesigned learning environments and artifacts embedded with theories about how people learn and studied people's experiences interacting with them, iteratively refining our pedagogies, designs, and theories based on our findings. The following sections summarize several iterations of this process.

ABOLITIONIST TEACHING AND ORGANIZING

Matthew taught Language Arts and Social Studies from 2008–2018 in a high school reengagement program serving young people who had been pushed out of Seattle-area schools, often because of racist and carceral school discipline policies. They and their colleagues facilitated abolitionist pedagogies, including transformative justice practices to resolve conflict without involving police. They also supported and marched with their students when they took action against police, prisons, and Seattle's youth jail, and they became involved in several related movements such as Occupy Wall Street.

These movements involved collective study and strategizing; Matthew and their friends and students wrote blog posts and made zines that helped cohere movement strategies. However, as social media platforms intensified their algorithmic controls, it became difficult to sustain these conversations, and they began to turn toward other mediums to theorize and strategize. Walidah Imarisha and adrienne maree brown (2015) offered one solution, reconceptualizing organizing as a kind of visionary fiction-writing, curating freedom dreams (Kelley, 2002) from current movements to imagine how they might unfold in the future. Inspired by this, Matthew switched from blogging to writing visionary fiction, assuming that speculative stories might hold peoples' attention more than theoretical prose. Also, speculative conversations are harder to surveil since they involve speaking in code; they imagine what people *could* do to liberate ourselves instead of telling oppressive forces what we are *planning* to do.

A confluence of events then inspired Matthew to focus on gaming as a medium for nurturing such stories. Many of their students were dynamic gamer intellectuals; for a Language Arts project, a Somali student wrote a brilliant design document for a first-person adventure game with anticolonial and antifascist themes. Matthew also began to design critical digital literacy games in the classroom, like *Facebook in Real Life*: Students imagined the platform had been abolished and they passed analog notes back and forth, liking and commenting on them, reflecting on what they would and would not miss about it.

In the wake of the 2014 antipolice protests, conversations emerged about how to cultivate joy to avoid burnout, and Matthew's friends began to propose games as a way to do this. When people blockaded the entrance to the port of Seattle to prevent an oil rig from shipping to the Arctic, Matthew codesigned a game prompting people on the picket line to describe what the rig could become if it stayed there permanently and were detoxified; they imagined the action as a portal from a liberated future. Similarly, organizers from the movement to abolish Seattle's youth jail asked Matthew's students what they would want to replace the jail with, and incorporated these ideas into movement strategies. In 2016, Matthew joined the ARTifACTS collective, a group of activist artists and theater makers; they helped design games for demonstrations and block parties outside of the youth jail, imagining what could replace it once it is abolished. ARTifACTS designed an alternate reality theater game called *Where Once There Were Cages*, imagining that the crowd is contacted by their descendants who live in a world without prisons, and that they are confused by why people back in the 21st century used to cage people (see Figure 4.1). ARTifACTS members acted out their attempt to decipher cryptic pictograms these descendants sent them, imagining these as complex emojis. They invited students and friends to respond to these prompts with hip-hop, dance, poetry, and theater pieces.

All of these activities inspired Matthew to imagine the world that would eventually become *Kai UnEarthed*. In this world, young people participate in a rite of passage ceremony where they become wildtenders, people who help a regrowing planet heal from the intergenerational traumas left behind by the capitalist era. During the ceremony, wildtenders receive energy tattoos that allow them to communicate with each other and with more-than-human relatives. These relatives include species like post-arachnids, spiders with an independent intranet that were bioengineered by the last capitalists

Figure 4.1. *Where Once There Were Cages.*

and then mutated, escaped, and reorganized themselves in feral ways as they adapted to climate change. Earth has become un-Earthed, feeling like an alien planet. Matthew began imagining young people preparing for the coming-of-age ritual by unearthing artifacts from the 21st century while exploring the ruins of a youth jail. They imagined this could become the basis for a video game.

However, instead of designing this game themself, Matthew invited their students further into the process through a series of participatory world-building activities in 2018. They invited students to write about wildtenders encountering artifacts they left behind, and several students wrote about them unearthing cell phones and basketball shoes, asking what these distracted people from. Matthew also invited them to develop details about the rite of passage. It involves being bitten by a post-arachnid, which makes someone hallucinate their ancestors' experiences. Students then wrote about how they would want to be remembered as ancestors in such visions, and illustrated what they thought the tattoos and post-arachnids should look like. Matthew facilitated two iterations of this participatory design process with two different classes, and their coworkers helped them improve the prompts for the second one by reflecting critically together on the results of the first one. Inspired by these activities, Matthew decided to attend the University of Southern California's PhD program in urban education to study critical digital literacies and game-based learning.

THEORIZING AFROFUTURIST DEVELOPMENT

During their time at USC, Dr. Brendesha Tynes was Matthew's advisor, and she was collaborating with colleagues at the Center for Empowered Learning and Development with Technology (CELDTech) to construct the theory of Afrofuturist development. Matthew joined these efforts, reading interdisciplinary Afrofuturist theories to support the team's theoretical synthesis and the further development of the games started in Seattle. As a design lens for creating learning experiences, AD involves nurturing technology-enhanced learning ecologies where young Black people can write and design themselves and their communities into possible liberated futures. The theory outlines 10 core principles that focus on "Black and/or Africana learning and development in homes, schools, communities, online, and at work across developmental stages" (Tynes et al., 2023). This theoretical work came together in synergy with the next iterations of Matthew's game design praxis, nurturing the development of the Seattle world-building into *Kai UnEarthed*.

DESIGNING AN ABOLITIONIST VIDEO GAME USING PLAYCENTRIC METHODS

Matthew took MFA game design classes in the USC Games program, where they met Olivia Peace and Claire Hu, and the three of them collaborated to turn the wildtender world into a video game, which can be found at KaiUnEarthed.com (see Figure 4.2). This is an interactive storytelling game where players role-play as Kai, an Afro-Indigenous-Asian teenager who is training to become a wildtender with their crush, Tempest. (Kai uses they/them pronouns.) Through branching narratives, the two face the choice of whether to fall in love in the reclaimed ruins of a youth jail. Through an interactive journaling process, Kai fantasizes about earning energy tattoos so they can use them to communicate intimately with Tempest. To do this, the player must guide Kai through meditations where they face their anxieties around the ceremony, stemming from the fact that one of their wildtender parents was killed by a mutant animal. They have to negotiate with one of their surviving parents, who does not want them to become a wildtender. There are multiple possible endings, including a walking-simulator-style minigame where Kai and Tempest do the ceremony together, navigating a 3D forest to encounter artifacts from the 21st century entangled in glowing

Figure 4.2. Screenshot from a prototype of *Kai UnEarthed*.

Your classmates are taking notes on an old image of the Minneapolis police station burning during the 2020 rebellion.

post-arachnid webs. When the player engages with enough artifacts, a post-arachnid bites them, opening a psychedelic time tunnel where they descend through multiple versions of the same room at different points in history, looking for unearthed artifacts that reveal a story of late-capitalist catastrophe, revolution, and healing.

This video game design process began as a project for classes with media artist Andreas Kratky and game designer Tracy Fullerton, where we learned playcentric design methods (Fullerton, 2019). These involve setting a player experience goal, creating a prototype of the game, and then playtesting it with players to see if their experiences are consistent with the goal (Fullerton, 2019). We wanted players to experience critical speculative imagination, and a sense that their decisions matter. After creating an initial prototype of the story branches with Post-it Notes, we created rough digital prototypes in the game engines Twine and Unity. We each led one aspect of the design process—programming and user interface design, art, and narrative design—while helping each other with the other aspects. This collaborative project-based learning created overlapping zones of proximal development (Vygotsky, 1978) where we learned a range of skills, including coding and using more features of the game engines. The process required us to overcome our perfectionistic tendencies and to be vulnerable, asking for feedback on prototypes while they were still rough so we could improve core aspects of our design before polishing the details.

Continuing the playcentric method, we paid most attention to feedback that showed us ways the game could better support our core player experience goals, as well as goals for specific minigames/scenes. We realized that we needed to better integrate the game's story, its world-building, and its game mechanics (interactive elements and challenges/objectives). Players liked the story, and enjoyed exploring an unpoliced future, but they did not experience the sense of shaping the world that we wanted them to experience. Informed by the AD framework, we wanted players to be able to write themselves into this liberated future, but we were limited in our technical capacity to code and model digital elements they could actively shape. To solve this problem, we created rough prototypes of new features that seemed within the scope of our abilities to produce. We discussed these until we came to a consensus as a team: We decided to pair the digital game with an analog journal that players can modify, and Olivia and Matthew designed this, mentored by Andreas.

The journal does not just include writing prompts, it is also multimodal, including its own game mechanics that prompt players to scribble, draw, tear the page, trace paths, put soil on the page, and draw on one's own body (see Figure 4.3). We conceptualized it as a kind of haptic interface. Its prompts and challenges correspond with those on the computer screen, with each medium directing the player back to the other one to complete activities. We added embodied elements to help alleviate anxieties some players might feel around the abstraction of writing, and to make the game feel less like a traditional school assignment. We want players to treat the journal the way wildtenders treat all things—as animate, contingent, decomposable, and impurely implicated in a web of unknown relations. We also want players to build a personal relationship with their journal, with it becoming a sharable record of their own journey, extending the game beyond the computer, and opening up multiplayer possibilities when players compare journals (which Kai and Tempest do on the screen). We integrated these multimodal mechanics with the game's narrative and world-building, imagining that the journal connects to the computer and both connect to the future wildtender world through bioenergetic networks of post-arachnid webs. The game's trailer video shows how the journal and computer-based mechanics relate.

In the narrative of *Kai UnEarthed*, the decomposition of the journal and the computer opens up space for the future to grow from our composted world and texts (Figure 4.3). The wildtenders and post-arachnids encounter the Internet and players' journals as mulched texts, remixed and recomposed by nonhuman beings (de Freitas & Truman, 2021). This is analogous to how people today encounter ancient texts—full of decomposed gaps, glitches, holes, and translation errors that open up creative possibilities for poetic reinterpretation and reiteration.

We also designed the journal to help situate *Kai UnEarthed* within critical game literacy learning spaces. Game literacy educators often position games as texts within learning environments, with gameplay analogous to reading, and game design analogous to writing; they invite people to play like designers, similar to how language arts teachers invite people to read like writers (Gee, 2013). Metacognition in language arts is similar to metagaming. Education researchers have shown that playing like a designer through

Figure 4.3. A page in the journal from *Kai UnEarthed*.

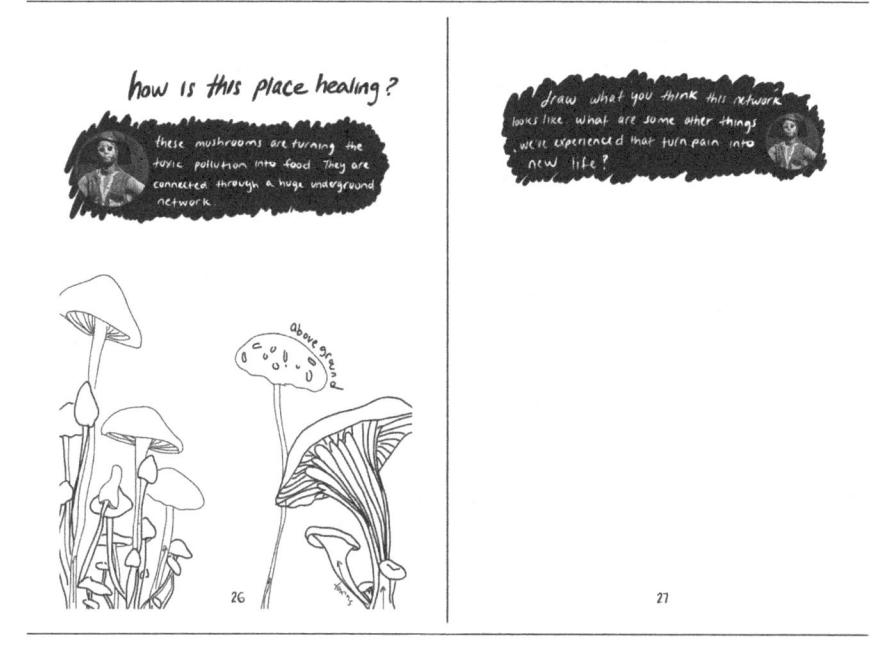

modifying games, probing glitches, and relating games to other media can help young people develop as historical actors producing possible futures (Gutiérrez et al., 2019). Building on these findings, the journal feature invites players to modify *Kai UnEarthed*, encouraging them to think like designers, and its analog metagaming interface invites this without the potentially intimidating barriers involved in technical game design tools.

At the time of this writing, we are still finishing the full video game version of *Kai UnEarthed*, making improvements based on playtest feedback from young people; again, we will focus on refining features most essential to meeting our player experience goals. In the meantime, we released a version of our interactive narrative prototype made in Twine, integrated with the journal. It can be played online in a web browser at https://kaiunearthed.itch.io/, making it accessible on school Chromebooks, older computers, and mobile devices. We hope it might appeal to young adult fiction readers who may not be into video games, and that it might contribute to a growing genre of Queer indie games made with Twine. It could also serve as a mentor text for people who want to make abolitionist games but do not yet have the capacity to code and create 3D art. We incorporated the full version of the video game into the Critical Game Jam.

DESIGNING AN AFROFUTURIST CRITICAL GAME JAM (CGJ)

Along with our colleagues at the USC Center for Empowered Learning and Development with Technology, all of the authors of this chapter were involved in organizing the CGJ. This is part of research that Matthew is leading for their doctoral dissertation, focused on the following research question: How can one design learning spaces, games, and game design activities that support critical game literacies and Afrofuturist development? To answer this question, we have designed and are studying the game jam, beginning with a week-long series of online workshops in the summer of 2021. Participant-researchers played, analyzed, and have begun to design games related to themes such as Black liberation and abolitionism. In particular, we have

- imagined liberated futures and reflected on our capacities to create these futures;
- critically analyzed existing games we play;
- reflected on how and why we play these games;
- imagined what kinds of games we would like to play and design;
- engaged in collective design prompts, discussions, presentations, and prototyping activities;
- engaged in interactive workshops with guest facilitators on critical character design and world-building;
- playtested prototypes of abolitionist games, including a new version of the full video game prototype of *Kai UnEarthed*;
- began to design games that could help challenge systemic oppression;
- gave feedback on each other's game ideas; and
- reflected on our learning process and gave feedback on the learning activities.

We designed loose curriculum scaffolding to support these activities and also altered it and improvised in real-time in response to learners' needs and desires.

Consistent with AD theory (Tynes et al., 2023), our team of participant-researchers was composed of educators and designers with extensive experience and training around how to support young Black people in learning and development. We put out a call for new codesigners to learn with us, and nine people in their early 20s chose to join. Most of them self-identified as Black, four as nonbinary, three as men, and one as a woman. We studied our shared learning experiences during these activities, through a range of research methods. These methods and findings will be shared in future publications, while this chapter focuses on the decisions we made in our design process, in the hope that other educators might be able to build on our practice while we continue to reflect on it ourselves.

Olivia and Matthew positioned the prototype of *Kai UnEarthed* as a proleptic design demonstration to suggest what kind of abolitionist design processes are possible, and to role-model how to conduct a playcentric design process (Fullerton, 2019; Vossoughi et al., 2021). We aimed to improve *Kai UnEarthed* by playtesting it, but we also wanted the process to be reciprocal, offering participants our support in creating their own games and offering our feedback on their prototypes in response to their feedback on ours. Also, while designing *Kai UnEarthed*, we found that there were a range of learning activities and design prompts that we wanted to incorporate into the game itself, some of them informed by the previous iterations in Seattle, but we did not have the capacity to include them all. Instead, we decided to move these activities to a broader metagaming culture we want to cultivate around *Kai UnEarthed*, in a move analogous to our decision to create the journal. The CGJ and our research on it became part of this metagame.

We hope this design process will generate other ideas for metagaming as well, such as abolitionist Tik Tok gameplay videos or transmedia storytelling. These could incorporate *Kai UnEarthed* and other abolitionist games that CGJ participants and friends are developing currently. To help cohere such possibilities, some of us launched an Abolitionist Gaming Network with a Discord server, workshops, and game nights. Past research has found that affinity spaces formed around shared passions can be environments where relative strangers build trust and learn from each other, bridging the gap between playing and designing games (Gee & Hayes, 2010). Our goal is to build an affinity space around a shared passion for abolitionism. Some participants in the game jam have chosen to develop their own concepts into playable prototypes. Others created pitches to their communities, imagining games that could be developed and played if people organize to change society and the game industry to make space for this kind of freedom dreaming (Kelley, 2002).

GAME DESIGN AS AFROFUTURIST WORLD-BUILDING

The Afrofuturist development framework involves designing contexts where people learn and play in ways that center their full humanity, fostering "Black aliveness and innovations of speculative futures void of oppressions" (Tynes et al., 2023). When designing such environments, educators should consider "the innovative use of technology for the purposes of liberation and world-building" (Tynes et al., 2023). This emphasis on critical world-building supports critical game literacy learning spaces where Black people can create game worlds to prototype liberated futures.

While learning to create various media might support these goals, games are particularly appropriate because they are ideological worlds (Squire, 2011), condensed models of the real world that focus attention on specific social dynamics and systems. The decisions around which aspects of the world to highlight in a game are ideological ones; they can either reproduce or challenge systemic oppression (Everett & Watkins, 2008). Moreover, games are tools for surmising the possibilities of different worlds, creating "niches in the real world" for these to inhabit (Gee, 2013, p. 153). For example, Cortez et al. (2022) found that young Black people developed speculative, abolitionist, and Afrofuturist worldmaking practices inside video games after the police murdered George Floyd.

A core theme that runs through our design process is that critical world-building can scaffold various aspects of abolitionist and Afrofuturist design-thinking. The participatory world-building in Seattle generated the world of *Kai UnEarthed*, which scaffolded the rest of our process designing the game. Then, that process scaffolded building the world of the CGJ, which, in turn, is a space where people are learning how to build Afrofuturist game worlds. The rest of this chapter analyzes this process.

From Abolitionist World-Building to Kai UnEarthed

While designing *Kai UnEarthed*, Olivia and Matthew adapted methods from the World Building Media Lab at the USC School of Cinematic Arts, which conducts world-building to support trans-media storytelling. The lab designs research-based, detailed worlds before writing stories, constructing a "space for multiple stories to emerge logically, organically and coherently from the coding" of the world (World Building Media Lab, n.d.). Similarly, we want *Kai UnEarthed* to be one among many possible stories that could emerge from the future world that Matthew and their friends and students imagined. While the lab aims to innovate new approaches to cinematic arts, we are applying similar methods from below and to the left, creating an open-source *UnEarthed* fictional/cinematic universe that other abolitionist designers, educators, and organizers can add to. *Kai UnEarthed* is one media project set in this world, but hopefully not the last. Our design process around it illustrates how world-building can scaffold collaborative and open-source storytelling.

Before writing a narrative or designing game mechanics, Matthew used Unity to create an explorable 3D world modeling the ruins of a youth jail that had been reclaimed and turned into a space called Abolition Playfield. They scanned and incorporated lore from the participatory design efforts in Seattle, for example, the emoji pictograms from *Where Once There Were Cages*. They then asked Olivia, Claire, and other friends what games and ceremonies might happen in such a world, and this began the brainstorming process that generated *Kai UnEarthed*.

Tracy Fullerton warned us that centering world-building in such ways might overshadow other key aspects of narrative design such as relatable conflicts and relationships among characters, which science fiction writer

Maureen McHugh told us are especially important to reach a young adult audience. We took this advice to heart and designed a game that focuses on relationships, mirroring young adult interactive fiction and Queer dating simulator games; Olivia's expertise, having directed the adolescent coming-of-age film *Tahara,* helped us get there.

While Matthew initially had been wary of taking up too much space in offering an already-developed world, we found that starting with world-building helped scaffold our collaborative design process: Because Olivia and Claire had a world to start with, it allowed them to jump right into narrative and user interface design based on the generative constraints of the world. It also allowed us to design game mechanics that make the world feel like a sentient character, not just a backdrop. Reflecting on this afterward, Olivia and Matthew realized that world-building is important scaffolding for learning critical design skills. When learners are asked to start from nothing, they sometimes freeze or start comparing their work to other peoples'. Because of past embarrassment and internalized oppression, many will not participate unless an environment is set for them, encouraging the creative process.

We also reflected on how our world-building process supported Afrofuturist visioning. For Olivia, Afrofuturism involves imagining forms of joy that exist outside of the political world of racialized capitalism and its lack, stinginess, absurdity, hatred, and fear. Our shared goal with *Kai UnEarthed* is to give people a different world to start with; on our website, we argue that it will be one of many abolitionist games that resonate with graffiti from the George Floyd Uprising: "another end of the world is possible." One goal of the CGJ was to support young adults in developing games that imagine such possibilities.

From *Kai UnEarthed* to the Critical Game Jam (CGJ)

We designed the CGJ informed by Afrofuturist development (Tynes et al., 2023) as a design lens, drawing on what we had learned from the previous iterations of abolitionist design described above. Olivia and Matthew began the curriculum design process with a reflexive, recorded conversation reflecting on our design process around *Kai UnEarthed*. We reflected on aspects of our own learning process that might inform the design of the broader learning ecology.

Through that conversation, we decided to scaffold world-building as a main feature of the game jam workshops. Olivia argued that the design prompts for the jam needed to be specific and generative constraints so that participants would not succumb to the tendency in the game industry to recreate existing game genre conventions. Echoing Bang and Vossoughi's (2016) argument that design-thinking is widely distributed, they argued that our prompts should validate the ways people already design games in their everyday lives, challenging internalized oppression and rethinking what games can be. In response to this, Matthew facilitated a playcentric design workshop where participants identified player experience goals drawn from their own sociocultural contexts, which they shared in a collaborative Google Doc. For example, Madu (one of the participants) said they wanted to make a game that felt like a Nigerian graduation party.

Olivia and Matthew decided that we should focus on scaffolding *critical* world-building in particular because otherwise people might limit their imagination of what is possible, using games to model and critique existing oppression or to narrate existing trauma rather than to model liberation and healing. People often perform being a good game designer, making games they think people want to play, and when we come from oppressed communities, this sometimes means making games about our oppression with no broader horizon. To address this, we positioned *Kai UnEarthed* as a demonstration of what is possible. However, in consultation with abolitionist game designers Brianna Mims, Christina Lelon, and Cecilia Sweet-Coll, we realized that we should put it toward the end of the workshops so that it would not set the expectation that the games people design need to involve coding and 3D graphics. We invited them to playtest their own analog game earlier in the week; it scaffolds speculative abolitionist world-building by structuring a process for groups to imagine communities without police and prisons. We all played the game and gave feedback on it, and we invited participants to incorporate aspects of the worlds they brainstormed into their own games.

The CGJ's scaffolding supported participants in imagining game worlds that depart from existing game industry conventions. For example, in response to a design prompt, a Brazilian participant named Gabriel imagined a game based on the Quilombos, the communities of enslaved people in Brazil who escaped and built autonomous camps at war with the plantations (similar to the maroons in the Caribbean). In a brainstorming document, he wrote:

> It got me thinking about a game like *Banished*. What if we could run and escape through a portal and build a new settlement. But in a new world, maybe escape to the future, maybe build some kind of Wakanda. Then send back expeditions and save our brothers without violence. In *Banished* you're only focused on building your society for balance, without militarization. The game could have a building like a museum where they teach about the history of Black and Latinx people. Even the buildings could be aesthetically different, inspired in Afrofuturism.

Just as we began with an unpoliced world and then created *Kai UnEarthed* around it, Gabriel responded to the world-building prompts of the game jam by imagining a world that could be the basis for an Afrofuturist game.

RECOMMENDATIONS FOR EDUCATORS

Based on the experiences narrated in this chapter, we offer these prompts as recommendations:

- *Get involved in abolitionist organizing, and ask your students what could replace youth jails.* This could help expand your critical speculative imagination, and theirs.
- *Start with world-building and use it to scaffold game design learning.* This might lower the barrier of entry for becoming a game designer, for both you and your students.
- *Imagining the future can be overwhelming, so scaffolding is crucial (e.g., design prompts and initial models of worlds).* Critical prompts can also help students avoid uncritically recreating existing game genres. You can invite your students to build on Kai UnEarthed if you want to (the Twine version runs on Chromebooks: https://kaiunearthed.itch.io/). Or you can make your own world for them to build on. Or you can provide prompts for them to create their own worlds.
- *Start with paper prototyping, so that intimidation around digital tools does not interrupt the brainstorming process.* Analog and digital games are equally valid. If you decide to prototype digital games, use game engines and templates like Twine and Unity to scaffold the design process. Be sure to remind students to assess all tools critically, especially around character design; many existing digital character templates reproduce racist, anti-Black, sexist, fatphobic, ableist, and colonial stereotypes and need to be modified or replaced.
- *Games can be used like reading and writing prompts as part of a broader learning environment, rather than as self-contained content delivery technologies.* Kai UnEarthed is a videogame but it is also a writing workshop consisting of a journal with accompanying multimedia meditative writing prompts. You can use it the same way you would invite students to read, discuss, and write about a short story or novel.

CONCLUSION

The design process described in this chapter was held carefully through multiple relationships and groups over many years, and across these contexts, abolitionist and Afrofuturist game design pedagogies have become a consistent and potent practice, reflecting a desire for critical game literacies adequate to this historical moment. This suggests that critical game design is an important speculative pedagogy that educators should consider. It is a way that young people can prototype futures where Black people—and all people—can thrive. We have found that scaffolding critical world-building is one way to do this, and we hope other educators and designers will build on our experiences to develop your own forms of playful abolitionist learning and Afrofuturist development.

REFERENCES

Bang, M., & Vossoughi, S. (2016). Participatory design research and educational justice: Studying learning and relations within social change making. *Cognition and Instruction, 34*(3), 173–193. doi:10.1080/07370008.2016.1181879

Boluk, S., & LeMieux, P. (2017). *Metagaming: Playing, competing, spectating, cheating, trading, making, and breaking videogames* (Vol. 53). University of Minnesota Press.

Cortez, A., McKoy, A., & Lizárraga, J. R. (2022). The future of young Blacktivism: Aesthetics and practices of speculative activism in video game play. *Journal of Futures Studies, 26*(3), 53–70. doi:10.6531/JFS.202203_26(3).0005

de Freitas, E., & Truman, S. E. (2021). New empiricisms in the Anthropocene: Thinking with speculative fiction about science and social inquiry. *Qualitative Inquiry, 27*(5), 522–533. https://doi.org/10.1177/1077800420943643

Everett, A., & Watkins, S. C. (2008). The power of play: The portrayal and performance of race in video games. In K. Salen (Ed.), *The ecology of games: Connecting youth, games, and learning* (pp. 141–166). MIT Press.

Fullerton, T. (2019). *Game design workshop: A playcentric approach to creating innovative games*. AK Peters/CRC Press.

Garcia, A., & de Roock, R. S. (2021). Civic dimensions of critical digital literacies: Towards an abolitionist lens. *Pedagogies: An International Journal, 16*(2), 187–201. https://doi.org/10.1080/1554480X.2021.1914058

Gee, J.P. (2013). *Good video games + good learning: Collected essays on video games, learning, and literacy* (2nd ed.). Peter Lang.

Gee, J. P., & Hayes, E. R. (2010). *Women and gaming: The sims and 21st century learning*. Springer.

Gutiérrez, K., Becker, B., Espinoza, M., Cortes, K., Cortez, A., Lizárraga, J., Rivero, E., Villegas, K., & Yin, P. (2019). Youth as historical actors in the production of possible futures. *Mind, Culture and Activity, 26*(4), 291–308. https://doi.org/10.1080/10749039.2019.1652327

Imarisha, W., & brown, a. m. (2015). *Octavia's brood: Science fiction stories from social justice movements*. AK Press.

Kelley, R. D. G. (2002). *Freedom dreams: The Black radical imagination*. Beacon Press.

Love, B. L. (2019). *We want to do more than survive: Abolitionist teaching and the pursuit of educational freedom*. Beacon Press.

Squire, K. (2011). *Video games and learning: Teaching and participatory culture in the digital age*. Teachers College Press.

Storm, S., & Jones, K. (2021). Queering critical literacies: Disidentifications and queer futurity in an afterschool storytelling and roleplaying game. *English Teaching:*

Practice & Critique, 20(4), pp. 534–548. https://doi.org/10.1108/ETPC-10-2020-0131

Tynes, B., Hamilton, M., Schuschke, J., & Stewart, A. (2023). Toward a developmental science that meets the challenges of 2044: Afrofuturist development theory, design and praxis. In D. P. Witherspoon & G. L. Stein (Eds.), *Diversity and Developmental Science—Bridging the Gaps Between Research, Practice, and Policy*. Springer, Cham. Preprint available for free at https://psyarxiv.com/6nj4g/

Vossoughi, S., Davis, N. R., Jackson, A., Echevarria, R., Muñoz, A., & Escudé, M. (2021). Beyond the binary of adult versus child centered learning: Pedagogies of joint activity in the context of making. *Cognition and Instruction, 39*(3), 211–241. https://doi.org/10.1080/07370008.2020.1860052

Vygotsky, L. S. (1978). *Mind in society: The development of higher psychological processes*. M. Cole, V. John-Steiner, S. Scribner, & E. Souberman, Eds. Harvard University Press. https://doi.org/10.2307/j.ctvjf9vz4

World Building Media Lab. (n.d.). Home. http://worldbuilding.usc.edu/

Part II

KINDLING COMMUNITY

CHAPTER 5

Dreaming Together
Exploring Youth–Adult Partnerships in Speculative Educational Design

Lauren Leigh Kelly

As a high school teacher and teacher educator, I spent a great deal of time advocating for attention to youth culture and imagination in the development of pedagogies that would support young people's freedom dreaming (Kelley, 2002) toward the building of their civic and social futures (New London Group, 1996). This approach to speculative education involves "imagin[ing] oneself or one's community into new modes of living and interacting" (Mirra & Garcia, 2020, p. 302) by engaging in critical reflection and dialogue about what has come before, what exists now, and what could be. Indeed, the latter, developing visions for a future free of oppression and injustice, is one of the goals of critical pedagogy and social justice education. Yet, I eventually came to realize that schools, as they currently exist, are limited in their ability to truly cultivate the type of "speculative dreaming" (Mirra & Garcia, 2022, p. 371) required for young people to engage in radical future-building. Thus, I began a project that invited young people to dream together to create a youth-led teaching and learning community rooted in youth imagination through art, activism, and popular culture.

Building on theories of youth speculative civic literacies (Mirra & Garcia, 2020) and social design experimentation (Gutiérrez & Jurow, 2016), this project examines how activist-oriented BIPOC youth engage in "generative world-making" (Garcia & Mirra, 2021) in their collaborative design processes. This project moves beyond the study of how youth imagine their social and educational futures by also exploring how they build toward these futures in their design and facilitation of a youth-led education, arts, and activist community.

In developing this initiative, I knew I would have to contend with my own positionalities as an educator, scholar, and adult as I worked with youth to engage in critical reflection and action, or praxis (Freire, 2000) regarding how they perceived their social and educational worlds and how they imagined their futures. What I did not expect was how much the presence of adults, including myself, would both limit and facilitate the youth leaders' speculative processes. As Garcia and Mirra (2021) stated, young people's speculative civic literacies "offer spaces for contesting and moving beyond the confines of adult-imposed" systems (p. 646); yet the presence of adults in these same spaces can contradict the goals of youth speculative design and future-building. This chapter thus explores the tensions and opportunities that can arise in youth–adult partnerships within speculative education projects.

Problems and Possibilities in Intergenerational, Social Justice Partnerships

Scholars in the fields of youth[1] activism and youth voice have begun to explore the role of adults in youth activism and leadership work, particularly in areas where youth participation is often limited or restricted (Kirshner, 2008). Across this body of literature, a distinction has emerged between programs in which youth are the recipients of adult leadership and facilitation and those in which youth work in partnership with adults. Zeldin et al. (2017) described the latter, youth–adult partnerships, as those in which multiple youth and adults collaborate in dialogue and action "as intergenerational partners, with interactions grounded in the principles of reciprocity, co-learning, and shared control" (p. 852). Whereas mainstream approaches to youth work often take the form of adult facilitation and guidance, with young people being apprenticed into existing forms of civic action or participation, youth–adult partnerships involve joint work in which youth and adults participate collaboratively, sharing power and responsibility in both decision-making and action (Kirshner, 2008; Zeldin, et al., 2017). As Zeldin et al. (2017) stated, "societal traditions, structural forces, community conditions, and age-related stereotypes limit the opportunities for youth to engage in collective leadership, especially those young people from the most vulnerable populations" (p. 871). Thus, youth–adult collaborations offer a powerful form of resistance against structures of oppression and provide a space for youth voice and agency to thrive.

In their cross-national study of youth participating in community-based programs, Zeldin et al. (2017) found that youth who are involved in decision-making and supported by adults in partnership are likely to demonstrate high levels of civic development and agency. In particular, the youth in their study reflected a significant link between partnerships with adults and their feelings of empowerment and community connectedness. Ramey et al. (2017) reported that youth participation in youth–adult partnerships increases their sense of credibility and legitimacy. Research also has found that partnering with adults can provide young people with increased feelings of support, safety, and belonging (Van Steenis & Kirshner, 2020) and that youth are more likely to "flourish when they experience the freedom to make decisions and carry them out, while concurrently, experiencing trust and power sharing from the adults with whom they are interacting" (Zeldin et al., 2017, p. 870). Additionally, involving both youth and adults in programmatic responsibilities allows for the various stakeholders to access "a full range of human resources" (Camino, 2005, p. 77), including resources only accessible to adults (Ramey et al., 2017).

Scholars have described youth–adult partnerships as positively impactful on young people's development (Mitra, 2009; Van Steenis & Kirshner, 2020), necessary for community-building (Camino, 2005), and "optimal for adolescent health and empowerment" (Zeldin et al., 2017, p. 852). However, research in this field has also unearthed the complexities and limitations of such partnerships in practice. For example, adults' reluctance to "overshadow" (Camino, 2005, p. 77) youth leadership or "undercut" (Larson & Walker, 2010, p. 342) youth ownership can compromise the success of a project. As a result, many youth–adult partnerships struggle with the choice between youth learning through trial and error and adults taking on more responsibilities in areas where youth lack experience, especially when facing "the complex demands of social action" (Kirshner, 2008 p. 89).

In addition to the logistical challenges involved in youth–adult partnerships, research also has highlighted the difficulties that adults often have in abdicating power and control to youth, especially in regards to decision-making (Ramey et al., 2017), since youth are not typically framed by adults as leaders or decision-makers. In fact, as Baldridge (2019) explained, "Adults, who designate the standards and conditions by which youth develop, shape the construction of youth as 'other,' and thus youth in America have often been framed as problems and burdens to society" (p. 15). Even when adults are willing to relinquish control to youth, existing structures of authority often lead to an unequal distribution of power within youth–adult partnerships (Mitra, 2009). Ramey et al. (2017) raised a concern that "in any [youth] organization that maintains adult-created mandates and structures, equal decision-making power and access to resources might be impossible" (p. 41). Larson and Walker (2010) similarly found that while youth workers have the freedom to decenter adult leadership in youth–adult partnerships, they cannot entirely relinquish the role of adult authority since there is a "tension between cultivating a democratic ethos and being the 'adult' who serves as the guardian and guarantor of that ethos" (p. 343). This tension also can cause youth to be hesitant or distrusting of their power to make decisions in youth–adult partnerships due to the presence of adult authority and youth's previous experiences with adults (Ramey et al., 2017).

Baldridge (2019) reminds us that "Although community-based youth work is crucial to the educational and social experiences of young people, it should not be romanticized" (p. 11) since youth programs, even outside of formal school spaces, are still subject to the disempowering forces that impact educational and social institutions, oftentimes through the words and actions of adult participants. Thus, the question of *how* adults show up for and work with youth is essential in exploring youth–adult partnerships that aim to support the agentive and speculative capacities of youth. Additionally, while extant research has explored how adults apprentice or facilitate youth participation within existing structures of political or social action, the study discussed herein is distinct in that it examines how adults support youth in the imagination, creation, and facilitation of their own structures for activism, including engaging with art, popular culture, and community-building as a vehicle for collaborative future-building.

Designing for Social Futures

Prior to beginning this project, I organized an annual 1-day youth summit that invited high school and undergraduate students to a college campus in New York City to participate in workshops and dialogues focused on the five elements of hip-hop: djing, breaking (aka b-boying/b-girling), emceeing/rapping, graffiti, and knowledge. This event came about as a result of my teaching a high school hip-hop literature class and wanting to connect my students to artists and youth who were engaged in hip-hop and activist communities. Each year, I invited teaching artists to facilitate these workshops as well as a scholar-activist to deliver a keynote address. After organizing this event for 5 years, it dawned on me that this event, which was developed to reimagine educational spaces for youth, did not center youth authentically in its design since I had not invited young people to participate in the design processes.

Oftentimes, in the practice of teaching for social justice, the distinction between youth-centered and youth-led can become distorted, with educators engaging themselves and each other in the thinking and reflecting components of activism and involving youth only in the action. Brazilian educator and philosopher Paulo Freire (2000) made the distinction between fighting for and fighting with the oppressed. He emphasized the need for those who are the subjects of oppression to be involved in the process of thought and reflection as they act against oppressive forces in their lives. Based on this premise, I aimed to reconfigure the youth summit in a way that decentered adult knowledge and instead highlighted the praxis and imagination of young people by inviting youth to co-develop an annual youth conference that engages young people as leaders, teachers, and change agents while fostering a community of youth at different stages of their academic, artistic, and activist development. These youth learn both from and with each other, co-constructing intergenerational knowledge and support networks that are grounded in youth culture, youth literacies, and youth imagination.

To document the processes and outcomes of youth speculative dreaming and future-building, I conducted a longitudinal, qualitative study of the annual conference, including its design processes, implementation, and impact on the youth leaders and attendees. As the director of the project and as a mentor to the youth involved, I conducted this study as a participant-observer, collecting data throughout the development of the conference to learn how the youth leaders develop and enact speculative pedagogies in their design and facilitation of the conference. An additional question that arose during this study, however, is that of the role of nonyouth in youth-led social justice education projects. More specifically, I wanted to explore how the participation of adults influenced the youth leaders' imagination, agentive development, and future-building within this project.

Engaging in Social Design-Based Research

The research approach of this study draws from social design methodology in that it seeks to build models for educational practice that are "theoretically and experientially informed" and are "co-designed, studied, and revised in the present" (Gutiérrez, 2016, p. 192). This study also utilizes structures of grounded theory in qualitative research since it examines participants' experiences of the processes, actions, and interactions (Creswell, 2007) involved in the development of speculative educational theories and practices.

Introducing the Youth Collaborators

The participants in this study are the 12 youth who were codesigners of the conference between 2019 and 2022. These youth volunteered to serve a 2-year term as a conference leader and community builder through an online application I created and circulated through emails, social media, and a program website. Although the only demographic requirement of the application was to be under the age of 21, all who have applied have been BIPOC high school youth. In addition to their activist and hip-hop identities, these youth have expressed their engagement with community-based endeavors, including visual art, music, poetry, dance, athletics, education, advocacy, and student government. While all of the youth were high school students when they applied and began their leadership of the conference, 7 of the 12 are currently in college, reflecting the layers of youth intergenerationality embedded in this project. Table 5.1 shares the names, ages, and self-identified race and gender identities of the members of the 2019, 2020, and 2022 cohorts of the youth leaders.

Table 5.1. 2019–2022 Youth Leaders

Name	Age	Race	Pronouns	Leadership Term
Chrissy	18	African American	She/Her	2019–2021
Sandra	14	Multiracial Latina (Dominican American)	She/Her	2019–2021
Donovan	14	African American	He/Him	2019–2021
Roya	17	Pakistani American	She/Her	2019–2021
Amanda	17	African American	She/Her	2019–2021
Rena	17	Black	She/Her	2020–2022
David	17	Hispanic	He/Him	2020–2022
Nico	17	Puerto Rican/ Dominican/ African American	He/Him	2020–2022
Denise	16	Black (Biracial)	She/Her	2020–2022
Sandy	14	Indian American	She/Her	2022–2023
Aurora	16	African American	She/Her	2022–2023
Shanice	16	African American	She/Her	2022–2023

Note: Demographic data based on first year of participation in program

Learning About Youth and Adult Partnerships Through Research Data

Data collection for this project primarily consisted of video and audio recordings of the 1- to 2-hour monthly conference planning meetings that took place between January and May each year via the video-conferencing application Zoom. I also audio recorded in-person meetings, conducted individual and group interviews with the youth leaders, and documented my observations and reflections as a participant-observer in my research memos. Table 5.2 shows the overview of data collected in the project. To analyze this data, I conducted multiple cycles of open coding, reading through the meeting and interview transcriptions to (1) highlight moments when the youth leaders engaged in dialogue with or about adults, including me; (2) identify the moments where the youth leaders were most engaged in offering new or creative ideas and perspectives; (3) note the youth leaders' descriptions of their experiences working with adults; and (4) look for patterns amongst the 12 youth participants regarding their individual and collective experiences of working with adults in their design and leadership of the annual conference. In the following sections, I share examples from this data and discuss the implications of this work for future research and practice involving youth–adult partnerships.

Table 5.2. Data Collection Overview, January 2019–June 2022

Data Collected	Amount Collected	Dates Collected	Participants
Virtual Conference Planning Meetings	15	January–August 2019; January–May 2020; January–June 2021; January–May 2022	Youth Leaders, PI, Mentors
In-Person Conference Planning Meetings	4	January 2019; January 2020; April 2022; May 2022	Youth Leaders, PI, Mentors
Group Interviews	10	March–June 2019; June 2020; February–December 2021; February–June 2022	Youth Leaders, PI
Individual Interviews	14	June 2019; June 2020; June 2022	Youth Leaders, PI
Researcher Memos	20	February 2019–June 2022	PI

Fostering Youth-Adult Partnerships in Speculative Educational Design

As I began the process of developing this project, I was in dialogue with Lisa, a scholar and teaching artist who had been hosting a hip-hop–themed education conference at her university for a number of years. I invited Lisa and our mutual colleague, Luz, to lend their experience and wisdom to the project by participating in planning meetings and serving as mentors to the youth involved. When I put out the call for young people to sign up for a 2-year term to be a leader of the youth conference, I was surprised to receive messages from several nonyouth, adults whose work spans the intersections of hip-hop, art, activism, and education, who reached out to express interest in the project and offer their support.

Although I had not initially envisioned the youth program to include more than the three of us (Lisa, Luz, and me), I considered how the combined resources and skills of multiple educators, scholars, and artists could provide additional support for the youth leaders, including providing mentorship that extends beyond conference organizing and into their academic and professional lives. I subsequently invited additional nonyouth to serve as mentors to the project for a total of six mentors who had either volunteered or whom I had sought out to serve in this capacity. Although my intention was for the adults, including me, to serve as supports to the youth leaders, there were moments over the course of the 4 years of this project in which the adult roles fluctuated between mentor and partner to the youth leaders.

"They Helped Us Sculpt": Adult Support of Youth Leadership

Through analyzing interview and meeting transcripts from this project, I discovered that the presence of adults in the program was viewed by the youth as supportive of their learning regarding community-building and social action. For example, in a planning meeting that I facilitated with the youth leaders before the second year of the conference, the group debated the age limits regarding who should be eligible to become a conference codesigner. In this discussion, Amanda described the role of adult mentorship in her Year 1 experiences: "I feel like I learned from Lisa . . . I felt like she was my mentor as well because she . . . had had her own conferences" (virtual planning meeting transcript, August 29, 2019). Within this discussion, Amanda reflected on her experiences with adult mentorship in the program in order to consider the impact of particular age groups on the youth leadership of the conference. Amanda also was very specific in explaining what, in particular, Lisa contributed to her learning experience; because Lisa had organized conferences before, Amanda invited and respected her mentorship.

In her postconference individual interview, when I asked what resources she found to be helpful in the planning processes, Chrissy also described adult participation (as well as Zoom) as supportive in conference planning, stating, "You and Lisa and Luz. Y'all had everything together. Just had it together even though it was like some stuff that was happening there wasn't expected. Y'all just had everything straight and together and still had the energy high, and had everything like amazing" (individual interview, June 16, 2019). Similar to what Amanda described, Chrissy's reflection highlights the importance of adult experience to the youth leaders' work. Chrissy's statement also implies that seeing the adults "have it together" and maintain our "high energy" in the face of unexpected issues helped her to navigate the planning processes and have a positive experience in the program. Many of the other youth leaders also discussed the impact of the adults' "energy" on their participation in the program.

During a group interview in 2022, Aurora shared her experience of Ricardo, one of the new mentors, stating, "I love Ricardo. . . . His reactions to everything is amazing. [His] energy overall. We could all be boring and all we need is Ricardo" (group interview, May 8, 2022). During the conference, when I asked the youth leaders who wanted to introduce Ricardo, they amiably argued over who would get to do it, with many exclaiming, "I love Ricardo!" In the subsequent postconference group interview, I asked the youth leaders what it was about Ricardo and Lisa that seemed to make them feel comfortable. Aurora explained, "Their energy is up no matter who they're with. . . . I feel like they're around youth a lot. They know how to act around youth. I think it really is just their energy though and they're funny too" (group interview, June 1, 2022). David added, "Yeah, I think it's energy as well. I think they're just fun people to be around with and they both have—them two and you as well, Lauren, you guys all have very interesting things to say and if I had the opportunity to take a class where any one of you were teaching, I'd totally take it without thinking about it" (group interview, June 1, 2022). In her individual interview, Sandy stated that Ricardo "was really helpful throughout the process" and that after meeting him it "felt like I knew him for a long time" (individual interview, June 8, 2022).

In addition to offering experiential wisdom and welcoming personalities, the presence of adult mentors also strengthened the youth leaders' connections to community. Over the course of the planning phases of the Year 1 conference, I noticed the youth leaders' excitement when Luz joined our virtual meetings, sometimes just to share greetings while on his way to work or to a meeting. There was an energy Luz brought into the space that was palpable. During our individual interview in 2019, I asked Roya about her meeting Luz in person for the first time at the conference. She shared, "I loved Luz being there. I feel like he perfectly hyped everyone up in the morning . . . we got to speak and then we also spoke after the conference. He DM'd me and just said, 'Thank you so much for everything,' and I was like, 'Stay in touch.' It's great because it fostered so many new relationships" (individual interview, June 19, 2019).

Across the 4 years of the program's development, the youth leaders clearly expressed wanting to learn from and work with adults whose energy they were drawn to, who were interesting, and who seemed comfortable being around youth. In addition to their connections with individual adult mentors, the youth leaders also described the conference and community of the program as a space in which youth voice was uniquely centered and uplifted, especially in comparison to their previous experiences with adults and with youth programs. After the 2019 conference, I asked the youth leaders how they perceived the role of adults in the program, including those who were not mentors but who had volunteered the day of the conference. Chrissy stated,

> Honestly the ones that I met were so open and just saw like for youth, like progression. It was like they really created, like, happy spaces. Like I feel like these were my aunties and uncles. Like they reach out, I'm just open and they didn't really try to have like any type of authority or anything. Like they were just like, there . . . to like uplift views.

Roya added,

> I think it was a really good ratio . . . because it didn't feel like we were being supervised, but it felt like we were being mentored. I feel like if there were more of them there, it would have felt like this was a field trip of chaperones.

Both Roya and Chrissy described adults as mentors and partners to the youth leaders based on the ratio of youth to adults and the adults' openness, uplifting rather than exercising authority over youth voice. In their individual interviews, the 2022 youth leaders further emphasized the conference community as youth-led in a way that is distinct from other youth programs or youth activities they participated in. For example, Sandy explained that in this program, "The mentorship is unique. I'm part of other clubs and stuff. We have people that are older than us, but they're not mentors or anything. They just tell us what to do, you know?" (individual interview, June 8, 2022).

Rena also described the program as a uniquely youth-driven space:

> It's actually student-led because a lot of the programs I've been a part of—yes, there are some students that do take charge, but a lot of us just sit in the background just kind of waiting, not being allowed to put input in, and not being able to express ideas without getting overshadowed, or there's adults in charge, and what they say goes. This one's actually student-led. (Individual interview, June 9, 2022)

Nico expressed similar experiences of the conference leadership being a space that decenters adult authority in contrast to other youth programs:

> The format for a lot of other youth development sort of things is that, it's very adult heavy. The youth are just kind of the pawn so to speak . . . they have this whole thing for them to do and then they just kind of put them in the system and then watch them kind of exit and enter. But this one is very youth driven, youth led. (Individual interview, June 6, 2022)

In this reflection, Nico indicates that adults in youth programs typically take advantage of youth, leveraging their participation as "pawns" to advance their own goals. In contrast, he describes the conference as a space that is invested in young people's development, rather than being a program that youth simply "exit and enter."

Like the other youth leaders, Aurora also described her experience of her work in this project in comparison to her previous experiences with adults in youth spaces:

> There was also a lot of adults who tended to be like, "Oh, well, this is how we've done it for previous years and it's worked, so let's continue." Or especially working with kids, a lot of adults don't tend to listen to the children first, and they want to tell us what to do. (Individual interview, June 8, 2022)

Despite being from diverse geographic regions and at various stages in their academic development, spanning high school and college, the youth leaders all shared similar past experiences with adults and with youth programs as being adult-centric and limiting to youth voice and imagination. In contrast, the youth leaders all described adults in our conference community as ones who flipped this dynamic by not only listening to youth but also partnering with youth and authentically encouraging youth imagination. For example, Shanice explained that having adults as partners helped the youth to "sculpt" their ideas: "Sometimes we didn't know how to put certain things in certain ways. And I felt like adults are there to help us just form what we wanted, but still let us have our own idea at the same time" (individual interview, June 9, 2022). Ultimately, each of the youth leaders expressed that they learned from adults as mentors and partnered with adults as collaborators in ways that supported their development of agency and their collective imaginings of their social and educational futures. However, even this "youth-directed" space was not without complications due to adult talk and authority.

"They Were Talking a Lot": Confronting Adult Talk in Youth Leadership and Imagination

As I shared earlier, Roya described her perception of adult participation at the first conference as being generally positive in that there were not too many adults and adults played the role of mentor rather than supervisor. However, she also shared the following experience from that day:

> I think the only, the only instance where I felt like maybe [adult presence] was a little overpowering was in the morning when we were signing up for workshops. . . . The adults, they like, as some people were signing up for the workshops, they were like, "Oh, like can you guys sign up for this one? They don't have as many people." And I know that kind of made some people feel uncomfortable cause they were like, "Ah, I really wanted to see this. But then they felt like authority, older authority telling me to sign up for this, let me go to that." And that kind of defeated the purpose of choosing what workshop you wanted to go to. I know they had the right intention, but I don't know if it came across the right way, if that makes sense. (Individual Interview, June 19, 2019)

What Roya is referring to here is an incident during the morning registration portion of the conference when attendees were asked to sign up for the breakout workshop they wanted to attend. According to the youth leaders, one of the adults, who was not a mentor but who volunteered to support the youth that day, was strongly encouraging the attendees to sign up for one particular workshop because they wanted that workshop's facilitator to feel supported. The impact, however, was that many of the youth attendees felt pressured to sign up for a different workshop from the one they wanted and the youth leaders felt their role as leaders being undermined by this adult's actions. Roya's reflection on this incident highlights one of the core tensions in youth–adult partnerships, wherein adult authority tends to overpower or undermine youth agency when the desires or motivations of each are not in alignment. Since youth are indoctrinated into a system in which they are told to defer to adult knowledge and authority, they often continue to do so even in spaces designed to challenge this hierarchical structure. This includes Roya, who in spite of being a co-organizer and designer of the conference, did not feel she had the authority to contradict or challenge an adult volunteer who inherently, at least according to the youth, wielded power as an "adult authority."

Another example of adult presence overpowering youth voice in this program occurred during the 2022 virtual conference envisioning meeting. For this first meeting of the 2022 youth leadership, I invited the adult mentors via email to attend briefly in order to introduce themselves and show their support for the youth. I added that they were also welcome to stay for the conference planning discussion. Subsequently, two things occurred that challenged my intentions for this first meeting: First, many of the youth leaders did not show up to the meeting. This meant that rather than there being an equal number of adults and youth, there were eight adults and five youth, one of whom arrived 45 minutes after the meeting began. Second, for the conference-envisioning portion of the meeting, I implicitly expected the mentors to listen to the dialogue between the youth and potentially contribute additional insights or resources after the youth had spoken, but I did not make this clear in advance of the meeting. I also underestimated the adults' eagerness to participate in this dialogue. Thus, when I offered the prompt to brainstorm ideas for the 2022 conference theme, it was the adult mentors *and not the youth* who began the discussion, immediately offering conference theme suggestions and building off of each other's contributions. Most of the mentors also knew each other from previous interactions and were immediately more comfortable in the dialogue than the youth, many of whom were meeting each other for the first time during this virtual session.

Once I saw that the mentors were leading the conversation, I attempted to redirect and also model what I wanted the other adults to do by offering a few questions rather than ideas or suggestions. However, when the mentors again kicked off the response I became more direct, naming the youth leaders and asking what thoughts they had. By this time, however, it was already too late. Adult talk had overpowered youth voice in this discussion and by the time the youth were explicitly invited to contribute, they felt it was too late to start over and simply agreed with what had previously been stated by the adults. For the next meeting with the youth leadership, I ensured that none of the mentors other than me were present. I also pointed out what had happened with the mentors in the previous meeting and asked the youth how they experienced that interaction. David shared the following:

> I did think it was a little overwhelming with all the mentors in the group. I mean, I found myself kind of struggling to add in something because I already felt like everything was kind of already said and that we already pretty much decided on a topic. (Planning meeting transcript, February 23, 2022)

Aurora shared a similar experience to David's in response to my question, stating that although "it kind of helped a little just to hear other ideas . . . it did feel, I guess, they were talking a lot . . . Not that I didn't want them to talk, but just that . . . majority of what could have been said was probably already said or already elaborated on" (planning meeting transcript, February 23, 2022). It is worth noting that Aurora credited the mentors in the dialogue with helping her own brainstorming process by sharing ideas and David also added that the conference theme that was arrived upon was something that he had already been thinking about and that he was happy with it. However, the fact that it was the adult mentors who initiated the theme and primarily participated in the dialogue rather than the youth undermines the agency and youth speculative imagination that the program was designed to cultivate. In particular, David's and Aurora's experience of feeling that they had nothing to contribute to the dialogue after the adults had already spoken reveals how adult talk can overshadow or limit youth imagination.

David further elaborated on this idea of adult talk months later in describing his experience of the 2022 conference, during which he facilitated an intergenerational panel with some of the adult mentors and youth leaders regarding generational and intergenerational connections to popular hip-hop music:

> One thing that I think about is the panel and how, at least from my perspective, being the facilitator of the panel, I felt like the contributions of Ricardo and Lisa, I feel like they contributed a little more or at least they talked more than [the youth leaders] and I feel like that's one way where having more adults in the room can be a negative. (Group interview, June 1, 2022).

Recall that Ricardo and Lisa are adult mentors whom the youth leaders deeply respected, cared for, and felt seen by. Thus, the youth leaders' criticism of adult talk is not a response to adult presence in general or to these mentors in particular, but to the extent to which adult talk can occlude youth voice, regardless of how wonderful and well-intentioned the adults are. Additionally, David immediately followed up the above observation by highlighting the important role of the adult keynote speaker to the conference and to his own learning and critical development, reaffirming the idea that adult participation is a welcome component of young people's future-building, provided that adult talk is not overpowering or disproportionate to that of youth.

Toward Youth-Led Intergenerational Collaboration

Whereas previous research on youth–adult partnerships in social justice projects found that adults tended to dominate the organizing processes when they were concerned about a project's success (Kirshner, 2008), the adults in this study had a tendency to dominate conversations when they were passionate about a topic or idea, even when the subject was youth-focused. To prevent youth–adult partnerships from being overpowered by adult talk, nonyouth should be mindful of the space that they take up in dialogue with youth and aware of when their cultural passions and knowledge become a dominating force rather than an asset for youth imagination.

Drawing from the data in this study, I offer the following recommendations for adult participation in intergenerational and youth-led spaces: (1) Prior to or at the beginning of the program, clear expectations for adult participation should be developed in collaboration with youth, allowing for all members to hold adults accountable to these expectations. This includes positioning adults as co-learners with youth and clarifying when adults are expected to take up the role of teacher or mentor versus partner. Opportunities for revisiting and revising these structures when needed should be built into the program also. (2) Before engaging in joint work with youth, adult partners must foster trust with youth participants by centering their voices and identities in generative dialogue. (3) When engaging in intergenerational dialogue, adults can mitigate the dominance of adult authority by first listening to the youth participants and encouraging youth contributions through problem-posing and question-asking. (4) This study reveals that how adults participate in youth-centered spaces early on can set the stage for youth participation throughout the program. Ramey et al. (2017) found that when youth voice is centered early on in the design phase of partnership projects, their feelings of empowerment are more likely to increase. Therefore, some youth–adult partnerships may benefit from introducing the majority of the adults later in the process, after the youth have begun to experience ownership over the space or project.

Supporting Youth Imagination in Social Action and Future-Building

In her interview, Sandy expressed feeling both intimidated and excited by the freedom she experienced as a youth leader working with adults, reflecting the reality that speculative future-building can also be daunting for youth. Sandy's experience also highlights the role that adults can play in balancing the power and possibility that comes with young people's future-building. This balance is perhaps best exemplified by the role of adults in the teen television series *Naomi* based on the 2019 comic book series of the same name.

In the speculative fictional world of *Naomi*, Naomi and her friends discover that she has superpowers and that there are dangerous people pursuing her who want to exploit these powers. Aware of Naomi's powers and the imminent danger, the adults in this community give these youth a great deal of space to self-discover, create, and problem-solve, supporting the teens' agency while also making clear that their only priority is to protect and support these youth. In one instance, the teens discover that a force field has been placed around their school, trapping them and their classmates inside. Naomi immediately recognizes that this challenge might be bigger than what the youth can solve on their own and says, "We need to contact some adults" (Bellotto & Gerima, 2022), reflecting her awareness that although she and her friends have agency in directing their lives and futures, they also have adult support in doing so.

Ironically, the adults find that they are unable to help and it is ultimately the scientific knowledge and radical imagination of Naomi and her friends that destroy the forcefield and save the student body. The forcefield thus presents a powerful metaphor for the limitations that are often placed on youth agency and imagination by existing hierarchical structures and the teens' success in defeating it reveals what is possible when adults provide love and guidance to youth while also giving them space to identify problems in their world and to activate their social imaginations in developing their own solutions and, perhaps, their own worlds.

Considerations for Teaching and Research

Although fictional, the examples of youth–adult partnerships reflected in *Naomi* are reminders of the limitations of adult knowledge, especially that which is derived from the navigation of or enculturation into longstanding systems of oppression. In contrast, the youth of *Naomi*, who are quite literally fighting for a better world, exemplify the need for youth knowledge and expertise to be invited into dialogue and action that attempts to address societal challenges, particularly those which directly impact young people and their communities. Teachers, in particular, are positioned uniquely to build community and problem-solve with young people, expanding students' capacities for speculative dreaming by curating classroom texts and dialogue that tap into youth knowledge, experience, and radical imagination.

At the onset of this chapter, I discussed the limitations of existing structures of schooling for the development of approaches to youth speculative literacies. Indeed, as bell hooks (1994) stated, "It's so difficult to change existing structures because the habit of repression is the norm" (p. 147). However, by bringing lessons learned from this project into the classroom, I believe we can work in partnership with youth to redesign school spaces in ways that honor young people's civic and speculative dreaming. For example, approaches to classroom teaching can benefit significantly from a reorientation of what students and educators bring to the classroom. Rather than viewing teachers as content experts and students as creators, what might it look like for teachers to exemplify their own creative capacities based on the knowledge and experience that students bring to the classroom? What might be gained from providing students with the opportunity to share their own expertise as youth leaders and pedagogical theorists? Rather than asking students questions to which teachers have already conceived the answers, perhaps teachers and students can work together to ask and engage with new questions, mirroring the bi-directional, dialogical processes of youth–adult partnerships. These approaches to classroom pedagogy might come across as discomfiting for teachers accustomed to exercising control over precisely what and how students will learn at each step; however, as the youth leaders' stories exemplify, much of their critical learning occurred in the unknowing and the unknown.

Of course, transforming hierarchical teacher–student relationships into restorative partnerships requires a restructuring of how teachers' and students' respective roles are constructed in the classroom. Many traditional approaches to youth work are rooted in the premise that youth will bring creativity, energy, and a passion for learning while adults bring knowledge and guidance through life experience (Camino, 2005). According to Camino (2005), "The pitfall lies in assuming that 'creativity,' 'authenticity,' and 'energy' are the sole qualities that youth can contribute, and that only youth can contribute them" (p. 79.) In contrast, the youth in this project explicitly described how the energy and creativity that adult mentors contributed to the group dynamics impacted the culture of the program as well as their own development. Consequently, research and practice involving youth must be expansive in viewing the various contributions of youth and adults in joint work and should begin to explore the role of youth–adult partnerships in adult learning and development with a particular focus on how adult partners learn both with and from youth (Ramey et al., 2017).

Finally, whereas research on youth learning and development often places most emphasis on the teaching and training of young people (Baldridge, 2019; Camino, 2005), research and practice must turn attention also to how teachers and mentors are impacted by and develop through their work with youth, building infrastructure that cultivates youth leadership, agency, and radical imagination in classrooms and communities.

NOTE

1. Although many organizations, including the United Nations, define youth as those between the ages of 15 and 24, the term "youth" herein refers to those between the ages of 14 and 21, since this range encompasses the average age of U.S. high school and undergraduate students as well as the ages of the participants in this research study.

REFERENCES

Baldridge, B. J. (2019). *Reclaiming community: Race and the uncertain future of youth work*. Stanford University Press.
Bellotto, R. (Writer), & Gerima, M. (Director). (2022, May 3). Worst prom ever (Season 1, Episode 11) [TV series episode]. In A. DuVernay, P. Garnes, & J. Blankenship (Executive Producers), *Naomi*. ARRAY Filmworks; DC Entertainment; Warner Bros. Television.
Camino, L. (2005). Pitfalls and promising practices of youth–adult partnerships: An evaluator's reflections. *Journal of Community Psychology, 33*(1), 75–85. https://doi.org/10.1002/jcop.20043
Creswell, J. W. (2007). *Qualitative inquiry and research design: Choosing among five traditions*. Sage.
Freire, P. (2000). *Pedagogy of the oppressed*. Continuum.
Garcia, A., & Mirra, N. (2021). Writing toward justice: Youth speculative civic literacies in online policy discourse. *Urban Education, 56*(4), 640–669. https://doi.org/10.1177/0042085920953881
Gutiérrez, K. D. (2016). 2011 AERA Presidential address: Designing resilient ecologies: Social design experiments and a new social imagination. *Educational Researcher, 45*(3), 187–196. https://doi.org/10.3102/0013189X16645430
Gutiérrez, K. D., & Jurow, A. S. (2016). Social design experiments: Toward equity by design. *Journal of the Learning Sciences, 25*(4), 565–598. https://doi.org/10.1080/10508406.2016.1204548
hooks, b. (1994). *Teaching to transgress: Education as the practice of freedom*. Routledge.
Kelley, R. D. G. (2002). *Freedom dreams: The Black radical imagination*. Beacon Press.
Kirshner, B. (2008). Guided participation in three youth activism organizations: Facilitation, apprenticeship, and joint work. *The Journal of the Learning Sciences, 17*(1), 60–101. https://doi.org/10.1080/10508400701793190
Larson, R. W., & Walker, K. C. (2010). Dilemmas of practice: Challenges to program quality encountered by youth program leaders. *American Journal of Community Psychology, 45*(3), 338–349. https://doi.org/10.1007/s10464-010-9307-z
Mirra, N., & Garcia, A. (2020). "I hesitate but I do have hope": Youth speculative civic literacies for troubled times. *Harvard Educational Review, 90*(2), 295–321. https://doi.org/10.17763/1943-5045-90.2.295
Mirra, N., & Garcia, A. (2022). Guns, schools, and democracy: Adolescents imagining social futures through speculative civic literacies. *American Educational Research Journal, 59*(2), 345–380. https://doi.org/10.3102/00028312221074400
Mitra, D. L. (2009). Strengthening student voice initiatives in high schools: An examination of the supports needed for school-based youth-adult partnerships. *Youth & Society, 40*(3), 311–335. https://doi.org/10.1177/0044118X08316211
New London Group. (1996). A pedagogy of multiliteracies: Designing social futures. *Harvard Educational Review, 66*(1), 60–92. doi:10.17763/haer.66.1.17370n67v22j160u
Ramey, H. L., Lawford, H. L., & Vachon, W. (2017). Youth-adult partnerships in work with youth: An overview. *Journal of Youth Development, 12*(4), 38–60. https://doi.org/10.5195/jyd.2017.520

Van Steenis, E., & Kirshner, B. (2020). Hip-hop music-making as a context for relational equity among youth and workers. In G. Brion-Meisels, J. T. Fei, & D. S. Vasudevan (Eds.), *At our best: Building youth–adult partnerships in out-of-school time settings* (pp. 183–198). Information Age Publishing.

Zeldin, S., Gauley, J., Krauss, S. E., Kornbluh, M., & Collura, J. (2017). Youth–adult partnership and youth civic development: Cross-national analyses for scholars and field professionals. *Youth & Society, 49*(7), 851–878. https://doi.org/10.1177/0044118X15595153

CHAPTER 6

Community-Engaged Culturally Sustaining Social and Emotional Learning as an Approach to Speculative Education

Jingjing Sun, Ronda Howlett, Debbie Hogenson, Lindsey M. Nichols, Anisa N. Goforth, Sisilia Kusumaningsih, Niki Graham, and Emily Brooke

It was a chilly day in May, the Séliš Month of Bitterroot in Flathead Nation in Montana (Greene & Sandoval, 2011). Elementary and high school students were lining up outside the new gymnasium where school staff and former administrators were cooking pancakes. Parents also showed up for this Community Day, helping their children get ready for the track events, cultural activities, and the afternoon pow wow and graduation celebration. The bright colors of girls' ribbon skirts and the jingling sounds of regalia created a sense of excitement against the gloomy sky above the Mission Mountains.

The drizzling rain did not stop young children from running with all their might on the slightly muddy field. Despite the shared eagerness to be the first to cross the finish line, many children encouraged their friends and classmates with yelps and cheers. At one point, all the 4th-grade boys decided to accompany a struggling peer. As the large group approached the finish line, several of them signaled to each other to slow down, so that their peer could cross the finish line first. The audience then burst into a thunderstorm of cheers. This heart-warming support reflected the spirit of inclusiveness of the day.

This spirit of inclusiveness continued after lunch, when students, teachers, caregivers, and community members gathered for the pow wow and graduation celebration. Housed in the renovated basketball gymnasium, championship flags were proudly hung on the walls. An Elder led the pow wow, explaining the sacredness of the drumming and the traditional teaching of their peoples of the Confederated Salish and Kootenai Tribes in the Flathead Nation. He emphasized the importance of the ongoing efforts in language revitalization, highlighting the nearby Nkʷusm Séliš Language Immersion School that would soon celebrate its 20th anniversary. Before the drummers sang, the Elder introduced the song's meaning and invited the audience to join the dance when appropriate. As soon as the drumbeat started, children flocked to the dance floor, some immediately dancing the rhythmic steps. In two large circles, each person greeted and shook hands with each other. Twenty high school graduates were honored, blessed by the Elder and the Indigenous teacher who helped organize the pow wow. Children, family, and community members joined the dance to shake each graduate's hands, honoring their accomplishment. Teachers—Indigenous and non-Indigenous alike—danced jubilantly alongside their students to embrace their students' cultural traditions and identity.

Community Day was one of blessings, laughter, tears, and dancing. It showcased the power of connection, community, and culture. The day also felt like a culminating experience for us as the Project SELA (Social–Emotional Learning in Arlee) team. As a team of Indigenous community members and non-Indigenous university scholars, our partnership was born in this school and has flourished over the past 5 years. Within this team, we are retired and current educators who have dedicated ourselves to children's well-being, tribal leaders and community members who work tirelessly to support our children's healthy development and academic success, and university-based interdisciplinary scholars who also train the next generation of teachers, school psychologists, and school counselors.

PROJECT SELA AS AN APPROACH TO SPECULATIVE EDUCATION

The purpose of this chapter is to share our team's journey in collaboratively building a space to dream in Project SELA as an alternative approach to education, an example of speculative education (Mirra & Garcia, 2020). We conceptualize speculative education as an educational system that is willing to leverage local culture and heritage to promote interest in learning (Khan et al., 2021), and as a space to provide flexible and creative approaches to learning for children from communities who have been systematically marginalized and oppressed within society. Specifically, we share how integrating speculative education into culturally sustaining social–emotional learning (SEL) can be a radical approach to addressing structural colonialism and racism that has shaped today's education policy and practices for Indigenous children (Brayboy & Lomawaima, 2018; McCarty et al., 2021; Sazbilian, 2019). In sharing our collaborative journey in building the partnership, and codesigning and implementing a place-based and culturally sustaining SEL program for students, educators, and families, this chapter presents an innovative approach to supporting Indigenous children's well-being that centers Indigenous knowledge, values, and stories. We argue that integrating speculative education into Indigenous ways of knowing provides opportunities to foreground the voices of Indigenous communities, therefore shifting away from the assimilation of Western notions of learning and pedagogy.

Project SELA originated from a collective response to a devastating suicide cluster that occurred in the community within a 2-year span. Across the United States, suicide has become the second leading cause of death among Indigenous People ages 10 to 34 (Office of Minority Health [OMH], 2019). Compared to white and other minoritized youth, Indigenous youth have disproportionately higher suicide rates and mental health concerns (OMH, 2019). The 2021 Montana Youth Risk Behavior Survey revealed that among Indigenous students attending secondary school, 49% reported feeling very sad or hopeless, 26.7% have seriously considered suicide, and 17.6% have attempted suicide. These disheartening statistics reflect the national data that 27% of Indigenous high school students seriously considered suicide compared to 22% of non-Hispanic white students (Centers for Disease Control and Prevention, 2023). In addition, Indigenous students experience significant inequity in academic achievement, with the lowest high school graduation rate among all ethnic and racial groups (Center for Native American Youth at the Aspen Institute, 2019).

The reasons for these disparities are multifaceted and complex. They reflect the systemic racism, white supremacy, marginalization, and oppression from the initial settler colonialism to Indigenous communities' contemporary experiences today (Brayboy & Lomawaima, 2018; Castagno & Brayboy, 2008). Intergenerational trauma from cultural genocide has disrupted the family system of Indigenous communities (Brave Heart et al., 2011). Further, the U.S. federal government's theft of Indigenous lands and persistent assimilation efforts dating back to residential boarding schools have led to Indigenous languages disappearing at an alarming rate (Evans-Campbell, 2008; Wolfe, 2006).

Despite these extraordinary difficulties, however, Indigenous families and communities persist in fostering resilience and resistance among their youth. This Indigenous survivance (Vizenor, 2008) has been realized through Indigenous language immersion schools like the Nkʷusm School in the Flathead Nation to connect children's identities, culture, and spirituality (McCarty et al., 2021; Whitesell et al., 2006). Indigenous communities also practice survivance with increased efforts in combatting settler colonialism to support Indigenous students' social–emotional well-being through culturally sustaining social–emotional learning (Sun et al., 2022).

Social–emotional learning (SEL) refers to the process through which children and adults acquire knowledge, attitudes, and skills to understand and manage emotions, create and maintain positive relationships, and make responsible and caring decisions (Weissberg, 2019). Meta-analysis of thousands of SEL studies has shown that SEL leads to better academic performance, emotional well-being, and long-term mental health (e.g., Durlak et al., 2011; Taylor et al., 2017). Most SEL programs, however, were developed for non-Indigenous populations and do not address inequities rooted in settler colonialism (Camangian & Cariaga, 2021; Jagers et al., 2019; Sun et al., 2022), ignoring the effects of intergenerational trauma and ongoing racism that shapes Indigenous students' lives (Brayboy, 2005; Mahfouz & Anthony-Stevens, 2020). Attending to these effects, transformative SEL was proposed by Jagers et al. (2019) to go beyond the focus on individual SEL competencies, and instead to center students' identity, culture, sense of belonging, and engagement in promoting culturally responsive SEL. This framework highlighted a critical need for culturally responsive SEL programs for Indigenous populations as well as culturally responsive approaches to measure the impact of such SEL programs. Additionally, although there have been numerous surveys developed to measure students' social–emotional competencies, such as the SAEBRS (von der Embse et al., 2016), most were developed for non-Indigenous children, potentially neglecting the critical values that Indigenous communities hold.

Embracing the transformative SEL framework, Project SELA presents a rare example where scholars are willing to work across disciplinary boundaries to collaborate around a shared goal. Initially, there were two separate but similar proposals for this project by the lead authors to a same grant: the American Indian-Alaskan Native Clinical Translational Research Program (AI-AN CTRP). Inspired by a conversation with the district superintendent on the urgent need to provide social–emotional support for every student in the school district, Sun proposed to develop a SEL program for the elementary school students. Meanwhile, Nichols and Goforth proposed a study focusing on a sequenced, placed-based professional development program to address the social and emotional needs of rural educators. Acknowledging the power of a multilayered SEL program for both Indigenous students and their educators, the three authors came together to propose Project SELA, which is grounded in the broader ecological system of the school, including the culture and values of the Indigenous community. As a result, Project SELA becomes one of the first SEL programs cocreated with an Indigenous community for Indigenous children and educators serving this population in the United States (Goforth et al., 2021, 2022; Sun et al., 2022).

Building a Space to Dream Through Community Engagement

Project SELA was conceived through culturally responsive community engagement (Goforth et al., 2021). Our initial phase of community engagement was guided by the Tribal Critical Race Theory (TribalCrit; Brayboy,

2005). Extending early critical race theories (CRT; e.g., Ladson-Billings & Tate, 1995), which argues that racism is endemic to the society, TribalCrit was developed to account for the unique historical context of settler colonization that has broadly impacted Indigenous Peoples (Brayboy, 2005). TribalCrit argues that, for Indigenous youth, not only do they endure the pervasive racism like youth from other racially minoritized groups, they also continue to be impacted considerably by colonialism in every aspect of their lives, including their identities as defined by legislature (e.g., blood quantum to decide tribal enrollment; Smith, 1999), and by an education system that largely serves the role of assimilating Indigenous youth to Eurocentric standards and civilization instead of honoring their own culture and values (Castagno & Brayboy, 2008). To counter white supremacy and endemic colonialism, TribalCrit emphasizes the importance of tribal sovereignty, knowledge, and culture as central to understanding the lived experiences of Indigenous People (Brayboy, 2005).

Guided by TribalCrit's position that Indigenous communities have a right to self-determination regarding their youths' education, we engaged in the Community-Based Participatory Research (CBPR; Collins et al., 2018) throughout Project SELA. Combining community-based engagement and shared leadership in research conceptualization and implementation, CBPR has the potential to decolonize research practice, create knowledge that is usable within the community context, and produce meaningful social change (Huffman, 2017). When centering Indigenous voices in research through CBPR, researchers can begin to address questions that are meaningful to the Indigenous community (Stanton, 2013). Thus, not only does CBPR have the potential to bring in a new level of attention to research ethics (Smith, 1999), it also has the potential to foster relationship building and catalyze sustained impact within the communities that have been historically marginalized (McCarty et al., 2014).

Indeed, Project SELA provides a pioneering approach to speculative education through CBPR. We adopted an orientation to research where community members are involved as equal partners and decision-makers through each step in the entire process (Ahmed & Palermo, 2010; Collins et al., 2018). Speculative approaches to education prioritize local relationships by "interweaving insider and outsider perspectives to craft the future education" and "provoking new ways of thinking" (Ross, 2017, p. 215). Project SELA shows how a participatory research structure enables future-oriented collaboration that embraces diversity and inclusion (Khan et al., 2021) and that allows egalitarian discussions among Indigenous community members and non-Indigenous university scholars. Underscoring the critical use of community engagement to decolonizing practices, we emphasize the preeminence of honoring tribal sovereignty and the essential role of our community liaison as a teacher, cultural broker, and confidant (Goforth et al., 2021). We urge our fellow researchers, educators, and other leaders to engage Indigenous community members respectfully throughout the entire research process to codesign and implement culturally responsive school-based intervention programs.

Project SELA also aligns with the speculative education philosophy in its iterative, practice-based approach to learning. As we reflected on the year of community engagement, through many shared meals in a local art gallery that features beautiful local artists' work and the place of our collaboration, we analyzed the research process using individual reflexivity of our experience, coupled with collaborative discussions. Through multiple iterations of analysis, we identified several critical themes during the community engagement phase, such as the centrality of context and relationships to build authentic partnership, learning through storytelling and metaphors, and challenges and rewards of immersion into community (Goforth et al., 2021).

In addition to cultivating local relationships and taking a reflective, experience-based approach to learning, Project SELA has presented community members with a space to think outside of typical boundaries and envision a future wherein their children are free from the harmful impacts of social injustice (Dunne & Raby, 2013). Through community dinners and focus groups, school and community leaders have been given the opportunity to envision education for Indigenous students beyond the current boundaries and limitations of the state's public education system. Educators have been encouraged to explore the "what ifs" for an alternative future beyond the constraints of our current reality, sharing their dreams of student learning through gardening and connecting with the environment, creating a space inside the school to welcome and connect with families and community members, building mentorships across age groups, and incorporating the community's spiritual values into the school's culture.

CODESIGNING AND IMPLEMENTING THE PLACE-BASED AND CULTURALLY SUSTAINING SEL PROGRAM

In Project SELA, tribal leaders, community members, school administrators, and educators collaborated with university researchers to identify research questions, examine community resources, cocreate a multilayered SEL program for elementary school children, educators, and families, implement the program, and evaluate its impact. This focus on Indigenous students, as well as the practice-research partnership with Indigenous communities, is perhaps unique, considering that only 16% of interventions in schools include Indigenous students (Gaias et al., 2020), and only 5% of public health research engages Indigenous communities at the inception stage of research (Lin et al., 2019). The unfortunately low level of community engagement may explain why many intervention programs for Indigenous youth,

Social and Emotional Learning as an Approach to Speculative Education   111

including suicide prevention programs, that were designed with good intentions and scientific rigor have failed to produce any long-lasting changes (LaFromboise & Malik, 2016). To reverse this trend and make sustainable changes, we followed recommendations from LaFromboise and Malik (2016), attending to unique strengths and needs of the Indigenous community and actively involve community members in intervention design, evaluation, and implementation.

Thus, informed by transformative SEL (Jagers et al., 2019) and TribalCrit (Brayboy, 2005), SELA was created to both integrate the new knowledge learned throughout the research process and to produce social change. To accomplish these goals, SELA embodies a synthesis of Indigenous and Western knowledge, guided by what Mi'kmaw Elder Albert Marshall refers to as Two-Eyed Seeing: "to see from one eye with the strengths of Indigenous ways of knowing, and to see from the other eye with the strengths of Western ways of knowing, and to use both of these eyes together" (Bartlett et al., 2012, p. 335).

Following the Two-Eyed Seeing, we facilitated open conversations with educators and community members to not only interrogate existing models for SEL, but also envision and construct a SEL model that would expand the

Figure 6.1. "Pathways to Wellness" poster.

normative understanding of SEL and be suitable for Indigenous students. In these discussions, CAB members shared their ideas about wellness and collectively dreamed a SEL model that is tailored to Indigenous values, culture, and interests. Such dreams include learning Indigenous language in public schools and creating a deeper connection with nature in the curriculum. The community's visions and dreams about wellness were then waved into the artifacts of the codesigned SEL programs, including the "Pathways to Wellness" poster (Figure 6.1), which is a cultural adaptation of the SEL framework developed by CASEL. Through this codesign process, community and school leaders redefined social–emotional competencies and explored groundbreaking ways to help *all* students appreciate the value of SEL and feel related in the learning process. The Two-Eyed Seeing that guided the cocreation of Project SELA offers a culturally responsive intervention that was successfully incorporated into a public school curriculum. Ultimately, it led to the multilayered SEL program that considers the ecological contexts and multiple systems of students, educators, and families (Bronfenbrenner, 2005; Garcia Coll et al., 1996).

Student SEL Program

Project SELA's student SEL program was developed and implemented through an iterative process over 2 years (Sun et al., 2022). Under the central goal of *Sicstmist* ("do one's best" in Séliš, the Indigenous language of the local tribe), SELA foregrounds the values emphasized by this particular Indigenous community—*Yoywals* (resilience), *Puteʔstxʷ* (respect), *Xʷčštwexʷ* (reciprocity), *NputeʔtnIEN* (reverence), and *Kʷše Olqʷšiʔit Esyaʔ* (responsibility)—into the teaching of social–emotional well-being. Community members collaborated with adult Séliš learners and first-language Séliš speakers to define and translate the core values from Séliš into English. When learning the Séliš vocabulary, students also understand how the core values are represented in daily life.

The program includes learning activities that are place-based and culturally responsive. For example, the program follows the seasonal round of the Flathead Nation where different traditional activities are carried out each month, such as Elders telling coyote stories in winter. When students learn about a core community value *Xʷčštwexʷ* (reciprocity), they discuss why it serves as the foundation for building relationships with others and how to practice it as giving back to oneself, to others, to the community, and to nature. Through teacher-led whole-class discussions, small-group activities, and individual journal writing, children identify daily practice of reciprocity, express their respect for the kinship of the community, and honor the sacredness of the surrounding Mission Mountains and the Jocko River that runs through their hometown.

Journal writing is an example of how students used dreaming and reflecting as a speculative practice in SELA project. Art, including drawing, writing, collecting mementos, and creating art books, is a powerful tool to engage in imagination to answer "what if" and "how might" questions (Bolin, 2009). Through journal writing, students reflected on current challenges and used their imagination to respond to the journal prompts. For example, believing that wellness can be achieved by spreading kindness and forgiveness, one student drew a picture of the world where SpongeBob lives and wrote "SpongeBob is always nice to people even if when they are mean." Additionally, when responding to the community members' vision for the collective path to wellness (see Figure 6.1), students perceived wellness from a communal orientation, and asserted agency when they confronted obstacles while walking on the path. For example, a 5th-grade student wrote, "I would change the teachers to learn to help," to involve adults as advocates when facing discrimination and unfair treatment in schools.

The initial two rounds of pilot testing of SELA with 3rd- to 6th-grade students demonstrated the positive impact of the program on children's well-being, resilience, and relationships across the age groups (Sun et al., 2022). Given the lack of culturally responsive measures for Indigenous children's well-being, we used qualitative analysis to examine their journals completed throughout the program. The children described in their journals how the program allowed them to deepen knowledge about the core values of their community, explore ways to honor these values while connecting to culture and land, and express themselves creatively. For example, when reflecting on the importance of reciprocity, one 3rd-grade student wrote: "When I take care of myself it makes me a better friend and student because when I take care of myself, I can spread kindness." Such a notion of reciprocity expands our current view of social–emotional competencies and provides additional evidence to the transformative SEL framework where identity, belonging, culture, and engagement are highlighted.

Educator SEL Program

Following a similar timeline, Project SELA's educator SEL program was adapted from a professional development (PD) program initially created by coauthors Nichols and Goforth for rural educators. The coadaptation of this PD occurred through a half-day retreat and a series of eight meetings with community members to provide opportunities for deep reflection and feedback on the original content of the PD. Meanwhile, educators in the Arlee School were consulted through small focus groups and follow-up interviews so that their social–emotional needs and the specific school context were considered in the coadaptation process.

The coadapted educator SEL program is thus a parallel curriculum of the student SEL program whereby educators are learning about culturally responsive SEL for their students, while also modeling those same SEL competencies themselves. Through this parallel curriculum, educators are supported to recognize that they do have a role in supporting students' SEL and are provided with strategies to integrate SEL into their pedagogy. The program also attends to the community's unique culture and values, aiming to enhance educators' empathy and understanding of this Indigenous community (Goforth et al., 2021, 2022).

The educator SEL program has gone through two phases of iteration. In Phase 1 (AY2020–21), we had to modify it to a remote PD led by the school counselor with a focus on educators' well-being due to the pandemic. Throughout the data-analysis process, we used inductive thematic analyses with a lens toward Indigenous research methodologies (Chilisa, 2020) to learn what would emerge from the data. Preliminary qualitative analyses showed that the PD sessions improved educator's knowledge of SEL for themselves and fostered empathy for their students (Goforth et al., 2022). More importantly, educators furthered their understanding of Indigenous resilience in the face of trauma and recognized the significance of context of working in a tribal nation in supporting their Indigenous students' wellbeing. These findings revealed the importance of challenging the normative understanding of SEL for educators who work in Indigenous communities.

In Phase 2 (AY2021–22), the educator SEL program was codesigned to be an in-person, full-day PD that included culturally specific training, with two tribal Elders as guest speakers. The addition of Elders was in response to ongoing conversations about the tension between the school and community, and educators' misunderstandings about the impacts of intergenerational trauma on parents and students (Sun et al., 2022). Although some educators reacted positively to Elders in the training, other educators expressed discomfort. We facilitated follow-up meetings, where discussions of racism, white privilege, trauma, and tribal sovereignty were brought forth, revealing further opportunities to strengthen communication and mutual understanding between school and community. Our Indigenous community members also followed up with the Elders, who reflected that they may have missed opportunities to hear from educators. Despite this challenging start, Phase 2 highlighted that not only did the PD support educators' SEL and culturally responsive practices, it also served as a bridge between adults in these students' lives: the educators, families, and community members. Nonetheless, the issues that arose through this PD also brought forward the generational harm from colonialism, and the longstanding tensions between school and community. Indeed, future phases of this project will focus on fostering positive relationships between the school and community.

Family SEL Program

In addition to codesigning and implementing the SEL program for students and educators, SELA also included a family outreach effort. Monthly newsletters were disseminated to homes that introduced a family-oriented SEL activity to extend SEL from school to home. Each newsletter begins with the Séliš name of the month and its meaning, referring to a children's book (Greene & Sandoval, 2011) that introduces the seasonal round of life that has always been an essential part of lifeway with the Confederated Salish and Kootenai Tribes. This book was written and illustrated by local Indigenous artists and produced by the Salish Institute as part of the ongoing efforts to revitalize their culture and language. Additionally, the newsletter includes a word of the month (e.g., "reciprocity"), representing the traditional values as well as the corresponding social–emotional competencies (e.g., relationship building) that are central to the SEL. Following the definition, a short and interactive activity is introduced to encourage parents to connect with their children, to honor the word, and to practice the skills at home. These family newsletters extend SEL beyond the school ground to individual families and the community at large. This deliberate interaction bridges multiple ecological contexts where children learn, including school, home, and the community (Garcia Coll et al., 1996). It fosters a communicative channel to unite school and families.

This intentional endeavor aligns with speculative education, which draws upon strengths, values, and crucial resources of the community to support children rather than dwelling on a deficit view of students' problems, barriers, and disparities. It also aligns with transformative SEL (Jagers et al., 2019) in emphasizing SEL needs to go beyond simply promoting individual SEL competencies that can be defined with a Eurocentric value system (Camangian & Cariaga, 2021). Instead, for SEL to sustain and create lasting impact, it needs to be participatory, actively involving youth from marginalized groups to be proud of their own cultural heritage, understand the systemic barriers, and mobilize them to disrupt the inequity. Project SELA advances the scholarship on creating a space for Indigenous students to flourish and cultivate their full potentials in poetic selves, brilliance, resilience, and cultural humility.

COMMUNITY-ENGAGED SEL AS A SPACE TO DREAM

In this chapter, we shared our journey of establishing a partnership between Indigenous community members and non-Indigenous university scholars to codesign and implement a culturally responsive SEL program for students, educators, and families. We argue that our story presents a practical approach to speculative education with concrete strategies that scholars and educators who work with Indigenous communities and other marginalized communities can employ.

Speculative education and reimaginative education carve out space to build upon the strengths of minoritized students, like Indigenous students. It envisions innovative practices and ideas into being (Ross, 2017) and promotes that what a community needs is not simply new knowledge; rather, what a community needs above all is lifelong education (Dahlstedt & Tesfahuney, 2010). As a result, it can lead to learning outcomes that include cultural humility (Pham et al., 2021) and appreciation for cultural multiplicity, as shown in our journey. In Project SELA, Indigenous voices, which emphasize that learning can happen in a variety of forms, and that schools should take advantage of numerous resources with which students may already be familiar, were centered and foregrounded throughout the codesign and implementation of the SEL program. As a result, other ways of communication and learning that have been cherished outside of school, such as telling stories, sharing rituals, and connecting with seasonal rounds, are celebrated in school as well.

In that space of acknowledging a variety of ways to communicate and learn, education also provides opportunities to dismantle the systemic issues that contribute to disparities among ethnic and racial minoritized students. Speculative education is an approach to move away from Western, Eurocentric assimilation of minoritized students and instead provides students with a space to bring the culture and values of their community into the learning environment. In that space, learning is diversified in that it does not require students to follow one standardized worldview or pedagogy. This space is in sharp contrast to the legacy of public education for Indigenous students, where they were expected to shed their identity, culture, and traditions, and residential boarding schools were used as one means to do so. The existing public school system continues to perpetuate this oppression, although much more implicitly (Sabzalian, 2019). For example, school textbooks neglect the real story of the Indigenous experience, and microaggressions continue in the curriculum as well as in school-based experiences (Holter et al., 2020). Project SELA highlights that the existing structures and systems must be changed to infuse identity and culture into school to promote Indigenous student learning and well-being.

Overall, Project SELA demonstrates a compelling example of how codesigning culturally sustaining SEL through community engagement can create a more equitable space for the future of education for Indigenous students. This learning environment that leverages local culture is similarly reflected throughout the Community Day, a day of culture, celebration, and inclusiveness. Teachers and staff joyfully participated in all the cultural activities regardless of being Indigenous or not. By doing so, they acknowledged that they value their students' cultural traditions and are willing to support them in embracing who they are and who their people are.

For many of these Indigenous children, it has always been "family and community before self." While this is often viewed negatively by school personnel as they were frustrated and wanted to see children succeed on an *individual* level, the Community Day provides an inviting space for everyone to realize the imperative beauty in children's hearts that strongly value connecting with others rather than "personal" achievement. This is the essence of actively engaging community in codesigning learning experiences as an approach to speculative education, to cultivate space to dream, envision, and celebrate culture and humanity.

REFERENCES

Ahmed, S. M., & Palermo, A. S. (2010). Community engagement in research: Frameworks for education and peer review. *American Journal of Public Health, 100*(8), 1380–1387. https://doi.org/10.2105/ajph.2009.178137

Bartlett, C., Marshall, M., & Marshall, A. (2012). Two-Eyed Seeing and other lessons learned within a co-learning journey of bringing together indigenous and mainstream knowledges and ways of knowing. *Journal of Environmental Studies and Sciences, 2*(4), 331–340. https://doi.org/10.1007/s13412-012-0086-8

Bolin, P. E. (2009). Imagination and speculation as historical impulse: Engaging uncertainties within art education history and historiography. *Studies in Art Education, 50*(2), 110–123. https://www.jstor.org/stable/25475894

Brave Heart, M. Y. H., Chase, J., Elkins, J., & Altschul, D. B. (2011). Historical trauma among indigenous peoples of the Americas: Concepts, research, and clinical considerations. *Journal of Psychoactive Drugs, 43*(4), 282–290. https://doi.org/10.1080/02791072.2011.628913

Brayboy, B. M. J. (2005). Toward a tribal critical race theory in education. *The Urban Review, 37*(5), 425–446. https://doi.org/10.1007/s11256-005-0018-y

Brayboy, B. M. J., & Lomawaima, K. T. (2018). Why don't more Indians do better in school? The battle between U.S. schooling & American Indian/Alaska Native education. *Daedalus, 147*(2), 82–94. https://www.jstor.org/stable/48563021

Bronfenbrenner, U. (2005). Ecological systems theory. In U. Bronfenbrenner (Ed.), *Making human beings human: Bioecological perspectives on human development* (pp. 106–167). Sage.

Camangian, P., & Cariaga, S. (2021). Social and emotional learning is hegemonic miseducation: Students deserve humanization instead. *Race Ethnicity and Education, 25*(7), 901–921. https://doi.org/10.1080/13613324.2020.1798374

Castagno, A. E., & Brayboy, B. M. J. (2008). Culturally responsive schooling for Indigenous youth: A review of the literature. *Review of Educational Research, 78*(4), 941–993. https://doi.org/10.3102/0034654308323036

Centers for Disease Control and Prevention. (2023). *Youth risk behavior survey: Data summary and trends report*. https://www.cdc.gov/healthyyouth/data/yrbs/pdf/YRBS_Data-Summary-Trends_Report2023_508.pdf

Center for Native American Youth at the Aspen Institute. (2019). *2019 State of Native youth report: Native youth count*. https://www.cnay.org/wp-content/uploads/2019/11/2019-State-of-Native-Youth-Report_PDF.pdf

Chilisa, B. (2020). *Indigenous research methodologies.* Sage.
Collins, S. E., Clifasefi, S. L., Stanton, J., The Leap Advisory Board, Straits, K. J. E., Gil-Kashiwabara, E., Rodriguez Espinosa, P., Nicasio, A. V., Andrasik, M. P., Hawes, S. M., Miller, K. A., Nelson, L. A., Orfaly, V. E., Duran, B. M., & Wallerstein, N. (2018). Community-based participatory research (CBPR): Towards equitable involvement of community in psychology research. *American Psychologist, 73*(7), 884–898. https://doi.org/10.1037/amp0000167
Dahlstedt, M., & Tesfahuney, M. (2010). Speculative pedagogy: Education, entrepreneurialism and the politics of inclusion in contemporary Sweden. *Journal for Critical Education Policy Studies, 8*(2), 249–274.
Dunne, A., & Raby, F. (2013). *Speculative everything: design, fiction, and social dreaming.* MIT Press.
Durlak, J. A., Weissberg, R. P., Dymnicki, A. B., Taylor, R. D., & Schellinger, K. B. (2011). The impact of enhancing students' social and emotional learning: A meta-analysis of school-based universal interventions. *Child Development, 82*(1), 405–432.
Evans-Campbell T. (2008). Historical trauma in American Indian/Native Alaska communities: A multilevel framework for exploring impacts on individuals, families, and communities. *Journal of Interpersonal Violence, 23*(3), 316–338. https://doi.org/10.1177/0886260507312290
Gaias, L. M., Duong, M. T., Pullmann, M. D., Brewer, S. K., Smilansky, M., Halbert, M., Carey, C. M., & Jones, J. (2020). Race and ethnicity in educational intervention research: A systematic review and recommendations for sampling, reporting, and analysis. *Educational Research Review, 31*, 100356. https://doi.org/10.1016/j.edurev.2020.100356
Garcia Coll, C., Lamberty, G., Jenkins, R., McAdoo, H. P., Crnic, K., Wasik, B. H., & Garcia, H. V. (1996). An integrative model for the study of developmental competencies in minority children. *Child Development, 67*(5), 1891–1914. http://www.jstor.org/stable/1131600
Goforth, A. N., Nichols, L. M., Sun, J., Violante, A. E., Christopher, K., & Graham, N. (2021). Integrating Indigenous evaluation framework in culturally responsive community engagement. *Psychology in the Schools, 59*(10), 1984–2004. doi:10.1002/pits.22533
Goforth, A. N., Nichols, L. M., Sun, J., Violante, A. E., Brooke, E., Kusumaningsih, S., Howlett, R., Hogenson, D., & Graham, N. (2022). Cultural adaptation of an educator social–emotional learning program to support Indigenous students. *School Psychology Review*, 1–17. https://doi.org/10.1080/2372966X.2022.2144091
Greene, J., & Sandoval, A. (2011). *Huckleberries, buttercups, and celebrations.* Npustin Press.
Holter, O. G., Goforth, A. N., Pyke, K., & Shindorf, Z. R. (2020). Cultivating perspective: A qualitative inquiry examining school history textbooks for microaggressions against Native Americans. *Journal of Educational and Psychological Consultation, 30*(3), 255–284. https://doi.org/10.1080/10474412.2019.1705162
Huffman, T. (2017). Participatory/action research/CBPR. In *The international encyclopedia of communication research methods.* https://doi.org/10.1002/9781118901731.iecrm0180

Jagers, R. J., Rivas-Drake, D., & Williams, B. (2019). Transformative social and emotional learning (SEL): Toward SEL in service of educational equity and excellence. *Educational Psychologist, 54*(3), 162–184. https://doi.org/10.1080/00461520.2019.1623032

Khan, A. M., Ejaz, M., Matthews, S., Snow, S., and Matthews, B. (2021). Speculative design for education: Using participatory methods to map design challenges and opportunities in Pakistan. In Designing Interactive Systems Conference (pp. 1748–1764). Association for Computing Machinery. https://doi.org/10.1145/3461778.3462117

Ladson-Billings, G., & Tate, W. F. (1995). Toward a critical race theory of education. *Teachers College Record, 97*(1), 47–68. https://doi.org/10.1177/016146819509700104

LaFromboise, T. D., & Malik, S. S. (2016). A culturally informed approach to American Indian/Alaska Native youth suicide prevention. In N. Zane, G. Bernal, & F. T. L. Leong (Eds.), Evidence-based psychological practice with ethnic minorities: Culturally informed research and clinical strategies (pp. 223–245). American Psychological Association.

Lin, C. Y., Loyola-Sanchez, A., Hurd, K., Ferucci, E. D., Crane, L., Healy, B., & Barnabe, C. (2019). Characterization of Indigenous community engagement in arthritis studies conducted in Canada, United States of America, Australia and New Zealand. *Seminars in Arthritis and Rheumatism, 49*(1), 145–155. https://doi.org/10.1016/j.semarthrit.2018.11.009

Mahfouz, J., & Anthony-Stevens, V. (2020). Why trouble SEL? The need for cultural relevance in SEL. *Occasional Paper Series, 2020*(43). https://doi.org/10.58295/2375-3668.1354

McCarty, T. L., Noguera, N., Lee, T. S., & Nicholas, S. E. (2021). "A viable path for education"—Indigenous language immersion and sustainable self-determination. *Journal of Language, Identity, and Education, 20*(5), 340–354. https://doi.org/10.1080/15348458.2021.1957681

McCarty, T., Wyman, L., & Nicholas, S. (2014). Activist ethnography with indigenous youth: lessons from humanizing research on language and education. In D. Paris & M. Winn (Eds.) *Humanizing research* (pp. 81–104). Sage.

Mirra, N., & Garcia, A. (2020). I hesitate but I do have hope: Youth speculative civic literacies in troubled times. *Harvard Educational Review, 90*(2), 295–321. https://doi.org/10.17763/1943-5045-90.2.295

Office of Minority Health. (2019). Mental and behavioral health—American Indians/Alaska Natives. https://minorityhealth.hhs.gov/omh/browse.aspx?lvl=4&lvlid=39

Pham, A. V., Goforth, A. N., Aguilar, L. N., Burt, I., Bastian, R., & Diaków, D. M. (2021). Dismantling systemic inequities in school psychology: Cultural humility as a foundational approach to social justice. *School Psychology Review, 51*(6), 692–709. https://doi.org/10.1080/2372966X.2021.1941245

Ross, J. (2017). Speculative method in digital education research. *Learning, Media and Technology, 42*(2), 214–229, https://doi.org/10.1080/17439884.2016.1160927

Sabzalian, L. (2019). *Indigenous children's survivance in public schools*. Routledge.

Smith, L. T. (1999). *Decolonizing methodologies: Research and Indigenous peoples*. Zed Books.

Stanton, C. R. (2013). Crossing methodological borders: Decolonizing community-based participatory research. *Qualitative Inquiry, 20*(5), 573–583. https://doi.org/10.1177/1077800413505541

Sun, J., Goforth, A. N., Nichols, L. M., Violante, A., Christopher, K., Howlett, R., Hogenson, D., & Graham, N. (2022). Building a space to dream: Supporting indigenous children's survivance through community-engaged social and emotional learning. *Child Development, 93*(3), 699–719. https://doi.org/https://doi.org/10.1111/cdev.13786

Taylor, R. D., Oberle, E., Durlak, J. A., & Weissberg, R. P. (2017). Promoting positive youth development through school-based social and emotional learning interventions: A meta-analysis of follow-up effects. *Child development, 88*(4), 1156–1171. https://doi.org/10.1111/cdev.12864

Vizenor, G. (2008). Aesthetics of survivance. In G. Vizenor (Ed.), *Survivance: Narratives of Native presence.* University of Nebraska Press.

von der Embse, N. P., Pendergast, L. L., Kilgus, S. P., & Eklund, K. R. (2016). Evaluating the applied use of a mental health screener: Structural validity of the social, academic, and emotional behavior risk screener. *Psychological Assessment, 28*(10), 1265–1275. http://dx.doi.org/10.1037/pas0000253

Weissberg, R. P. (2019). Promoting the social and emotional learning of millions of school children. *Perspectives on Psychological Science, 14*(1), 65–69. https://doi.org/10.1177/1745691618817756

Whitesell, N. R., Mitchell, C. M., Kaufman, C. E., & Spicer, P. (2006). Developmental trajectories of personal and collective self-concept among American Indian adolescents. *Child Development, 77*, 1487–1503. https://doi.org/10.1111/j.1467-8624.2006.00949.x

Wolfe, P. (2006). Settler colonialism and the elimination of the native. *Journal of Genocide Research, 8*(4), 387–409. https://doi.org/10.1080/14623520601056240

CHAPTER 7

"I Think a Song Would Be Good"
Grounding Youth Speculative Practices in Theories of Relationality and Desire

Lee Melvin M. Peralta and Joanne E. Marciano

> Alex[1]: I think we should just say something new that we've done over the week . . .
> Jasmine: Like a new song or a new book or poem. I don't know. I think a song would be good [. . .] a song that puts us in a good mood.

This exchange between Alex (10th grade) and Jasmine (11th grade), high school student participants in a community-based research initiative called The Youth Voices Project, took place on April 15, 2020, one month after the community center in their subsidized housing community closed as a result of the COVID-19 pandemic. Unable to meet in person, Alex, Jasmine, and their peers chose to pause their place-based attempts to improve conditions of lighting and the basketball court in their community. Yet they and the additional middle and high school students involved in The Youth Voices Project wanted weekly meetings of the initiative to continue online, opening up new possibilities for engagement and action as indicated in the youths' comments above.

Since March 2020, the COVID-19 pandemic, alongside events involving racial, economic, political, and environmental injustice and unrest, dramatically shaped the context and conditions of education in the United States and globally. The changes that occurred within The Youth Voices Project were no exception. The initiative began in September 2019 in collaboration with community educators in a subsidized housing community, before the appearance of COVID-19, with youth choosing and pursuing action research projects focused on issues relevant to their lives and community. The collaborative work of the project has since transformed and evolved into a space for building and maintaining community, pursuing shared interests, having discussions, and providing mutual support in the context of COVID-19 and other events, including the murder of George Floyd and the attack on the

U.S. Capitol. Ladson-Billings (2021) called for educators to take the global pandemic as an opportunity to disrupt persistent educational inequities, particularly those experienced by marginalized youth, through a "hard re-set" (p. 68) in education that actively draws from students' diverse and evolving cultural practices. Unfortunately, the pandemic led to the opposite effect of a hard reset in certain respects. Instead of seeking out new possibilities for education, some researchers and other educational reformers focused on the "learning loss" that occurred during the first several years of the pandemic, citing test-score gaps before and after the pandemic (Kuhfeld et al., 2022). This focus on learning loss can reinforce notions that equate learning with success on standardized exams and frame the purpose of schooling in terms of job preparation and competition. To the extent that a focus on learning loss echoes past calls to remediate so-called "at-risk" students, a focus on learning loss is regressive, representing a step back rather than a step forward in the direction of imagining new educational possibilities for marginalized youth. Darling-Hammond (2021) argues, "If we focus only on 'learning loss,' we will walk down a familiar road, one paved with repetitive remediation, disengaged students, and reluctant families who are disillusioned with impersonal, inauthentic learning" (para. 13). In this chapter, we consider how informal youth-led spaces such as The Youth Voices Project can disrupt considerations of youth's experiences during the pandemic that focus merely on learning loss.

Accordingly, we examine select moments from The Youth Voices Project to understand how youth participatory action research (YPAR) may inform new possibilities for schooling that foreground relationality and desire as one path toward a reset in education. In this chapter's epigraph, Alex and Jasmine were seeking "something new" in their lives and the opportunity to share their discoveries, interests, and sources of inspiration with others. Their words not only point to practices of everyday flourishing in the midst of crisis but also represent moments that can be considered speculative. Their words represent speculative practices grounded in relationality and desire that can serve as a powerful yet underappreciated source of wisdom as educators seek to reset education toward the disruption of racial and other forms of inequity. This chapter focuses on youth speculative practices to examine what happened when youth shifted their focus from their YPAR projects after COVID-19, transitioned from in-person to online meetings, and imagined new ways of being and doing in the youth-centered research space. In doing so, this chapter provides a "snapshot" of youth's experiences at the onset of COVID-19 in the United States, during a time when closures and social distancing necessitated new forms of interpersonal connection, relationship building, and dreaming of otherwise possibilities for oneself and one's community.

Our work in The Youth Voices Project (Marciano et al., 2020) is guided by theories of culturally relevant and sustaining education (Ladson-Billings,

2014; Paris & Alim, 2014) and educational research about YPAR and student voice (Cook-Sather, 2006). These frameworks help us make sense of data collected throughout the project and align with our goal that the project become a humanizing space (Paris & Winn, 2013). In response to the drastic changes in education and beyond that have occurred since March 2020, as well as the contributions of the youth participants and adult collaborators with and from whom we have learned, we seek to develop an ongoing conceptualization of the speculative to understand our time in the project in new and expansive ways. In particular, YPAR as a methodology is rooted in the Freirean notion of reading and writing the world through education (Freire, 1970), with a particular focus on embracing youth-led ideas and initiatives as a way to honor the agency of youth and learn from and alongside them. Embracing youth-led ideas and initiatives always entails uncertainty. Indeed, as Miller (2017) states, "[T]hose of us committed to PAR endeavors need to consider implications of the unknown, the unpredictable and the unmeasurable as aspects of always entangled but never fully conscious or static subjectivities" (p. 495). YPAR is ripe for speculative approaches to education and educational research because it is intended to embrace uncertainty and the unknown that comes from validating and creating space for knowledge production by youth, who often possess expertise about their local communities and who are often willing to transgress boundaries found within many educational settings.

In this chapter, we examine the following questions: How might our evolving conceptualization of the speculative, grounded in theories of relationality and desire, inform how we make sense of youth practices in The Youth Voices Project? How might new ways of making sense of The Youth Voices Project speak to broader questions about education in a (post)pandemic world? We begin by providing a sketch of our ongoing conceptualization of the speculative. Then, we describe the context of the Youth Voices Project and our methodological approach. Lastly, we explore how youth demonstrated speculative practices during the project that were grounded in their diverse cultural practices and that point to possibilities for enacting a hard reset in education for marginalized youth.

AN ONGOING CONCEPTUALIZATION OF THE SPECULATIVE

In March 2020, the COVID-19 pandemic and resulting school closures required us to transition The Youth Voices Project from weekly 2-hour-long in-person meetings at the Pondside Houses community center to online sessions via Zoom. The disruption led us to move away from traditional approaches to YPAR, where youth and adults collaborate on research projects relevant to youths' lives, and toward a messier, nonlinear, and improvisational approach to research. It was at this point we began to turn our thinking toward the speculative. In some sense, all research begins as a speculative endeavor (Truman, 2022). Every researcher uses their imaginations to engage in the "not-yetness" (Ross, 2017, p. 215) of a what-if question and explore how things might be as opposed to beginning with the guarantee they know how things already are. Research can lose its speculative force once the researcher settles on a choice of methodologies that prescribe formulae for bridging the gap between their hypotheses and settled conclusions. Practices such as coding, while developed as an analytic tactic for organizing and making meaning out of data, can foreclose new possibilities from emerging within research. However, given the disruptions to schooling caused by the pandemic, new possibilities within research are particularly urgent and, following Ladson-Billings (2021), opportune.

Researchers interested in speculative approaches reopen themselves to possibilities rather than foreclosing them out of some belief in analytic necessity. The speculative involves imagination, risk-taking, an openness to consider radical hypotheses, and a belief that even false propositions can be interesting if they stimulate thought (Debaise & Stengers, 2018; Shaviro, 2019). In our thinking around the speculative, we build with scholars who discuss or use speculative methods in a range of educational studies, including digital education (Ross, 2017), walking methodologies (Springgay & Truman, 2019; Truman, 2022), writing praxis (Truman, 2019), climate change education (Rousell et al., 2017), design research (Ehret et al., 2019), STEM education (McGee & White, 2021), and civic literacy research (Mirra & Garcia, 2020). Because the speculative evokes the past, present, and future, we also build with artists, scholars, and activists involved in futurist movements such as Octavia Butler (1993), Aimee Bahng (2018), and José Esteban Muñoz (2009). These futurist creators and scholars provide an alternative to a mainstream Western approach to thinking about the future, which "perpetuates linear versions of time and universalized futures that continue to abstract the material conditions of race" (Springgay & Truman, 2019, p. 548). Mainstream futurisms present cis-heteronormative, white, middle-class life centered on productivity within a capitalist regime as the only possible future (Bahng, 2018). In contrast, futurisms such as Afro- and Indigenous, Latinx, Asian, and Queer futurisms seek to pique our imaginations and expand our sense of the possible so as to widen who the future may be for.

In its reliance on the fantastic, the speculative can be used to "explode" traditional understandings of the past, interrogate dominant ways of knowing, and imagine new possibilities (Mirra & Garcia, 2020, p. 316). The current challenge is to consider how to tailor our conceptualization of the speculative to be most responsive to the collective hopes, dreams, and needs of the youth participants and adult collaborators in The Youth Voices Project as our collaborative work continues to evolve in response to the COVID-19 pandemic and ongoing barriers to racial justice. The transition from in-person gatherings to online Zoom meetings—coupled with the hope, dread, opportunities, and challenges that youth participants and adult collaborators experienced since March 2020—inform how we view the role of the speculative in our work and the lives of the project's participants. This theoretical work is ongoing and continuously developed as we make sense of data and continue to experience and reflect on our time in the research space.

We find it helpful to ground our ongoing thinking around the speculative in terms of relationality and desire. Relationality is a broad term that can encompass a range of approaches to understanding the relatedness or connectedness of people, things, and concepts. We adopt Bingham and Sidorkin's (2004) nine principles of relation, which guide our thinking about relations as a key element in the speculative since if all things are relational, the speculative exists within our relations with each other. If the speculative is about pursuing the not-yetness of a what-if question, relationships are where the answers to such questions are pursued.

Desire is another concept that grounds our emerging conceptualization of the speculative. Like relationality, desire is a far-reaching term. We build with Tuck's (2009) formulation of desire within a framework of desire-based research. Desire is a lens for understanding youth in terms beyond a pathologizing, damage-centered narrative and toward understanding their "differing joys, pains, dreams, and desires" (Gahman et al., 2020, p. 626). These joys, pains, dreams, and desires include their agentic responses to the "not yet" and "not anymore" (Tuck, 2009, p. 417). Tuck (2009) explains that desire-based research is "concerned with understanding complexity, contradiction, and the self-determination of lived lives" (p. 416). Her formulation draws not only from Deleuze and Guattari (1987), who understands desire as a plurality, but also from Gordon (1997), who foregrounds the idea of "complex personhood" whereby "all people . . . are beset by contradiction, and recognize and misrecognize themselves and others" (p. 4, as cited in Tuck, 2009, p. 420). Like relationality, desire is a key component of the speculative because, in its embrace of risk taking and daring hypotheses, it arises within the complexity, contradiction, and full personhood of individuals and communities living in relation to one another. Desire becomes a way of disrupting mainstream approaches to the future and the "linearity of straight time" (Muñoz, 2009, p. 25) that seek to pathologize people of color and other historically marginalized groups who are seen as having failed to conform to the normative demands of the current moment. Instead, the speculative emphasizes the agency and affective excesses of people seeking what Muñoz (2009) might refer to as queerness, which he describes as a "[utopian] formation based on an economy of desire and desiring" (p. 26). In the next section, we describe the context of our project in greater detail and our methodological orientation toward what Jackson and Mazzei (2011) call "thinking with theory."

THE YOUTH VOICES PROJECT

The Youth Voices Project is a multiyear sustained YPAR initiative at Pondside Houses, a subsidized housing community in the Great Lakes region. At the time of this writing, Pondside Houses was home to 436 residents living in 135 apartment and townhome units. Although data about residents' racial identities are not collected at Pondside Houses, the community is racially and ethnically diverse and includes residents who are Black, white, and refugees from countries in the Middle East. Pondside Houses has a community center that provides programming and resources for all residents, including an after-school program for youth staffed by community educators and undergraduate student volunteers from the local university, a college preparatory program led by the community's youth director, a community garden, a computer learning center, and weekly food distribution.

For the past several years, there has been a mutual development and nurturing of relationships between Lee Melvin, Joanne, additional members of the university-based research team, youth participants, community educators, and undergraduate volunteers at Pondside Houses. The project began in 2019 when Joanne, who spent 13 years as a high school English teacher at a New York City public school, met with Patricia, the youth director of Pondside Houses, to discuss possibilities for collaborating to design, facilitate, and research free after-school programming with youth living at Pondside Houses. Patricia shared her perceptions of youths' interests and needs, and Joanne shared examples of literacy programming she previously facilitated. After multiple conversations, Patricia and Joanne agreed to start The Youth Voices Project as a weekly YPAR initiative with students who participated in a preexisting college preparatory program at Pondside Houses. During the early stages of The Youth Voices Project, youth participants and adult collaborators met in-person every Wednesday from 6–8 p.m. at the Pondside Houses community center. Each meeting began with participants gathered around tables sharing a meal prepared by Patricia and an AmeriCorps Vista member. These "family dinners," a term coined by several of the youth participants, consisted of informal conversation followed by a routine where participants took turns sharing "rants" and "raves" from their week. Following dinner, the youth engaged in research activities that included learning about research methods, piloting research methods, and forming research teams around topics of their choice. Many of these activities were initially facilitated by Joanne, but as the youth developed their collaborative research projects, they chose how time during each session was spent. During this time, Lee Melvin, a Filipino male graduate student, approached Joanne to express his interest in participatory methods, which he developed as a middle school mathematics teacher in a primarily APIDA (Asian Pacific Islander Desi American) school in Queens, New York. In January 2020, he joined The Youth Voices Project and supported youth participants as they worked to take the actions they recommended when presenting their YPAR projects to the community at the end of the Fall 2019 semester.

In March 2020, the pandemic caused a dramatic shift in the lives of youth participants and adult collaborators and in the project itself. School closures and social distancing requirements raised questions about whether and how the project would continue. On March 25, 2020, the Wednesday evening meetings resumed over Zoom at the request of youth participants. Dinners could no longer be served, but the rants and raves routine continued. Instead of taking turns around the dinner table, people "popcorned" to the next person, calling on them to share their rant and rave since the previous week's meeting. Because of pandemic-related constraints, the youth chose to pause their place-based action research projects. Instead, Lee Melvin, Joanne, and the other adult collaborators (graduate student researchers, Patricia, and the AmeriCorps Vista member) planned and facilitated online weekly meetings focused on relationship building and supporting youth during their transition to online school. During the early months of the pandemic, the adult collaborators planned each meeting on a week-by-week basis, with many portions of the meetings left open-ended to create space for activities and discussions based on how youth wanted to spend their meeting time. Based on the initiative of the youth participants, several meetings became a supportive space for discussing and responding to current events. For example, in response to the murder of George Floyd, some of the youth participants began to plan for a book club to increase awareness of the Black Lives Matter movement among residents of the Pondside Houses community. This idea was led by Andrea, Jasmine, and Elizabeth, with the adult collaborators taking on a supportive role. To pilot their book club, they facilitated sessions by engaging the other youth participants and the adult collaborators in socially distanced arts-based literacy activities. Since the start of the pandemic, the project has welcomed new youth participants, a new youth director, a new AmeriCorps Vista member, and new research team members. In-person activities resumed in Fall 2021, with some youth participants resuming their original YPAR projects, other participants starting up new projects, and additional participants continuing their work with the Black Lives Matter book club and arts-based literacy activities for the community. A total of 12 youth participants enrolled in grades 7 through 12 have participated in The Youth Project through Spring 2021 (see Table 7.1 for participant demographics).

THINKING WITH THEORY

To examine our research question, we reviewed a combination of audiovisual recordings, notes, and youth-generated artifacts from our weekly meetings with youth. We chose to closely examine five sessions of the project (April 22,

Table 7.1. Youth participants.

Name	Gender	Race/Ethnicity	Joined the Youth Voices Project in . . .	Grade Level
Aaliyah	F	Black	Fall 2021	7
Alex	M	White	Fall 2019	10
Andrea	F	Black	Fall 2019	11
Bobby	M	Black	Fall 2021	9
Caden	M	White	Fall 2020	8
David	M	Black	Fall 2019	11
Desiree	F	Black	Fall 2021	7
Elizabeth	F	Black	Fall 2020	9
Jake	M	Lebanese American	Fall 2019	10
Jasmine	F	Lebanese American	Fall 2019	11
Qwaine	M	Black	Fall 2021	9
Bruce	M	Black	Fall 2021	11

Note: The following pairs are siblings: Jasmine and Jake; Andrea and David; Alex and Caden; Aaliyah and Desiree. Elizabeth and Andrea are cousins. All names are pseudonyms. Gender and race/ethnicity are self-identified. Grade level indicates the student's grade level when they joined The Youth Voices Project.

2020; March 17, 2021; January 19, 2022; January 26, 2022; February 2, 2022). Four of the sessions occurred on Zoom. The sessions were chosen for analysis as illustrations of our ongoing conceptualization of speculative thought and as an opportunity to make sense of powerful moments during which we came to understand the youth participants, and the project as a whole, in new ways. In our methodological approach, we lean on Jackson and Mazzei's (2011) work on "thinking with theory," which describes a nonpositivist approach to research where "data interpretation and analysis does not happen via mechanistic coding, reducing data to themes, and writing up transparent narratives that do little to critique the complexities of social life" (p. 261). In lieu of coding and themes, Jackson and Mazzei draw on Deleuze and Guatarri's (1987) "plugging in" one "literary machine" into another. The concept of a literary machine broadens our understanding of "text" to include "interview data, tomes of theory, conventional qualitative research methods book that we were working against, things we had previously written, traces of data, reviewer comments, and so on *ad infinitum*" (Jackson & Mazzei, 2011, p. 1). The literary machine stresses how texts function in their production of truths rather than what preexisting truths exist within a text. Given this emphasis on the function of texts over their form or content, plugging in texts into one another is an ongoing activity that continuously results in the creation of something new.

We find thinking with theory useful because it allows us to consider how the "texts" of our data and ongoing theorizing around the speculative mutually inform one another. Instead of developing a theoretical framework before applying it to data, we view our ongoing conceptualization of the speculative and our understanding of the project's data as co-constitutive. In the remaining sections, we "think with" our ongoing conceptualization of the speculative to refine our understanding of it and understand what new ideas can be produced by putting theory in conversation with data. In doing so, we seek to explore how the speculative practices of youth within the context of a YPAR project can inform the reset that, as the pandemic has made even more clear, has always been needed in education.

A SONG WOULD BE NICE

Throughout their time in The Youth Voices Project, youth participants demonstrated speculative moments that point to otherwise possibilities for thriving outside the usual constraints of school. To illustrate one such moment, we consider the role music played as a repeated theme throughout the project as we sought to maintain community during the initial stages of the pandemic. Music served as a way to build connections among youth and adult participants in the midst of social distancing requirements, to share stories about our pasts, presents, and desired futures, and to create a comfortable and inspiring atmosphere during several of the project's activities. Music became a medium through which moments of desire and relationality could surface to reveal the speculative potentialities of the project.

The first time music became a significant aspect of the project was shortly after the pandemic necessitated the closure of youths' schools and the Pondside Houses community center. These closures resulted in the youth deciding to pause the place-based YPAR projects they began in Fall 2019. In searching for a way to build and maintain community, we engaged in an activity where youth and adult participants could share a song with the group and talk about why they chose it. The prompt was open-ended and the activity itself was largely improvised. Song choices could be a person's favorite song or a song that resonated with them. Using Zoom's share screen feature, participants took turns playing their songs on YouTube while the rest of the group listened. Participants explained why they chose the song, how they felt when they listened to it, when they first heard it, and what connections they made between the song choice and other song choices or occurrences in their lives. The epigraph that begins this chapter motivated this activity.

Youths' song selections consisted of many well-known tracks such as "Everything's Gonna Be Alright" by Bob Marley, selected by David, "Lean on Me" by Bill Withers and others, selected by Jasmine, and "Never Too Much" by Luther Vandross, selected by Andrea. The youth participants' musical choices point to what Muñoz (2009), drawing on the work of philosopher Ernst Bloch, refers to as "educated hope" (p. 3). They represent educated hope because unlike naive approaches to hope, they are tethered to youths' consciousnesses and cultural repertoires. David chose Bob Marley's song because "I thought of like, kind of what's going on in the world, like Corona and stuff. Personally, I think like, I think it's gonna end soon." Andrea drew a connection to David's song choice, noting "it reminds me of when I was younger 'cause my mom played Bob Marley a lot." Likewise, Jasmine recalled listening to "Lean on Me" when "my mom was playing it when we were cleaning the house. And then she was telling me about how good it is. And I was just crying when I was vacuuming." Lastly, Andrea chose Luther Vandross's song because "it's very upbeat and when I listen to it, it puts me in a better mood, especially during this time, so yeah . . . Like when we were able to go outside, I listened to this song a lot, so it reminds me of outside." Notably, Andrea's comments came at a time when youth were not able to freely go outside due to restrictions and uncertainty experienced at the start of the pandemic.

Music enabled the youth to express their desires and draw connections with one another and their relational ties with family in ways that exceeded mere speech. What we can glean from their song choices is that utopic striving, grounded in desire and relationality, is just as much an aesthetic practice as it is a cognitive and affective one. In using the term aesthetic, we consider it to be a phenomenon not only related to art, beauty, and taste but also tied to broader politics of perception and recognition. The aesthetic is a quality of experience that determines what is recognizable, where politics can take place, and what is considered at stake in politics (Ranciere, 2004). Music was an expressive tool youth participants could use to make sense of their lives and consider possibilities of connection and hope in the context of a pandemic. It was also a means by which affective attachments and aspirations could be recognized as such. By invoking "Everything's Gonna Be Alright," for instance, David not only let the group know how he was feeling at the moment, but through his sharing of the song, created the conditions for which "Everything's Gonna Be Alright" became a possibility that we could feel and collectively strive toward in the face of the pessimism and dread that many people experienced at the beginning of the pandemic. As educators seek to understand how YPAR can inform efforts to make schools more culturally relevant and authentic for students, it is not enough to focus on the ideas and feelings youth express through words alone. Instead, educators can also attend to the aesthetic forms of youths' speculative practices as they suggest possibilities that have always been present but not adequately recognized as legitimate and generative practices in education.

David explained his song choice during the Zoom session by noting "I think it's gonna end soon," a hope that ultimately did not come to fruition. David's hopes were expressed in April 2020, but the pandemic (has) continued well beyond that time. Despite the growing literature on speculative approaches in education, there is a need for more critical attention toward how scholars think about the "never-happened-ness" of "predicted change which does not play out as envisaged" (Ross, 2017, pp. 220–221). Because utopian feelings "can and regularly will be disappointed" (Muñoz, 2009, p. 9), we do not despair in seeing David's prediction that "it's gonna end soon" contradicted by the passage of time. Rather, we remain optimistic because even when educated hope results in disappointment, such hope was and will always be necessary for transformation. To expect that hope and the speculative *must* result in one's desired outcome is to believe in a narrative of progress and conception of linear time that artists and authors such as Octavia Butler (1993) spoke back against. Lauren Olamina, one of Butler's most well-known fictional characters from the *Parable of the Sower* and *Parable of the Talents*, writes, "We shape God. In the end, we yield to God. We adapt and endure. For we are Earthseed. And God is Change" (Butler, 1993, p. 27). Butler (1993) offered a vision of radical hope where we must acknowledge the indeterminate nature of the future in the face of historically situated struggle while simultaneously holding onto the belief in our individual and collective agency. The musical selections and accompanying explanations by David, Jasmine, and Andrea, as well as those by the other youth participants, suggest that radical hope can be found in desire and relationality.

Music continued to play a significant role throughout the project. In response to the murder of George Floyd and subsequent Black Lives Matter protests in Summer 2020, several of the youth participants facilitated a collaging activity via Zoom in Spring 2021. The youth-led activity began with a video of Kwame Alexander's reading of his children's book *The Undefeated* (2019), followed by a group discussion of the book's themes led by Jasmine. Andrea followed up by sharing a playlist of songs she, Jasmine, and Elizabeth curated reflective of themes related to the Black Lives Matter movement, including "Glory" by Common and John Legend; "Rise Up" by Andrea Day; "Brown Skin Girl" by Blue Ivy, SAINT JHN, Beyoncé, and WizKid; and "The Family Madrigal" by Stephanie Beatriz and Olga Merediz. The songs were played while we created collages reflective of our understanding of the Black Lives Matter movement. We used art materials—magazines, glue sticks, and canvas—that Joanne dropped off at the Pondside Houses community center the previous day. Youth picked up the items and brought them home for the session. Because the activity occurred on Zoom, some of the participants' cameras were turned off while others could be seen with their head down intently creating their collage. Everyone listened to the same curated playlist, which served as an anchor that joined the participants in a shared experience despite the context of social distancing. Indeed, while Jake was offering suggestions for how the activity could be improved for future participants, he noted the role music played for him: "Hearing the song as I did it [the collaging activity], kind of, like, helped. It helped me get in that mood . . . The music was excellent."

The important role music has played throughout The Youth Voices Project challenges us to reconsider how we think about youth "voice." Scholars often describe YPAR in terms of elevating youth voice by taking youth's words and ideas seriously and treating them as knowledgeable experts about their schooling and life experiences (Cook-Sather, 2006). The term "voice" not only connotes youth are present and participate in research but also suggests youth have the capacity and power to influence the outcomes of research (Cook-Sather, 2006). Through its emphasis on voice, YPAR becomes a way to push back on traditional research practices that position youth as mere passive recipients of knowledge. But what exactly constitutes voice, and where is it located? It is natural to turn toward youth's words as evidence of their contributions and agency within a research space. The role of music in our project, however, challenges us to consider how youth's utopic strivings, found within the music they curated and played at various points throughout the project, might also constitute youth voice. Music can be seen as a speculative act, a way for youth to express themselves through a playlist that evokes a mood rather than through words alone.

GENERATING PATHMAPS

To demonstrate another moment of speculative possibility within The Youth Voices Project, we recall when youth shared their personal interests and journeys in a pathmapping activity[2] organized in Spring 2022. In a pathmap, participants used text and images to create a "map" of some aspect(s) of their lives. Embracing the idea of maps as subjective and coconstructed, pathmaps might depict a personal journey, aspirations for the future, or reflections about the past and present. The purpose of the activity was to extend vision boards the youth generated the previous semester. Due to a university requirement that classes be held online for the first 3 weeks of Spring 2022, we chose with community educators to host the first three sessions of The Youth Voices Project in 2022 online as well. As a result, we began the first two sessions of the pathmapping activity on Zoom and completed the last session of the activity in-person back at the Pondside Houses community center. During the Zoom sessions, youth participants and adult collaborators created their pathmaps using Google Jamboard. Meanwhile,

Jasmine, a former youth participant who now serves as a member of the university-based research team, played music from the curated playlist described above.

Youth participants and adult collaborators made rich pathmaps displaying images of their communities, their social relations, their hobbies and interests, and their aspirations for the future. Because the pathmaps contain numerous instances of identifying information, we chose not to include images of them in this chapter. We nonetheless provide a brief description of the pathmaps of sisters Aaliyah and Desiree. Their pathmaps featured images and references to their school and hometown as well as the icon for the social media app SnapChat. Aaliyah's pathmap included an image of the title card to the television show *Friends* and a note next to it stating, "I love and respect all my friends." Her map had photos of the singer and actress Aaliyah and the rappers Cardi B, Rod Wave, and Pooh Shiesty, labeled with the note, "People that inspire me." Next to a photo of Louisiana State University was the note, "My dream college," and next to a picture of tropical islands was the statement, "My dream place to go to is the bahamas." Desiree's pathmap had an image of a friend labeled "my best friend" and a note that stated, "i love all my friends and family." Her map included a note and accompanying photo of "my idle Taraji P. Henson" as well as photos of Rod Wave and WNBA player Nneka Ogwumike.

One might misinterpret the pathmapping activity as a mere icebreaker or "get-to-know-you" exercise. On the contrary, we argue that Aaliyah and Desiree's pathmaps support Muñoz's (2009) argument that "the mark of the utopian is the quotidian . . . the utopian is an impulse we see in everyday life . . . This quotidian example of the utopian can be glimpsed in utopian bonds, affiliations, designs, and gestures that exist within the present moment" (pp. 22–23). On the surface, Aaliyah and Desiree's references to their hometown, their school, their sources of inspiration, their interests, and their friends appear merely quotidian; they belong in the everyday and mundane in that they do not draw on the fantastical imagery found within speculative fiction or speculative design, and, therefore, they are unimportant. We disagree. Building with Muñoz, we see within Aaliyah and Desiree's pathmaps a striving toward utopia, both in the present and for the future, that challenges popular images of the ideal school-aged youth as someone who is defined solely in terms of their motivation and autonomy (see Harkness et al., 2007). This is not to say that motivation and autonomy are not valuable traits. Muñoz's (2009) reference to the utopian raises questions about what priorities youth surface in their words and actions. Aaliyah and Desiree prioritized their bonds to family, friends, and people they look up to. They defined themselves not by a list of personal accomplishments (of which there are many) but by their relational ties to loved ones and inspirational figures. These relational ties represented the "utopian bonds, affiliations, designs, and gestures that exist within the present moment."

Aaliyah and Desiree's pathmaps challenge us to reconsider what speculative practices look like in the context of the everyday lives of youth. During a portion of the meeting when youth shared their pathmaps and responded to youth participants and adult collaborators' questions, Aaliyah noted, "I've had the same friends since elementary but some new friends have been added to the group." As Aaliyah shared her pathmap, Lee Melvin asked her why she thought both her and her sister's maps featured the music artist Rod Wave. Aaliyah explained, "His music is just emotional, I guess. It's understandable . . . It's about just feelings . . . He puts all his feelings . . . It's like he puts all his feelings into one song." How might we make sense of these references to friendship and emotion? Traditional research methods might search for findings that lead to generalizable conclusions useful for identifying interventions that can produce measurable increases in student achievement. In contrast, speculative thinking strives for possibilities beyond the present moment. In a climate of education and schooling marked by an increasing focus on individual achievement and accountability, the references to friendship and emotion exceed this present moment by hinting toward a desire by Aaliyah and Desiree to step outside of themselves and see their lives in relation to others. In their striving for emotional connection, they "enliven[ed] worlds of possibility in everyday practices of care" (Bahng, 2018, p. 132). The idea of creating new possibilities through everyday practices of care is an important lesson that Aaliyah and Desiree can teach educators seeking a hard reset in education. Instead of seeking to optimize learning outcomes at any cost, classrooms can become a space where students' feelings, friendships, and desires are recognized and embraced not only because they improve engagement and enthusiasm for school but also because they are valued as ends in themselves.

RELATIONALITY AND DESIRE AS COUNTERSPECULATIVE PRAXIS

Considerations of the speculative across this chapter are timely given disruptions to education caused by the pandemic. The speculative is an appropriate conceptual and methodological intervention for seeking the hard reset in education Ladson-Billings (2021) urges educators to pursue. Further, the speculative can speak back against reactionary calls to increase accountability measures in education in the face of learning loss research that has arisen in a (post)pandemic world. Learning loss research seeks to "take the risk out of education" (Biesta, 2016, p. 1) by seeking to minimize uncertainty in classrooms so that education becomes secure and predictable. Schooling practices that seek to recover learning loss in a (post)pandemic world are premised on the idea that students can be tracked, measured, and remediated according to predictive models about student learning and behavior. In this sense, such schooling practices are inherently speculative in nature.

The youth-led practices described in this chapter represent a different form of the speculative, one that is culturally situated, affective, and emancipatory to the extent that it embraces education as a risky endeavor. These youth-led practices can be said to be counterspeculative because they resist the already speculative logics of traditional schooling. These youth-led counterspeculative practices offer modes of thinking about the past, present, and future that reject the fetishization of traditional school success foregrounded by learning loss research in a (post)pandemic world. Instead, the youth demonstrated practices of care grounded in everyday desires and relationships. The song selections of David, Jasmine, and Andrea, as well as the pathmaps of Aaliyah and Desiree, provide a window into otherwise possibilities for marginalized youth. These possibilities foreground the inherent value of feelings, familial connections, friendships, hopes, and aspirations as forms of practice youth use to survive and thrive in the midst of crisis.

Returning to Ladson-Billings's (2021) call for a hard reset in education, recent crises offer educators renewed opportunity to reject dominant paradigms of schooling that treat education as a business whose sole function is to maximize student productivity and minimize the risks inherent in schools. Youth-led counterspeculative practices—particularly those enacted within informal after-school spaces—can serve to disrupt business as usual by steering the focus of education away from productivity and risk minimization and toward the dreaming of new possibilities for marginalized youth.

The practices by youth participants in The Youth Voices Project provide concrete lessons for reimagining in-school and after-school programming in a (post)pandemic world. First, their counterspeculative practices are a continued reminder to take an asset-based orientation when working alongside and collaborating with youth. Youth practices are culturally situated, place-based, and representative of a repertoire of strengths that are not always recognized within traditional schooling settings. Second, the song selections of youth participants point to the importance of attending to desire and relationality as an everyday aesthetic practice. In The Youth Voices Project, music provided a shared experience and point of connection that allowed the youth participants and adult collaborators to overcome the challenges of social distancing, particularly during the onset of the pandemic. Nonetheless, as classrooms and other educational programs move back to in-person settings in a (post)pandemic world, the role that music can serve for building connection and for self-expression continue to be relevant. Music is a powerful site for recognizing speculative practices that do not rely on words alone. The song selections by Andrea and David teach us to listen to students, not only by paying attention to the words they use but also by attending to what they are able to communicate through their aesthetic practices. These aesthetic practices encompass more than music to include students' artistic, stylistic, and other preferences and practices. Lastly, the pathmaps of Aaliyah and Desiree teach us that hope and desire can be found and should be sought for in the mundane. It is true that dreaming can and should be found in youth's desires for significant cultural, political, economic, material, and structural change. However, the speculative can also exist in the mundane desires of youth, where everyday dreaming can build toward lasting change.

In short, the speculative is a call for educators to create space for, listen to, and be responsive toward what youth strive for in the present and for the future. It is a methodology and an orientation to education that challenges visions of school as a site for achieving predetermined learning outcomes and maximizing test scores and seeks to rework education from the ground up, the new foundation of which is built on everyday practices of care and the embrace of the complexity, contradiction, and self-determination of youth.

ACKNOWLEDGMENTS

We are thankful for the contributions of youth, their families, and community educators for generously sharing their time and experiences with us. We are also grateful to the following university-based research team members for their contributions to the work of The Youth Voices Project: Alecia Beymer, Beth Herbel-Eisenmann, Audriyana Jaber, Lauren Elizabeth Reine Johnson, Ji Soo Lee, and Hannah Rosemurgy. We further appreciate grant funding support for The Youth Voices Project provided by the American Educational Research Association Division K Re-envisioning Teaching and Teacher Education in the Shadow of the COVID-19 Pandemic small grants program; the American Educational Research Association Division G small grants program; the Engagement Scholarship Consortium; the Education Research Service Projects Program of the American Educational Research Association; the Michigan State University College of Education; and Michigan State University English Education Program.

NOTES

1. All names, including those of locations, are pseudonyms.
2. Pathmapping was adapted from an activity organized by the hosts of a virtual learning lab that Lee Melvin attended in his own time, and it shares many characteristics with the qualitative method of Education Journey Mapping (Annamma, 2016).

REFERENCES

Alexander, K. (2019). *The undefeated*. Versify.
Annamma, S. (2016). Disrupting the carceral state through education journey mapping. *International Journal of Qualitative Studies in Education, 29*(9), 1210–1230. https://doi.org/10.1080/09518398.2016.1214297

Bahng, A. (2018). *Migrant futures: Decolonizing speculation in financial times*. Duke University Press.
Biesta, G. J. (2016). *The beautiful risk of education*. Routledge.
Bingham, C. W., & Sidorkin, A. M. (Eds.). (2004). *No education without relation*. Peter Lang.
Butler, O. E. (1993). *Parable of the sower*. Four Walls Eight Windows.
Cook-Sather, A. (2006). Sound, presence, and power: "Student voice" in educational research and reform. *Curriculum Inquiry, 36*(4), 359–390. https://doi.org/10.1111/j.1467-873X.2006.00363.x
Darling-Hammond, L. (2021, April 5). Accelerating learning as we build back better. *Forbes*. https://www.forbes.com/sites/lindadarlinghammond/2021/04/05/accelerating-learning-as-we-build-back-better/
Debaise, D., & Stengers, I. (2018). The insistence of possibles: Towards a speculative pragmatism. *Parse Journal*, 12–19.
Deleuze, G., & Guatarri, F. (1987). *A thousand plateaus: Capitalism and schizophrenia*. University of Minnesota Press.
Ehret, C., Ehret, L., Low, B., & Čiklovan, L. (2019). Immediations and rhythms of speculative design: Implications for value in design-based research. *British Journal of Educational Technology, 50*(4), 1603–1614. https://doi.org/10.1111/bjet.12802
Freire, P. (1970). *Pedagogy of the oppressed*. Continuum.
Gahman, L., Penados, F., Greenidge, A., Miss, S., Kus, R., Makin, D., Xuc, F., Kan, R., & Rash, E. (2020). Dignity, dreaming, and desire-based research in the face of slow violence: Indigenous youth organising as (counter)development. *Interface: A Journal for and about Social Movements, 12*(1), 616–651.
Gordon, A. (1997). *Ghostly matters: Haunting and the sociological imagination*. University of Minnesota Press.
Harkness, S., Blom, M., Oliva, A., Moscardino, U., Zylicz, P. O., Bermudez, M. R., Feng, X., Carrasco-Zylicz, A., Axia, G., & Super, C. M. (2007). Teachers' ethnotheories of the 'ideal student' in five western cultures. *Comparative Education, 43*(1), 113–135. https://www.jstor.org/stable/29727818
Jackson, A. Y., & Mazzei, L. (2011). *Thinking with theory in qualitative research: Viewing data across multiple perspectives*. Routledge.
Kuhfeld, M., Soland, J., Lewis, K., & Morton, E. (2022, March 3). The pandemic has had devastating impacts on learning. What will it take to help students catch up? *Brookings*. https://www.brookings.edu/blog/brown-center-chalkboard/2022/03/03/the-pandemic-has-had-devastating-impacts-on-learning-what-will-it-take-to-help-students-catch-up/
Ladson-Billings, G. (2014). Culturally relevant pedagogy 2.0: A.k.a. the remix. *Harvard Educational Review, 84*(1), 74–84. https://doi.org/10.17763/haer.84.1.p2rj131485484751
Ladson-Billings, G. (2021). I'm here for the hard re-set: Post pandemic pedagogy to preserve our culture. *Equity & Excellence in Education, 54*(1), 68–78. https://doi.org/10.1080/10665684.2020.1863883
Marciano, J. E., Peralta, L. M., Lee, J. S., Rosemurgy, H., Holloway, L., & Bass, J. (2020). Centering community: Enacting culturally responsive-sustaining YPAR during COVID-19. *Journal for Multicultural Education, 14*(2), 163–175. https://doi.org/10.1108/JME-04-2020-0026

McGee, E. O., & White, D. T. (2021). Afrofuturism: Reimagining STEM for Black urban learners. In R. Milner & K. Lomotey (Eds.), *Handbook of urban education* (pp. 384–396). Routledge.

Miller, J. L. (2017). Neo-positivist intrusions, post-qualitative challenges, and PAR's generative indeterminacies. *International Journal of Qualitative Studies in Education, 30*(5), 488–503. https://doi.org/10.1080/09518398.2017.1303215

Mirra, N., & Garcia, A. (2020). "I hesitate but I do have hope": Youth speculative civic literacies for troubled times. *Harvard Educational Review, 90*(2), 295–322. doi:10.17763/1943-5045-90.2.295

Muñoz, J. E. (2009). *Cruising utopia: The then and there of Queer futurity.* New York University Press.

Paris, D., & Alim, H. S. (2014). What are we seeking to sustain through culturally sustaining pedagogy? A loving critique forward. *Harvard Educational Review, 84*(1), 85–100. https://doi.org/10.17763/haer.84.1.982l873k2ht16m77

Paris, D., & Winn, M. T. (Eds.). (2013). *Humanizing research: Decolonizing qualitative inquiry with youth and communities.* Sage.

Ranciere, J. (2004). *The politics of aesthetics: The distribution of the sensible.* Continuum International Publishing Group.

Ross, J. (2017). Speculative method in digital educational research. *Learning, Media, and Technology, 42*(2), 214–229. https://doi.org/10.1080/17439884.2016.1160927

Rousell, D., Cutter-Mackenzie, A., & Foster, J. (2017). Children of an Earth to come: Speculative fiction, geophilosophy and climate change education research. *Educational Studies, 53*(6), 1–16. https://doi.org/10.1080/00131946.2017.1369086

Shaviro, S. (2019). Defining speculation: Speculative fiction, speculative philosophy, and speculative finance. *Alienocene: Journal of the First Outernational, 23,* 1–11.

Springgay, S., & Truman, S. E. (2019). Counterfuturisms and speculative temporalities: Walking research-creation in school. *International Journal of Qualitative Studies in Education, 32*(6), 547–559. https://doi.org/10.1080/09518398.2019.1597210

Truman, S. E. (2019). Inhuman literacies and affective refusals: Thinking with Sylvia Wynter and secondary school English. *Curriculum Inquiry, 49*(1), 1–19. https://doi.org/10.1080/03626784.2018.1549465

Truman, S. E. (2022). *Feminist speculations and the practice of research-creation: Writing pedagogies and intertextual affects.* Routledge.

Tuck, E. (2009). Suspending damage: A letter to communities. *Harvard Educational Review, 79*(3), 409–427. https://doi.org/10.17763/haer.79.3.n0016675661t3n15

CHAPTER 8

Participatory Methodologies to Transform the Project of Schooling
Student Voices Leading

Leyda W. Garcia, Edwin Cruz, Jaune Reyez, Aliza Manalo, Eduardo Galindo, Adriana Rios-Cruz, Alex Alejo, Nareli J. Lopez, Le'kie Hatfield-Whitlock, Claire Matias, and Walter Hernandez Mejia

INTRODUCTION

Context | Setting

The streets around our public school are home to human beings who march, not just walk, to school, work, bus stops, factories, pushing *changarros* with freshly squeezed orange juice, tamales, scrambled eggs, *atoles* of all kinds, donuts, hot Cheetos, and coffee. Brown and Black faces, still masked, move swiftly to their destinations. A constant movement of bodies from street to street, from territories to territories. All saunter with a purpose in mind. You hear Spanish, Mam, K'iche', English, Korean, Filipino, Chinese, Arabic, Bangla, Hindi, Russian, Urdu—world languages transcending continents, space, and place. Almost a thousand young bodies converge at a school site with students ages 4 to 21, a space where dual-language programs thrive, open-door policies reign, and a laser focus on social justice and emancipatory practices shines. This is schooling rooted in community, communities forged from struggle, marginalization, and exclusion. Except that is not how they define themselves, not how we define ourselves. We would say we are scholars, thinkers, philosophers, inventors, magicians, and creators. The mission and vision of our school call for a whole community to embrace the richness in the traditions and languages of our ancestors. Adults are called to know their students well to help them thrive on their own terms.

Flashback

Our school was founded in 2009 as the UCLA Community School, a public school in partnership with the University of California–Los Angeles (François & Quartz, 2021). That inaugural year we opened our doors to serve students in grades kindergarten to 5th grade. Families gathered in the multipurpose room eager to meet the staff and hear about the plans for the year. The community shared in the joy of being part of a larger story of struggle—struggle to alleviate overcrowded schools and subpar educational opportunities, a struggle for equal access. There was much controversy about the opening of a brand-new multimillion site for students of color. A not-so-subtle message made clear that certain students, our students, did not deserve such an investment. The questionable deservingness of our students permeated the media coverage. But for students and families who had been part of focus groups and community town halls to discuss what they envisioned for their new school, that September day represented deliverance and hope. In 2010, the school welcomed secondary students grades 6 to 11, and by 2012, the school graduated its first class. During those challenging first years, the school focused on building a sense of community that elevated the student experience and centered the margins. Over the next 10 years, the school grew its inclusion program, an infrastructure of support for newcomer immigrant students, additional services for families, a legal clinic, as well as multiple partnerships to continuously redefine what public schooling could and should be.

Present Time

Today, the school exists in the praxis of (1) operationalizing educational theories that often reside in faraway spaces, away from the reality of urban schools, and (2) the action required to redefine the project of schooling. We—students, educators, families—embrace the challenge to operationalize theories around social justice, abolitionist teaching, reality pedagogy, healing pedagogies, translanguaging stances, and the speculative—the dream-making. Love (2019) reminds us that "theory is a practical guide to understanding injustice historically, the needs of people, and where collective power lives within groups of people" (p. 132). She reminds us that only action coupled with solidarity can solve issues, and at our school we problematize issues so we can solve them and improve upon our community schooling practices. Our work is marked by constant iterations that seek to chip away at oppressive systems of education to reveal emancipatory approaches that center the voices of our youth and their families. This work showcases the epistemology and leadership of our young people as they create the school anew, with their wisdom and ways of being. Reality pedagogy within our way of schooling affirms students' experiences and communities and helps us ground our work in our ratchet selves—the selves that are expansive and complicated, the selves that keep marginalized communities out of the clean spaces of settler-colonialism education (Emdin, 2016, 2021).

Embracing the Speculative

The episodes presented in this chapter are weaved by threads of our lived and yet-to-be-lived experiences—they are explorations and declarations of what is happening within our school. Some might call them speculative—as they are indeed experimental in nature, a probe into new possibilities. Some explorations were born out of the pandemic and a collective commitment to stay connected and not accept a diminished educational experience, nor a return to "normal." The Student Advisory Board redirected our trajectory as a school and redefined student leadership in the midst of a pandemic that shut down our physical doors, but opened up other pathways for learning and connecting. The coteaching spaces that developed from a student-run club to a history elective reshaped the role of student and teacher. A coteaching classroom, where student and teacher hold parity and a supportive environment elevates student knowledge and wisdom, now informs how we view pedagogy and instruction, differentiation and engagement. Young students looking for better ways to coexist with fellow creatures, like raccoons, offer a glimpse of a future where humans are not above any others. These captured moments in our school are explorations because the future will be iterations of these initial steps in redefining schooling. The episodes are also declarations because they are living proof of what is possible now, and perhaps what may be doable tomorrow "if only we're brave enough to see it/if only we're brave enough to be it" (Gorman, 2021).

Our lived praxis demonstrates that it is possible to create such contexts that turn the speculative into a daily experience. As a community school, we aim to construct and live in "fantastic paradigms of collective thriving," spaces where speculative education can tether us to the stories of our communities while providing us with wings to fly above the mundane and overdone, the regimented and bounded (Garcia & Mirra, 2023, p. 4). We sustain that our students hold the expertise and experience to redefine schooling (Bertrand & Rodela, 2018). Our school embraces its *oppositional imagination* to fight against old narratives (Furman, 2012).

We dwell in the *speculative* to guide transformative work in instruction, teacher leadership, student leadership, research and practice (Garcia & Mirra, 2023). We appreciate that our school is in good company and the storytelling we craft reminds us that:

> It is from this unchosen history of collective and suppressed knowledge that we posit that the recognition of other universes, on our imaginative horizon, have

always been with us. In dreams, in the stories shared from our elders as we stared at stars, and in the inertia that compels us to continually question the status quo, we are constantly skating on ice that separates us from the icy depths of an always unknown and always so close elsewhere. (Garcia & Mirra, 2023, p. 17)

We are dream weavers and sharers. Our school is accompanied by the speculative and imaginative work transpiring at Social Justice Humanitas in the San Fernando Valley in the Los Angeles area (Saunders et al., 2021), and across the nation with Fannie Lou Hamer Freedom High School in the Bronx (Strauss, 2015). Spaces do exist where communities are braiding their knowledges and leveraging partnerships to cocreate rich contexts for learning and teaching in dialogical ways. Through this compilation of testimonies we present possibility. What if students had a real seat at the table? What if students were the ones conducting research at their schools and leveraging the power of their findings to enact change? What if young scholars determined the school's green initiatives to create more sustainable practices? What if school communities were allowed to work together in ways that they valued, and thus forged a future that was genuinely affirming for those who have been at the margins for too long? What if we answered the call "to agree on collective, liberatory freedom as a fundamental purpose of education?" (Garcia & Mirra, 2023, p. 9).

As we ponder the questions aforementioned, we imagine that if students had a seat at the table more classes would be codesigned and cotaught by student scholars. We speculate that if young people were conducting their own research projects, their findings would yield irrefutable data about the appropriate course of action given any problem the school may be facing. If student voices were fully amplified, schools would have many teams, not just one Green Team, to address issues impacting not just the school, but humanity and the planet as a whole and thus multiple universes of possibility would coexist.

OUR STORIES: EPISODES IN THE LIFE OF OUR SCHOOL

Our chapter is an offering of stories, stories representative of the integral role students play in how we choose to school and how we choose to learn from one another. You will find us using our names because we have all accepted the challenge to share our stories in the first person. Parents were informed and consented to their children being coauthors, narrating aspects of our school's development and portraying their learning in their own words. High school students, some of whom will be in college by the time this volume is published, wanted to be the narrators of the audacious possibilities they coconstructed in their school.

EPISODE 1: STUDENT ADVISORY BOARD: STUDENTS INFORMING THE SCHOOL'S RESPONSE TO THE PANDEMIC

In this first account Alex Alejo, Eduardo Galindo, Nareli J. Lopez, and Adriana Rios-Cruz describe their role as student leader-researchers, engaged in community-based research methodologies to better understand the impact of the pandemic on our school. The knowledge they shaped through their project led to a deeper and richer understanding of what the school's response needed to look like to truly support students and teachers.

The Conditions

During the 2021–2022 school year, we represented a corps of student workers who supported the school in the daily routines of COVID-19 protocols, greeting families and students with bright smiles, and other projects like summer retreats for incoming students. We open this section with the introduction to a blog we authored relating our reflections on virtual learning during the 2020–2021 school year:

> In a year that many have considered lost, we have learned much. We learned that we have many gifts and talents. We got better at our hobbies and discovered new hobbies, too. We learned that we are good at chipping in—we can cook for our families and take good care of our siblings. We learned how to fix things and do chores properly. We also learned how to manage our time, avoid procrastination, practice self-care and love, and appreciate and enjoy the present. Our school lives were transformed just as much. We are members of the Student Advisory Board of the UCLA Community School. When the coronavirus changed life as we knew it, we came together to be sure that student voices were heard as our school moved to online learning. (Aguilar et al., 2021)

The Process

We, Adriana, Alex, Eduardo, and Nareli, are all part of the Student Advisory Board. During virtual learning we embarked upon a research journey to learn about the impact of the pandemic on our community and to share our findings with teachers, students, and families. Our work centered student experiences and revealed what strategies students found helpful and what areas the school could improve upon. We shone a light on the student experience through surveys and focus groups. In the focus groups, we convened students in the same grade level to have them answer a series of questions we created. One of us took care of the chat to keep the discussion moving and ensure we heard from everyone. The answers we captured were very honest and open. We heard stories about job losses and sick family members. We also heard stories of triumph as older students recounted how much their families depended on their assistance and work. Many students were working in businesses like supermarkets. There was a lot of loss, pride, and moments of joy, even in the most difficult situations. We really wondered what the best way to share our findings would be and how we could influence how our school was responding to the challenges the pandemic brought to students and their families.

In terms of our data analysis, we used spreadsheets to organize and synthesize the data from surveys and focus groups. Some of us loved sharing the formulas we learned to code our data and sharing short cuts with the team. We decided to share our findings with the teachers during one of their Wednesday professional development sessions. For our process, we separated the teachers into various breakout rooms where pairs of us presented the data about the student experience through charts, graphs, and quotes. Our teachers listened openly to what we described. There were student quotes about long hours of work, helping siblings, and appreciating a modified school schedule. Presenting our findings to our teachers was one of the hardest things we did, but it helped our school community realize the impact of the pandemic on students and families. We also designed a feedback form that helped us ascertain what teachers made of our findings and what recommendations they had for us as the advisory group. The most powerful piece of this exchange was realizing that teachers also were craving a space to share their own lived experience during the pandemic and online teaching. Teacher questions and feedback helped us expand our project to include the voices of our teachers. We worked on a teacher survey that sought to reveal the teacher experience during online schooling.

The teacher survey revealed similarities across the groups. Teachers expressed similar feelings of isolation and also a newfound creative energy given the different schedule our school had. Teachers were very candid about how hard it was to teach to black tiles with names, not quite knowing who was actually on because it was rare to hear someone's voice or see someone's face. Teachers described feeling like they were just putting on "a show" where the feedback was sometimes coming in only through the chat. Our process helped the students and the teachers connect around a very difficult situation. Through our research we humanized each other by honestly sharing what we were going through during virtual learning.

The Impact

The first wave of impact involved students wanting to turn on their camera during advisory classes as a sign of appreciation for our teachers. Our turn-on-your-camera campaign helped connect students and teachers. Families, who saw the data through meetings with the school's staff, were moved also by what students and teachers shared. As the in-person return materialized in the spring of 2021, part of our work involved creating recommendations for that return. A few of us were also part of our school governance council and during budget development we posited the possibility of the school becoming a community partner in employing students. Our families had suffered tremendous income loss and many students were now working to contribute to their families. What if the school hired student workers? Our knowledge and advocacy gave way to the Student Workers Corps, a team of students who are hired by the school to lead a variety of projects. Some student workers designed and ran summer retreats for incoming 9th- and 10th-grade students. Others worked on creating a podcast and other sources of information for our school community. Today, all of us serve our community by supporting safety protocols. We welcome our fellow schoolmates at the gate and help create a sense of unity. Our smiles and positive attitudes give a warm welcome to students and families. Things are not quite back to normal but we know our knowledge and actions have enriched our school community. Our voices matter.

EPISODE 2: STUDENTS AS COTEACHERS: BRAIDING PERSPECTIVES TO ENRICH LEARNING

Edwin Cruz, Aliza Manalo, and Jaune Reyes present their learning as coteachers of a course called Japanese History and Culture. Their work in the seminar (an elective course) will continue to inform the current standards of what our elective spaces look and feel like for students and teachers. Several students presented their journey as coteachers at the National Community Schools and Family Engagement Conference in June 2022 at the Los Angeles Convention Center.

The Conditions

In March 2020, a terrible plague afflicted the nation with worry and unease. This prompted schools to transition to an inferior form of education—virtual learning. Both teachers and students alike dreaded Zoom as a means of teaching. Students would not unmute themselves, the class sessions felt empty, and worst of all, the myriad technological issues that arose as a result of using Zoom as a means of teaching were exhausting for all. As days wasted away, like many teenagers with newly found free time, we spent our time watching anime and thought about how we could share this interest with others. We found it pretty interesting and we ended up researching Japanese history and culture in our own time.

    One of our teachers, after hearing about our interest in Japanese history and culture, decided to sponsor a club dedicated to this topic of interest.

What made this club interesting for both the teacher and students was the structure of what felt more like a class. For each day of the club, we made presentations for students to learn about different aspects of Japan—the mythology, the gender inequalities in the workplace, the history of Nintendo, clan wars, and more. After hearing that we would be going back to school in-person, our advisory teacher, Mx. K, reached out to propose the idea of transitioning our club to a seminar class to teach other students what we had learned.

The Process

We started by recruiting eight dedicated club members to coteach alongside us. These members were passionate about teaching others, and their expertise in the subject was high. To optimize our time, we decided to work on our curriculum right away. Many of us found that researching in preparation for a class would be far more difficult than imagined.

We also created core agreements. First, we had people work on their own lesson and made it their responsibility to finish it. Second, we agreed on collective collaboration to decide on lessons and overall activities. Third, we aimed for equal division of labor. We really wanted to show our contribution to the seminar by making sure it was not the guiding teacher doing everything. The final core agreement was that everyone would be a teacher and a student, including our advisor. Whenever we were not teaching the class, we were students who would participate in the activities that were presented. We all turned in the work just as any other student would, and Mx. K was also a student whenever they were not teaching.

We met weekly on Zoom to work on the development of our course. In these meetings, we communicated our aspirations, our troubles, and our solutions. We talked about logistics, content, and students. Most recently, after seeing how some of our students were struggling in the class, we all agreed to split up and help struggling students improve their grades. Since we believe that the best learning takes place not just in the classroom, but outside of it as well, we planned and fundraised for field trips and scavenger hunts for our students.

The Impact

Going into the seminar, many of the coteachers had to learn that it is okay to rely on others. To have the best course we could have, Mx. K, a history teacher, brought their own expertise to the seminar along with us providing our expertise as students. We have always been awestruck by the way that teachers approach their occupations and how much dedication they have for the field. With this in mind, we were able to bring all the experience we have accumulated from two perspectives. We have student-teachers who have gained years of experience being taught by teachers and understand what students find compelling in class. With both of our expertise brought to the table, we were able to make the lessons for everyone be the best for students to have them stay engaged and learn. We were able to bounce off each other's ideas on what might be effective and what could be improved. We asked Mx. K about any questions or concerns that might come up since we relied on their years of experience. Every step of the way, Mx. K was really supportive of our aspirations.

Throughout the semester, we improved our knowledge of teaching and what comes with being a teacher. Having an experienced teacher check in with us and give advice on how to improve was an immense help for us all throughout the year. Whether it be helping us communicate our needs to the administration or communicate with others on a more professional level. We might not feel as comfortable speaking to someone who holds great power, but with the guidance of Mx. K, we felt more confident when approaching adults at our school. We are now experts in this field since we were able to learn from past experiences and observe how our seminar advisor dealt with these situations.

As first-time student-teachers, we would say that challenges of teaching include knowing what content to plan, the timing between activities, grading assignments, and time management in general. There are a lot of aspects to take into consideration when it comes to making something engaging for students: visuals, videos, and hands-on activities, which are a few of the many learning techniques that our school implements. Although these are valid areas, our main concern was how to connect with the students. We constantly wondered: How can we make this lesson fun and engaging for them? Will they learn, remember, and/or share this knowledge with people outside the classroom? Every day was a challenge in itself. During our first semester, something we remember in particular was confronting a student who made a homophobic comment toward a film we were watching. This was something new to us, and at first we did not know how exactly to deal with it. As coteachers we decided the best course of action would be to pull the student aside and have a conversation about what they had done. Even though things were resolved in a favorable manner, it was still an experience that was new, and it was a challenge to come up with a way to approach the incident.

We love being student-teachers. With all our teachers, it is clear that they teach because they like to guide students to their own adventures and paths; it is that fact that has made us admire and respect them all the more. We must remain determined and dedicated to this work. We must teach in a way to fit all the learning needs present in our class. Aspiring teachers should keep this in mind because developing a relationship with your students is key to having a worthwhile experience not only for the students, but also the teacher.

EPISODE 3: VOICES FROM THE GREEN TEAM: CARING ECOSYSTEMS FOR ALL

In this section, elementary students and Green Team leaders Le'Kie, Claire, and Walter share words about their perspectives about recycling, the Green Team, and our overall responsibility to the ecosystems that thrive on our campus. Their leadership helped revamp our elementary recycling program. Their words are taken from informal interviews and brainstorm sessions with Principal Garcia. Although this section is structured similarly to the last two stories, in this segment there are direct quotes from the students to capture the richness of their thinking.

The Conditions

For the last several years, our school has engaged elementary-age students in what we call the "Green Team." The Green Team's mission is to handle all the recycling during breakfast and lunch. The goal is to reduce the trash while recycling materials that should not end up in a landfill. Milk cartons and trays are recycled while other items are thrown away. Fruits are saved for after-school snacks. The community-parent center passes out fruit to students and families. The after-school program also relies on the fresh fruit for students who stay in the program. This simple act reduces trash tremendously and the school actually earns recycling money that gets invested into physical education equipment. Our custodial staff appreciates seeing students and staff involved in this manner and the sense of community across students and staff is deepened. The closures caused by the COVID-19 pandemic eliminated the need for the Green Team. Fortunately for the 2021–2022 school year, our site welcomed all students back to campus and the Green Team was revived.

The Process

Students from 2nd to 5th grade joined the team after an announcement was made during one of our assemblies. Students were eager to learn how to support their school. Parents received a letter recognizing their children for their decision to participate in this program. Students were broken up into shifts during recess and lunch to help all classes recycle and reduce trash. The students were divided into two teams by grade levels; 2nd- and 3rd-graders supported their own grade and breakfast for TK through 1st-graders. The older students, 4th- and 5th-graders, helped their own grades and the lunch period for our youngest students. Monthly meetings were held with the teams to check in and update schedules. Through these informal spaces student, ideas and leadership naturally emerged and informed new initiatives for the Green Team.

The first manifestation of student leadership came through content creation about recycling. The older students (4th and 5th grade) decided it was important to create informative content that could be shared schoolwide. Student-created videos and slides were shared during virtual assemblies reminding the community why recycling matters to students, custodians, and furry friends like squirrels and raccoons. Some of the content also included fun facts about the environment and human impact on climate change. Classmates enjoyed seeing their friends on the screen and more students wanted to join the Green Team.

The process of recycling was informed by students also, who often would have suggestions about how to best recycle materials and enhance collaboration across a particular "shift" of Green Team members. Students asked for schedules to be posted close to the recycling areas. At recess and lunch, students loved checking for their names to learn if it was their turn to assist. Several students became leaders and they supported new members by sharing their expertise in emptying out opened milk cartons into a big bucket with wheels, stacking all the trays, and disposing of food items in a separate receptacle. The fresh fruit, unopened milk, and dry snacks like crackers were put into baskets later taken to the community-parent center. Students themselves decided who would take the baskets and who would take the trays to the large recycling bins. Initially, students used paper trays to carry these goods, but inspired by the student leadership, the supervision staff donated baskets to facilitate the process. Custodians also helped students by making sure brooms and other cleaning supplies were available to them. The exchanges across students and staff members ensured the recycling process ran smoothly and also augmented the feeling of community and shared responsibility for our campus.

The Impact

As the recycling system got underway, Green Team members advocated for a Green Team shirt to be worn by all Green Team members. Students wanted to highlight the importance of the work students were engaged in and inspire additional students to join the team. Students felt it was important for them to design the shirt, and thus a process was created. Students submitted their design ideas and 3rd-grader Claire and 2nd-grader Walter won the competition. Their design was turned into a T-shirt that was proudly worn by all the Green Team members. The enthusiasm generated by the T-shirt design inspired 5th-grader Le'Kie to initiate schoolwide clean-up days. Le'Kie's concern was over the animals that live in our school's big planters and near the various trees. He felt birds and insects deserved a clean habitat to thrive, just like their human friends. In his own words:

> I saw so much trash and I wanted that to change; there have been so many animals living here, like squirrels and raccoons, and I wanted to clean the

environment for them, so the animals could come back to the school and feel welcomed. [I would love to] have weekly, bring animals from rehab centers to see what animals can come back to the school to live in our habitats. Like kiwi birds used to be around but if it's too dirty they won't come back. I want to partner with organizations to support animal life in our own school.

To this end, he organized pods of students to clean on a biweekly basis; he also asked his teammates to wear their Green Team shirts every Wednesday they had a clean-up day. Seeing Green Team shirts around the campus ignited an appreciation for these student leaders and their advocacy for the campus and other species that call our school home—from ladybugs to butterflies, to redtail hawks and kiwi birds. The students' activism enriched our sense of community and gave dozens of students the opportunity to participate in a cause that was meaningful to them. The students' actions inspired our custodians and supervision staff to lend a hand also and assist the students. Even students who had been hesitant to fully participate in the team's actions were moved to actively support the clean-up days.

For Walter, a shy 2nd-grader with black-rimmed glasses and a stylish haircut, participating in the Green Team opened up opportunities to engage with peers and share an important message. In his words:

> My dream . . . I would like to keep it all clean, make sure there's no trash, we need more people to help out with trash. A clean environment means we all are healthy, humans and animals. Green Team needs a bigger table to sort items and recycle. And I wish we had peacocks, like the ones we saw at the Arboretum.

Walter echoes Le'Kie's interest in the animals that coexist with us on our campus and also presents a vision for a richer ecosystem that would allow for animals like peacocks to roam around the school campus. Walter's vision calls for a complete redesign of learning and schooling spaces, much like Le'Kie's interest in having rescue animals be brought to our campus to live and thrive. This shared idea that schools could become a welcoming home for animal species other than humans points to students' capacious view of what a learning environment can and perhaps should be, and the impact that may have in how we maintain those spaces.

Claire, a vivacious and friendly 3rd-grader whose mentorship really inspired the staff to become more involved with supporting the Green Team, expresses how helping others is her driving force. In her words:

> I want to help to clean the community and to help others. I helped them with the Green Team, the schedule showed someone was working but if they were absent, Ms. Alicia asked me if I would help.

I would tell them to join to help others. Other students need to care about keeping their school clean!

Claire's advocacy comes through in her words and actions. Ms. A, a supervision staff member, was very taken by the students' hard work and leadership. She counted on Claire as much as Claire counted on Ms. A to make the system work. This readjustment of roles and authentic collaboration between students and staff offers another window into what is possible when those rigid boundaries are broken. The added capacity of students and school staff, beyond classroom teachers, can contribute to active engagement throughout a campus and in a variety of spaces that enrich the learning experiences of both students and staff.

In many ways opening spaces for our youth to lead the way is simple. Their connection to the world and school community is enriched by their curiosity and openness. Their words, advocacy, and actions are inspiring. Le'Kei's keen concern about animal friends, Walter's wish to have a space similar to a beautiful outdoor museum, and Claire's collaborative work with staff give insight into how important spaces (physical and relational) are for students to learn and grow. If we positioned ourselves in a way that genuinely allows for student voices to direct how we work, teaching and learning truly would be enriched. The process of schooling would be so much more liberatory for young people and adults alike.

FINAL REFLECTION

This section I humbly approach as the formal leader of the UCLA Community School for the last 10 years. I must begin by acknowledging and appreciating the student contributions to this entire chapter. For me, hearing their voices in the work is what gives meaning to a life in education. Students and their families always have been the point of origin; the community always has nourished our development and identity as a community school. As a school in partnership with a public university we

> yearn for, believe in, and commit to opening the public university [public school] to concerns of the common good, and to carving with others delicate spaces of collective criticality and public science where we interrogate privilege and argue through differences, forging what Audre Lorde called "meaningful coalitions" and designing research collectives drunk on a wide range of expertise and experience. (Fine, 2018, p. 117)

We want to ensure that the learning and teaching spaces are fertile ground for imagining and creating a more affirming and just space for all students, especially those whose experiences are often seen through deficit lenses. We seek to leverage all our resources, including students, families, our university partner, our community-based partners, our entire staff—from teachers to foodservice workers, our histories and languages, our traumas, and our healing practices. Based on the stories above, some of this lived praxis is revealing what is possible already, but we hold steadfast to the idea that we are just beginning to uncover those possibilities. And, we want to hold on to that liminal space and thus never forget that learning and liberatory practices are not places you arrive to, but rather dimensions you explore and inform, reshape and reconfigure with shared knowledge and experiences that both anchor and propel the work toward freedom in and through education. The journey is cyclical in nature and reflection is an essential part of measuring progress.

As I stepped down as the principal of the school in 2022, I welcomed a group of alumni who were entering our school as new teachers, new instructional aides, and researchers. That moment of recognition and reunion was magical, filled with memories of connection and audacious hope. Assigning classrooms and passing out keys to a new generation of teachers for whom community schooling meant fulfilled dreams and breaking barriers was extra-ordinary. Extra, in the best sense of the word, because there was so much mutual appreciation and deep respect in our encounter. Ordinary because we have always belonged in those formal spaces where teaching and learning is part of a long history of resistance. As I moved to another phase of my own journey, I also bid farewell to our inaugural class. In 2009, the students of the class of 2022 began their educational journey in our newly constructed building in the heart of the Pico-Union-Koreatown area of Los Angeles. The graduates embodied hope and possibility, profound love, and a deep sense of responsibility to remain active participants in their community. Shaking hands as we handed off diplomas, I was moved by the stories behind every student. Our paths had crossed and coexisted for 10 of those 13 years they had spent at the Community School. We were in each other's lives and in accompaniment of each other's dreams and aspirations. We were, in fact, one community.

To dream, to reimagine, to operationalize equitable and just education is the work of the collective. Opening up spaces for student and family voices to fill rooms requires commitment and perseverance. I know this entire book can help us all shift a bit more toward enacting liberatory practices that rectify the wrongs of the past and present, and center a continuous focus on what can be and already is in some places. We are there, at the threshold of possibility.

REFERENCES

Aguilar, G., Alejo, A., Laureano Carranza, G., Juco, J. L., Lopez, N. J., Rios-Cruz, A. (2021, May 13). Finding our voices and our research skills during the pandemic. EdSource: Student Voices. https://edsource.org/2021/finding-our-voices-and-our-research-skills-during-the-pandemic/654552

Bertrand, M., & Rodela, K. C. (2018). A framework for rethinking educational leadership in the margins: Implication for social justice leadership preparation. *Journal of Research on Leadership education, 13*(1), 10–37. https://doi.org/10.1177/1942775117739414

Emdin, C. (2016). *For white folks who teach in the hood and the rest of y'all too.* Beacon Press.

Emdin, C. (2021). *Ratchetdemic: Reimagining academic success.* Beacon Press.

Fine, M. (2018). *Just research in contentious ties: Widening the methodological imagination.* Teachers College Press.

François, A., & Quartz, K. H. (Eds.). (2021). *Preparing and sustaining social justice educators.* Harvard Education Press.

Furman, G. (2012). Social justice leadership as praxis: Developing capacities through preparation programs. *Educational Administration Quarterly, 48*(2), 191–229. https://doi.org/10.1177/0013161X11427394

Garcia, A., & Mirra, N. (2023). Other suns: Designing for racial equity through speculative education. *Journal of the Learning Sciences, 32*(1), 1–20. https://doi.org/10.1080/10508406.2023.2166764

Gorman, A. (2021). The hill we climb: An inaugural poem for the country. Viking Books.

Love, B. (2019). *We want to do more than survive: Abolitionist teaching and the pursuit of educational freedom.* Beacon Press.

Saunders, M., Martínez, L., Flook, L., & Hernández, L. E. (2021, May 10). *Social Justice Humanitas Academy: A community school approach to whole child education.* Learning Policy Institute. https://learningpolicyinstitute.org/product/social-and-emotional-learning-case-study-humanitas-report

Strauss, V. (2015, June 11). A rare 'defy the odds school' where learning isn't driven by high stakes test. *The Washington Post.* https://www.washingtonpost.com/news/answer-sheet/wp/2015/06/11/a-rare-defy-the-odds-school-where-learning-isnt-driven-by-high-stakes-tests

CHAPTER 9

"Is This How It's Always Going to Be?"

Speculative Teacher Education With(in) Community Toward Liberatory Praxis

Kristen Jackson and Rubén A. González

It was another uncharacteristically hot summer day and we (Kristen and Rubén) were taking one of many sweaty strolls through our tree-lined university campus on our way to the teacher candidate social gathering—the first of the upcoming academic year. While we were excited to be working with the teacher candidates, we were lamenting our recent experiences laboring in separate university summer programs.

> *Rubén:* "Damn [exhale], it's been a super long week. I'm getting tired of this shit and we *just* started doing some of this work!"
> *Kristen:* "Yes! I'm teaching my first class and already having issues! They expect so much and don't support, I can't be held responsible for fixing the entire teacher education program here overnight!"
> *Rubén:* "I'm sorry. How can I support you?"
> *Kristen:* "I'll be fine, thanks for supporting as usual. How are you holding up?"
> *Rubén:* "Same old thing. How can these undergrad program administrators say their goal is to serve first-gen, low-income students but then admonish me and disregard my input as a first-gen, low-income staff member?"
> *Kristen:* "Yeah, it makes no sense. I'm sorry."
> *Rubén:* "You're good, thank you for supporting me while I was going through it."

The conversation took shape in the way many would in the coming months: Kristen contemplating the difficulty of teaching in a historically violent, year-long teacher education program and Rubén navigating the challenge of speaking up without being perceived as "the angry Latino" in a summer bridge program. These walks became staples in our relationship: processing the day/week/month on a walk back to graduate housing, after a lunchtime pizza and pasta meeting with colleagues, on a boba run, or on the field outside one of our dorms. These short debriefs and strategizing conversations became necessary to persist in our precarious conditions.

Our initial meeting happened the previous year, prior to committing to and enrolling in our current doctoral program. Our early meeting in 2020 occurred on a snowy weekend at a Midwest university during a recruitment visit, directly prior to the COVID-19 shut down. This moment proved to be incredibly fruitful. Our initial bond was strengthened by the fact that we were both current classroom teachers with plans to close out our brief but rich teaching careers before transitioning to graduate study. The uncertainty of 2020 coupled with the layered transitions proved incredibly challenging. Against the backdrop of COVID-19 and the "racial uprisings" in the summer of 2020, we found solace in the community we built when we first met. That chance meeting continued to prove that the only way to overcome the isolation and the violence that comes with aligning with the academy is through community.

In this chapter, we briefly reflect on our experiences transitioning from K–12 classrooms into the higher education space of teacher education. One notable reflection that continues to arise in our conversations is the sheer solitude of academic spaces. We both come from community-oriented spaces; building, communing, and organizing with like-minded people comes naturally to us. The vignette above occurred after our first year of graduate study, where we quickly realized this process is not one that can be embarked upon alone. Moreover, contrary to its design, success in forging ties with(in) the communities we serve in schools and the academy cannot be done in solitude. It is the solidarity we fostered with one another, and by extension the future teachers of color we now support, that fortifies our ability to engage in a speculative tomorrow while navigating the violent today of higher education.

We see the speculative as a way to dream about the community we desire most—one where teacher educators of color are not siloed in the university but surrounded by the organizers and organizations that truly power radical education. The tension we felt was alleviated quickly after every brief conversation—regardless of the medium, being in community offered immediate respite. If the revolution is a journey, then it is, as the saying goes, better to go far together than to go fast solo. Furthermore, we offer this chapter as an introspective look into where we came from because radical pedagogy isn't found in texts but in people, in community, and in being. Knowledge generated among comrades should be central to powering the work of teacher education, for that is where teachers go when they leave the academy. We engage in the speculative as an uncertain answer to systemic violence as a way to honor the past while dreaming forward. Thus, we put this forth as a way to consider the skin we have in the game, and hope that it prompts deep reflection by the reader to consider how their roots and origins were planted to move them forward.

SPECULATIVE EDUCATION

Mirra and Garcia (2020) define the youth speculative civic literacies as "expansive, creative forms of meaning making and communication aimed at radically reorientating the nature and purpose of shared democratic life toward equity, empathy, and justice" (p. 297). We build on their work and the Freirean approach of "reading the word and the world" (Freire & Macedo, 1987, p. 12) to turn our attention to the speculative praxis of teacher educators of color. We draw on Indigenous (Grande et al., 2015; San Pedro, 2015) and Black (Hartman, 2019; Kelley, 2002; Otieno, 2018) epistemologies to inform the speculative praxis of creating meaning, knowledge, and illuminating alternative present and future lifeworlds rooted in collaborative struggle and possibility toward liberation. This speculative act provides an approach to communal praxis rooted in reflection, (re)imagination, and action toward alternative present and future realities is informed by the act of communal dialogue and narratives. We draw on what San Pedro (2015) calls the Indigenous practice of "storying," which serves to converge theory and practice in a relational act of communal listening and giving back to shared questions and stories that arise with others. We are also informed by Otieno (2018), who demonstrates the practice of Black communities engaging in narratives to create alternative and affirmation knowledge and ways of being despite persistent institutional (extra)judicial forms of violence.

We offer here a layered definition of speculative: *the verb, noun, and adjective*. Engaging in speculative methods requires indulging all three to confound the generally expected certainty. Accepting the speculative in teacher education opens the door to dreaming for and with radical futures for dispossessed communities. This is the action/verb where we encourage teacher educators to invite dreaming into their collective learning spaces. Speculative, the noun, is the uncertain space in research and teaching wherein feelings, emotions, and dreams are not dismissed for their lack of scientific clarity. And speculative, the adjective, is used to describe the space between where we are and where we could be and engages those who desire to freedom dream (Kelley, 2002) in that space with us.

We build on this work to engage in a speculative praxis with(in) teacher education, which centers community, reflection, and action toward the (re)imagination of how to prepare and support future K–12 classroom teachers to work with students of color and other marginalized youth. A speculative praxis calls for teacher educators to draw on their past, present, and future selves in an act of vulnerability and reflection of individual and collective challenges, defeats, triumphs, and possibilities. In drawing on these experiences, a speculative praxis serves as an approach to counter the often solitary and violent spaces of teacher education for teacher educators of color. In particular, doing so with(in) community and toward a liberatory present and future possibilities in the preparation and support of future teachers. We engage with a speculative praxis to demonstrate how teacher educators of color fuse collective past experiences with our dreams and actions of alternative present and future worlds.

THE LANDSCAPE OF TEACHER EDUCATION

Teacher education, literally and figuratively, has an overwhelming presence of whiteness (Carter Andrews et al., 2021; Matias et al., 2018; Sleeter, 2001), which has resulted in racism being normalized within the structures of teacher education (Sleeter, 2017; Souto Manning, 2019). Within these structures saturated in white epistemologies, ontologies, and axiologies, scholars (Kohli & Pizarro, 2022) have documented the layered toll of racism on teacher educators of color. In addition, while sparse, there is nascent literature focused on the value and struggles of Black (Dixon & Dingus, 2007), Latinx (de los Rios & Souto-Manning, 2015), and Asian (Matias, 2013; Shim, 2018) teacher educators in racially hostile professional contexts (Kohli & Pizarro, 2022). Drawing on this literature and our individual and collective lived experiences, we employ a co-autoethnographic (Coia & Taylor, 2009) approach to our work and to this chapter, and do so to counter the trend to work individually within the academy, recognizing that "identity is dialogical [and] we maintain our identity in relation to others" (p. 3).

We engage in this endeavor through the perspective of our shared identities—people of color (Black and Chicano), former classroom teachers, and current teacher educators—and our differing identities—race, gender, sexual orientation, and geographic origin backgrounds. We do not offer these as a list of our marginalities, but instead as a hopeful invitation in the ways other teacher educators of color may see themselves in our story and how teacher educators of color may engage in work within and beyond differences in their past, present, and future lived experiences. As we collaboratively engage in a speculative worldmaking and "criminal" action within and at war with the academy (Moten & Harney 2013) and in teacher education, we do so with what Arellano et al. (2021) call "shadow work": work in response to a problem, work that emerges wherever there are haunting circumstances, "work carried out for another person in the name of care, love, and leaning without certainty or guarantee for what that work might yield" (p. 31). The place and space of the "undercommons," and the literal and figurative "shadow work" that is the impetus for our work with future classroom teachers is not new. Our shared commitments are informed by the speculative (re)imagining of our individual and collective past and present experiences, and our work toward a more liberated present and future.

THE FOUNDATION OF OUR SPECULATIVE PRAXIS

Rubén

As a son of Mexican immigrants, and as someone who experienced K–12 schooling as a literal and figurative violent space at the hands of white teachers and a few teachers of color who trafficked in whiteness, I have always employed my critical sociopolitical disposition of reading the word and the world (Freire & Macedo, 1987) through an understanding and analysis of race, gender, and class, among other factors. This way of engaging with the world has influenced my personal epistemologies, ontologies, and axiologies. Foundationally, this was further informed by my work as a classroom teacher, which now drives my work as a teacher educator toward seeking to engage future classroom teachers in work toward liberatory practices at the classroom, school, and larger community levels.

As a first-year English teacher in Sacramento, California, I recall eagerly teaching a lesson about institutional racism and sexism with my 9th-grade students. We collectively explored the racialized and gendered historical, contemporary, and future experiences of the local community where the school was located. After a 75-minute lesson, which included multimodal individual, pair, group, and whole-class reading, writing, speaking, and listening activities, we concluded our time together. Janny, a Hmong student whose parents immigrated to Northern California as a result of the "Secret War" in Laos, raised her hand and asked, "Ok, Mr. G., but so what, now what?"

At this moment, I remained speechless. Staring back at 25 Black, Latinx, and Southeast Asian students, I realized the limitations of my lesson, regardless of my critical and good intentions. Janny, and her peers, pushed me to realize that it was not enough to explore, understand, and analyze various critical sociopolitical issues in community with key stakeholders. There must be collective action. This group of students pushed my work as an educator into the realm of activism and organizing, and we began not only to engage in the speculative of (re)imagining alternative lifeworlds in schools, but to engage in collaborative action toward that work in the classroom (González, 2018) and beyond (Macdonald, 2016, 2018). In short, my students helped me to engage in the speculative of my work as a classroom teacher, and pushed me to become a community-engaged teacher–activist–organizer.

Kristen

My grandmother was an educator. A Black educator committed to the education of Black kids. She spent decades teaching elementary school in Detroit, Michigan, and eventually got her master's degree in special education. She would always lament to her children the importance of meeting kids where they are. My mom often tells stories of helping to set up my grandmother's classroom, conducting coat drives, and the late nights my grandmother spent away from her family to support others. She will always say, in these moments, "Kristen got the gift from my mother." There is something incredibly sacred to me, to have bestowed upon me the responsibility of carrying forward her dreams of serving the community through the classroom.

Since her recent passing, I have learned the most about my grandmother's pedagogy from my mother, and I can definitively say that she was a dreamer. She dreamt of a future where Black children in Detroit were nurtured in their schools by educators with a shared fire (shut up) in their bones. She envisioned a time where young Black teachers clamored to work in classrooms full of Black children learning, growing, and thriving. In her retirement, she observed and coached student teachers until she couldn't anymore. In my family, she was the teacher educator that I didn't know I wanted to become. I remember going to observation debrief meetings at the McDonald's near Wayne State that doubled as her satellite office—I did not know it at the time but she was also showing me that you must meet teachers where they are. My grandmother laid a framework of community-based pedagogy—she did not operate out of an institution but took her work into the community. She knew, as I have discovered, that the only way to do this work is in and with the community. I often think of her and wonder, "What would she tell me to do next?" She encouraged me to dream, and in her death, I continue to envision a community-based approach to teacher education that meets at the point of communal need.

Our calls to action and invitations to reimagine the world are vastly different, but the end result is almost identical. We were pushed in our respective experiences to reconsider what it means to pursue justice through classroom pedagogy. First as K–12 teachers, and now as evolving teacher educators, the mission has remained the same. We both stand on the shoulders of ancestors who imagined radical futures for their communities. Together, we take up that imagining and collective dreaming (Kelley, R. D. G. (2002). Freedom dreams: The Black radical imagination. Beacon Press, 2002) to continue to push for systems that meet students where they are and never stop asking, "So what, now what?" "We argue that co-constructing knowledge, co-creating relationships, and exchanging stories are central to educational research" (San Pedro & Kinloch, 2017).

It is in the intersection of our disparate ontologies and shared epistemologies that we are able to foreground future careers shaped around a radical futurity. Before we were teachers, we were students and small humans who encountered an unfriendly world. Those identities do not and should not take a backseat upon entrance to the academic field. We continue to call the young teacher who was challenged by his student to dream forward, and the young girl who traveled with her grandmother to support new teachers in every space we occupy. Together, we have forged a professional and personal relationship that centers mutual respect and a deep trust in a shared vision toward liberation in and beyond educational settings. These axiological agreements—informed by our K–12 student and teacher experiences with oppression but more importantly with joy—have birthed several projects that serve as the backdrop of our current co-autoethnographic work.

SPECULATIVE PRAXIS WITH(IN) COMMUNITY

Back to our opening dialogue, as we grappled with our racialized and gendered positionalities, this was a profoundly pivotal collective moment in our development as teacher educators. In response to our recent individual plights within the academy, and informed by our individual values of community, dialogue, and working toward liberation, we began to collectively engage in a speculative praxis regarding our work together as burgeoning teacher educators. It is important to note here that the opening interaction is merely a speculation of the precise dialogic exchange. For the sake of this chapter, we interrogated our individual and joint memories of the interaction to document it as the introduction, as it was a formative conversation that resulted in generative building. But it is necessary to acknowledge that it is far from precise, but that does not preclude its accuracy. In the speculative (noun, adjective, and verb), uncertainty is where beautiful clarity resides. Whereas we do not know exactly what was said, we know the essence of the conversation and, more importantly, the resulting emotions and reflections.

We can be certain that on this hot summer day, we were informed of the institutional creation, design, and upcoming implementation of newly formed student-led affinity groups in the teacher education program. The focus of these two groups included supporting Black, Indigenous, and People of Color (BIPoC) candidates and white candidates interested in becoming antiracist educators. Due to our own, often difficult, K–12 schooling experiences as the result of how our racialized and gendered bodies were positioned, we discussed the potential and possibilities of such spaces. We began to speculate about what these spaces might be in the present and future, specifically what we, the institution, and the teacher candidates might want from these present and future spaces. While we recognized our lived experiences in the field of teacher education as violent and oppressive, we used these experiences as fodder to seek and work toward alternative present and future spaces. More importantly, we always came back to what K–12 students of color and other marginalized youth *needed* these spaces to be for the teachers they will soon have in their classrooms.

As we arrived for this teacher candidate social gathering, we exchanged pleasantries with students, faculty, and program administrators. Over free pizza and beer, we engaged in a speculative praxis about our collective role within and beyond these affinity spaces.

> *Rubén:* This might be cool to check out and to be a part of this upcoming year.
> *Kristen:* I agree—it would be dope to tap in with the teacher candidates in this space. What do you think it'll look like?
> *Rubén:* I think it is an opportunity to support the candidates this year in their own sociopolitical and pedagogical development, and to research the larger spaces to think through how to change how future teachers are prepared and supported.
> *Kristen:* We didn't come here to sit on the sidelines and leave it up to the university to support teacher candidates.
> *Rubén:* I do worry the BIPoC space will focus on free pizza and beer. We should be more involved in what happens in the BIPoC space, maybe design and facilitate aspects of the meetings?
> *Kristen:* I don't think pizza and beer is a bad thing. Marginalized people also need healing spaces where their peace is prioritized.
> *Rubén:* You're right [pause] but I still worry. Maybe frame it as a critical space from the beginning, to set the intention so it doesn't become BIPoC yoga.
> *Kristen:* Have you supported preservice teachers before?
> *Rubén:* Only informally, I never had a student teacher. My principals never trusted me. They likely thought I'd radicalize the candidates [laughs].
> *Kristen:* I hear you, but if we push too early and too hard, they might resist and not want our support. We can let them do their thing, and if it becomes a critical space, cool. If it doesn't become a critical space, they might get frustrated and then come to us for support, wanting our support. I hear you, but we can't always be Rambo and just bust down the door and rush in.
> *Rubén:* [laughs] Yeah, you're right, you're right. I can definitely come off too harsh. I appreciate you calling it out. I don't know.
> *Kristen:* I got you. We got this.

The dialogue above reflects the first of several conversations in which we begin to grapple with a speculative (re)orientation to our work as teacher educators and our work with teacher candidates. While we had divergent approaches, we both held the belief that the current teacher education experience was not enough for racially minoritized teacher candidates. We had to (re)imagine and (re)configure, and do so with community, approaches to prepare and support teacher candidates. Our conversations led to the formation of an ongoing research project for and with the teacher candidates who would engage in critical dialogues as a part of racial affinity spaces (González & Jackson, observation debrief Jackson & González, observation debrief).

We engaged in a speculative praxis in divergent yet similar ways as our work progressed. Rubén spoke with two candidates about their mid- and long-term goals in their teacher education experience and how the BIPoC affinity group would serve as a vehicle toward those goals. In essence, how such a space could serve as the undercommons for the teacher candidates. The shadow work that Rubén engaged with included multiple phone and in-person conversations about strategizing how to build a coalition with their peers and how to redirect institutional space, place, and resources. In contrast, Kristen formed a deep connection with one teacher candidate with a very similar background, and together they soothed the aches of existing as Black women in violent spaces. She was once asked, "How do you do this and stay happy? I always see you smiling." Kristen told her simply, "They aren't the cause of my joy, so they can't take it." Together, they dreamed of a joy that could not be stolen by the spaces they existed in, one that persisted like the joy of their grandmothers. Through frequent text check-ins that were never longer than 2–3 messages, they uplifted each other, both a reminder to the other that the loneliness was a fabrication.

Extending the concept of uncertainty in a speculative praxis, we each invoked dreaming in powerful ways. Whereas Rubén engaged in vision-building around how to support teachers of color, Kristen offered centering joy as both an aspiration and a daily practice to usher in the possibilities of existing in potentially violent educational spaces without crumbling. The difference in approaches, however, mirrors the aforementioned separate but powerful experiences that spurred them to this moment. While Rubén often is looking for the next move—or the "so what, now what?"—Kristen likes to lead from behind and allow students—of all ages and experiences—to dictate their approach. These divergent perspectives regarding vision and action, while they could have been a debilitating clash for others, instead served as a "choque" that instead of destroying created a new and better existence (Torre & Ayala, 2009).

Our continued speculative praxis has helped the project grow into a space where we both interrogate the experiences of teacher candidates in critical affinity group spaces, while simultaneously offering a space for teacher candidates to process the growth they have experienced and the shortcomings of a student-led critical collaborative space. Some preliminary findings show that the two spaces—one is modeled after BARWE (Building Anti-Racist White Educators) out of Philadelphia, and the other is a BIPoC affinity group—presented more tensions than solutions. Students found themselves puzzling more than critically processing and ultimately turned their attention back to the institution for falling short.

In the words of one teacher candidate who attended the BIPoC affinity group, "I feel like it's good to have a social group to just decompress." A frequent point of contention was the general purpose, a finding that echoed conversations shared by the two authors early in the year. The question of what students wanted versus what they needed was never resolved, as some teacher candidates wanted a critical praxis in the affinity group, while others wanted to do yoga, eat pizza, and to heal. In response, Kristen continually tried hard to honor and validate that those desires are warranted—being marginalized in schools comes with an incredible cost and space to undo the harm and violence of schools is important. However, the lack of cohesion led to further tensions. Another teacher candidate, reflecting on the difficulty encountered when trying to organize a critical cohesion to the BIPoC affinity group, stated ". . . it's like, every step that we took forward, we were immediately like stomped to the ground . . ." While some wanted the pizza and beer, those willing and ready to do the work found themselves "stomped to the ground."

We have reflected extensively over the formal interview data and informal reflections from students around the fissures in the BIPoC affinity spaces. Although we disagreed on the level of input we should have had in the planning and supporting of the student-led affinity spaces, one thing that never wavered was our commitment to listening to and validating each other's perspectives and the perspectives of the teacher candidates with whom we both worked. This is where our paths converge. We are wholly committed to continuing to do work that centers the voices of the marginalized, but there is no roadmap for how to do that work as a marginalized graduate student/teacher educator. The barriers we face feel larger and more insurmountable because of our own marginalities. In our collaborative (re)imagination of a speculative present and future for the preparation and support of future classroom teachers, we strive toward more liberatory schooling experiences for K–12 students of color and other marginalized youth.

Rubén

My conversations with the teacher candidates who made up the BIPoC affinity group planning committee, who I will refer to as Danny and Jessica, were rooted in preparing and supporting them to engage in a speculative praxis toward justice in their work in various settings. First, in response to their critique of various teacher education structures and barriers to their work, while I listened and reassured them, I would also lovingly nudge them to go beyond rhetoric and to take action. This included conversations about rooting the BIPoC affinity group in a Freirian act of praxis, in which participants engage in "reflection and action upon the world in order to transform it" (1970, p. 52), rather than simply focusing on free pizza and beer. Second, I lovingly encouraged them to engage in a speculative praxis in their student teaching placement, focusing on what and how they taught their students. These conversations were also dialectical, not limited to myself telling them what they should or should not do, or engaging them in reflective questions and strategizing conversations, but also moments of them pushing my own thinking. While I would have loved for them to engage in certain critical stances in their work within their teacher education program, and within their student teaching placement, they pushed me to engage in a speculative praxis of self-care and sustainability, and not simply focusing on the activist aspect of this work. They reminded me that this work was not about me, and it was not about them, but it was about a collective *us* engaging in speculative acts of what teacher education can be for all of us.

Kristen

My conversations with the teacher candidate I'll call Sarai deeply embodied a legacy of Black feminist sister circle practices. Neal-Barnett et al. (2011) define sister circles as "support groups that build upon existing friendships, fictive kin networks, and the sense of community found among Black women" (p. 267). Though the conversation was initiated for the purpose of data collection, they ventured far from the scripted interview guide when Sarai expressed distress about her experience in the teacher education program and at the university we both attend. Superseding the data collection protocol was Sarai's need for space to feel supported and encouraged, and an unplanned sister circle was formed; evoking the speculative practices often called on when Black womxn come together to brainstorm the survival strategies necessary to navigate institutions designed to prevent their thriving. At the end of the meandering conversation, we both agreed to center joy and love in our daily practice for students and for ourselves. When Sarai asked me how I stay joyful, I told her that it is a choice. I loosely recall telling her (a refrain I offer in various iterations with frequency), "In a world trying to kill me, I can have joy that it hasn't worked." I hope that Sarai has held onto the challenge to bring joy and love into her classroom every day, and I have immense gratitude that she lovingly reminded me to hold onto this even when things become challenging.

We offer the above excerpts from a larger corpus of data not to do traditional academic analysis but instead to demonstrate how our ongoing interactions, with(in) each other and the teacher candidates of color in this project, continues to reorient us to the past, present, and future, and urges us to continually reimagine how we receive the concerns and struggles of teacher candidates of color as more than just data points. To engage in the speculative also requires what Wong (2019) refers to as a reflexivity of uneasiness. Our invitation into conversations and vulnerable spaces with anyone demands an ongoing reflection of power and positionality in that space. We argue that all moments are pivotal; they teach you something about yourself, the person on the other side of the conversation, the space, the structure, and the institution. We learned an incredible amount in our first full year as teacher educators engaging with teacher candidates hoping to do critical social justice work in their classrooms and beyond. Although we did not offer those vignettes/anecdotes for analysis, we can share how they oriented us toward a deeper engagement with ourselves and the work we desire to do.

MOVING FORWARD

A speculative praxis in teacher education calls for a (re)imagination of our present and future lifeworlds toward liberation, with specific attention to future teachers and the impact they will have on K–12 students of color and other marginalized youth. We posit such work must begin with teacher educators and our preparation and support of future teachers, and must stem from a critical (re)imagination and (re)orientation to our past, present, and future experiences. We must take inventory of our individual and collective experiences, and do so in a manner that privileges dialogue, community, and praxis. The speculative with(in) community—the self, teacher candidates, youth, and community members—allows for the (re)imagination of an alternative present and future for teacher candidates and the youth they will serve. As demonstrated in this chapter, our work toward a speculative preparation and support of future teachers is strengthened by our communal, and at times different yet similar, approaches and values. Said differently, the solidarity fostered between the two of us served as the catalyst for our work in the historically violent and constraining space of teacher education for scholars of color, and served as the impetus to lovingly disagree and push one another in our individual and collective speculative praxis.

Ultimately, speculative as a methodological praxis is simply an invitation. We are inviting you, our readers, into the learning space we have created and will continue to cultivate with our students, teacher candidates, and future mentees. We view every stakeholder in education as a potential dream partner. There is hope in imagining new ways of being, and the solidarity formed in the collective will ground us in the uncertain. We also posit that this space, though fluid, is not a transitional place. It is not a steppingstone into the next phase of research. Perhaps the speculative space, the fluid, alternative, ever-changing ambient space, is one where we can and should exist in perpetuity. We will always extend new invitations for dreams and dreamers to tackle the newest phases that the evolving teaching landscape may bring, and we vow to stay put to embrace those who heed the call. Amidst the uncertain abstractness of speculation, it is the coalition building among partners that will provide solid ground and consistency. That collective will hopefully serve to sustain hope during the journey. Thus, it is our hope that this desire-centered practice continues to evolve, and that remaining in a speculative praxis brings more questions than it does answers, in an ever-evolving attempt to reach the point of equity saturation.

REFERENCES

Arellano, S., Cortez, J. M., & García, R. (2021) Shadow work: Witnessing Latinx crossings in rhetoric and composition. *Composition Studies*, *49*(2), 31–52.

Carter Andrews, D., He, Y. Marciano, J. E., Richmond, G., & Salazar, M. (2021). Decentering whiteness in teacher education: Addressing the questions of who, with whom, and how. *Journal of Teacher Education*, *72*(2), 134–137. https://doi.org/10.1177/0022487120987966

Coia, L., & Taylor, M. (2009). Co/autoethnography: Exploring our teaching selves collaboratively. In D. L. Tidwell, M. L. Heston, & L. M. Fitzgerald (Eds.), *Research methods for the self-study of practice* (pp. 3–16). Springer.

de los Rios, C., & Souto-Manning, M. (2015). Teacher educators as cultural workers: Problematizing teacher education pedagogies. *Studying Teacher Education*, *11*(3), 272–293. doi:10.1080/17425964.2015.1065806

Dixon, A. D., & Dingus, J. E. (2007). Tyranny of the majority: Re-enfranchisement of African-American teacher educators teaching for democracy. *International Journal of Qualitative Studies in Education*, *20*(6), 639–654. https://doi.org/10.1080/09518390701630775

Freire, P., & Macedo, D. (1987) *Literacy: Reading the word and the world*. Praeger.

González, R. A. (2018). "Students with big dreams that just need a little push": Self-empowerment, activism, & institutional change through PAR *entremundos*. In J. Ayala, M. Cammarota, M. Berta-Ávila, M. Rivera, L. Rodríguez, & M. Torre (Eds.), *PAR EntreMundos: A pedagogy of the Américas* (pp. 169–200). Peter Lang.

González, R. A., & Jackson, K. (2022, April 21). *The ideological becoming of teacher educators of color in BIPoC affinity group spaces* [Roundtable presentation]. American Educational Research Association (AERA) Annual Meeting, San Diego, California.

Grande, S., San Pedro, T., & Windchief, S. (2015). Indigenous peoples and identity in the 21st century: Remembering, reclaiming, and regenerating. In K. Koslow & L. Salett (Eds.), *Multicultural perspectives on race, ethnicity, and identity* (pp. 105–122). NASW Press.

Hartman, S. (2019). *Wayward lives, beautiful experiments: Intimate histories of riotous Black girls, troublesome women, and Queer radicals*. W.W. Norton & Company.

Jackson, K., & González, R. A. (2022, April 26). *Exploring the critical development of teacher educators of color through collaboration & shared positional analysis* [Paper presentation]. American Educational Research Association (AERA) Annual Meeting, San Diego, California.

Kelley, R. D. G. (2002). *Freedom dreams: The Black radical imagination*. Beacon Press.

Kohli, R., & Pizarro, M. (2022). The layered toll of racism in teacher education on teacher educators of color. *AERA Open*, *8*(1), 1–12. https://doi.org/10.1177/23328584221078538

Macdonald, C. (2016, June 24). Florin High students call for restored bus service. *Elk Grove Citizen*. http://www.egcitizen.com/news/florin-high-students-call-for-restored-bus-service/article_04797d89-f2b7-5713-bc7e-34de38091b9f.html

Macdonald, C. (2018, September 5). Busing to be restored for Florin High. *Elk Grove Citizen*. https://www.egcitizen.com/news/busing-to-be-restored-for-florin-high/article_ec25d87c-b139-11e8-a3fd-dbc824408d9c.html

Matias, C. E. (2013). On the "flip" side: A teacher educator of color unveiling the dangerous minds of white teacher candidates. *Teacher Education Quarterly*, 40(2), 53–73. https://www.jstor.org/stable/43684739

Matias, C. E., Nishi, N. W., & Sarcedo, G. L. (2018). Teacher education and whiteness and whiteness in teacher education in the United States. *Oxford Research Encyclopedia of Education*.

Mirra, N., & Garcia, A. (2020). "I hesitate but I do have hope": Youth speculative civic literacies for troubled times. *Harvard Educational Review*, 90(2), 295–321. doi:10.17763/1943-5045-90.2.295

Moten, F., & Harney, S. (2013). *The Undercommons: Fugitive planning & Black study*. AK Press.

Neal-Barnett, A., Stadulis, R., Murray, M., Payne, M. R., Thomas, A., & Salley, B. B. (2011). Sister circles as a culturally relevant intervention for anxious Black women. *Clinical Psychology: Science and Practice, 18*(3), 266. https://doi.org/10.1111/j.1468-2850.2011.01258.x

Otieno, E. (2018, October 22). The Black speculative arts movement and Afrofuturism as an Afrocentric, ethnocultural social philosophy. *Griot*. https://griotmag.com/en/the-black-speculative-arts-movement-afrofuturism-as-an-afrocentric-technocultural-social-philosophy/

San Pedro, T. J. (2015). Silence as shields: Agency and resistances among Native American students in the urban Southwest. *Research in the Teaching of English*, 132–153. https://www.jstor.org/stable/24890030

San Pedro, T. J., & Kinloch, V. (2017). Toward projects in humanization: Research on co-creating and sustaining dialogic relationships. *American Educational Research Journal*, 54(1), 373–394. https://doi.org/10.3102/0002831216671210

Shim, J. M. (2018). Working through resistance to resistance in anti-racist teacher education. *Journal of Philosophy of Education*, 52(2), 262–283. https://doi.org/10.1111/1467-9752.12284

Sleeter, C. E. (2001). Preparing teachers for culturally diverse schools: Research and the overwhelming presence of whiteness. *Journal of Teacher Education*, 52(2), 94–106. https://doi.org/10.1177/0022487101052002002

Sleeter, C. E. (2017). Critical race theory and the whiteness of teacher education. *Urban Education*, 52(2), 155–169. https://doi.org/10.1177/0042085916668957

Souto-Manning, M. (2019). Toward praxically-just transformations: Interrupting racism in teacher education. *Journal of Education for Teaching*, 45(1), 97–113. https://doi.org/10.1080/02607476.2019.1550608

Torre, M. E., & Ayala, J. (2009). Envisioning participatory action research *entremundos*. *Feminism & Psychology*, 19(3), 387–393. https://doi.org/10.1177/0959353509105630

Wong, C. P. (2019). *Pray you catch me: A critical feminist and ethnographic study of love as pedagogy and politics for social justice* (Publication No. 28113530). [Doctoral dissertation Stanford University]. ProQuest Dissertations Publishing.

CHAPTER 10

Education as a Fundamental Right
A Speculative Narrative About Educational Dignity

Raquel Isaac, Maria Karina Sanchez, Duy Tran, Tania Soto Valenzuela, and mandy wong, with Remi Kalir, on behalf of the Right2Learn Dignity Lab[1]

INTRODUCTION

The Constitution of the State of Colorado was drafted in the spring of 1876 and approved by voters on July 1st of that year. Only 19,505 ballots were cast in that election—most, if not all, presumably by white men (Dunham, 1959). Article 9 of the Colorado Constitution concerns education, with Section 2, the "Establishment and Maintenance of Public Schools." It states:

> The general assembly shall, as soon as practicable, provide for the establishment and maintenance of a thorough and uniform system of free public schools throughout the state, wherein all residents of the state, between the ages of six and twenty-one years, may be educated gratuitously. One or more public schools shall be maintained in each school district within the state, at least three months in each year; any school district failing to have such school shall not be entitled to receive any portion of the school fund for that year.

We write 146 years after the Colorado Constitution was approved.[2] Article 9, in our estimate, is anemic for it lacks any mention of learning, equity, or dignity. Ambiguity of the "thorough and uniform" mandate has, for example, been referenced when upholding school finance policy that perpetuates funding disparities and other statewide inequities (Engdahl, 2013). We represent the Right2Learn Dignity Lab, or R2L, a community-based research and political advocacy group. Our practices center educational dignity (Espinoza & Vossoughi, 2014; Espinoza et al., 2020), and include efforts to create more dignity-affirming classrooms and school policies (i.e., Childress et al., in press; Sanchez, 2022). Furthermore, we seek to amend Article 9,

Section 2, of the Colorado Constitution through a citizen-driven ballot initiative process, so that it may read:

> Education is a fundamental right held by all human persons; it is a means for achieving social equality and necessary for the fulfillment of freedom, justice, and peace. The Colorado General Assembly shall protect, respect, and support this right. Public schools are sanctuaries, spaces where the inherent and inalienable dignity of the human person is inviolate, spaces where compassionate guidance abounds. In its effect, education for human growth and dignity strengthens the individual and community, it fosters agency rather than servitude, and promotes solidarity among all human persons. Furthermore, education enables the actualization of human potential through the arts, sciences, and humanities. The Colorado General Assembly shall create and maintain public schools as safe and healthy spaces where all human persons will experience their inherent dignity and understand the rights flowing from it. Guided by the principles of integrity and equity, the Colorado General Assembly shall ensure that all public school students have ongoing and diverse opportunities to meaningfully participate in their education. As a paramount requisite of education, meaningful participation fulfills the promise of the public schools as havens for learning and growth, crucibles for inquiry and experimentation, forums for dialogue and dissent.

We imagine that the forthcoming vignettes presented in this chapter take place in 2074, 50 years after the Colorado Constitution has been successfully amended.[3] It is necessary to amend our state constitution for many reasons, including the fact that students living in underresourced districts may not prosper to their fullest potential; we believe that everyone deserves an education that affirms their human dignity and worth regardless of race, ethnicity, social class, ability, nationality, sexual orientation, gender expression, and religious affiliation. We present educational concepts proposed in our amendment—such as actualization of human potential, meaningful participation, and educational dignity—as they may manifest in reality for people of different ages and backgrounds. We write in the speculative tense (Toliver, 2020) inspired by examples of counterstory (Martinez, 2020) and youth activism (e.g., Mirra & Garcia, 2020; Tivaringe & Kirshner, 2021). We presume that the state's education clause has come to include the language of human dignity for half a century, and that it serves as a foundation for fulfilling the promise of freedom, justice, and peace for current and future generations (UNICEF, 1990).

A HISTORY OF R2L

> The following conversation occurs in 2074 among a class of students about the Right2Learn Dignity Lab, and what these students have learned about the group's efforts. It is narrated by Luis, a 10th-grade student.

Education as a Fundamental Right 171

"R2L started their work in the early 2000s. They believed everyone deserved an education that recognized and affirmed their dignity and worth. They amended our state's educational clause to include the language of dignity. Today, on the 50th anniversary of that amendment passing, we continue their efforts and fight to secure a fundamental right to education that centralizes our inherent worth as human beings all over the world," Ms. Padilla-Chavez began as she relaxed into her swinging chair, the ropes attached to the ceiling taut in her hands as she gracefully rocked back and forth.

To the class, she posed a question, "Does anyone have any more important background on R2L before we share some of our favorite highlights from what we've learned?"

A pause overtook the room as we all sunk into our ruminations. I didn't have much to add, since I would be hosting the ceremony commemorating the anniversary later in the day. I was itching to hear what everyone else had to say.

Sweeping my eyes across the room, I looked across the circle at my friend, Frida, eyes unfocused, lost in thought, body slack in the big bean bag. The light from the afternoon sun shone through the big windows as similar looks of concentration filled the room.

To gain our attention, another student, Diego, raised his hand before carefully adding, "I thought it was so cool that their leadership in educational dignity was a product of agency to change the conditions around marginalization, isolation, and oppression within the U.S. public school system at that time. All R2L members were students, family members, and educators whose zip codes, immigration status, home languages, skin colors, family education, genders, or abilities determined the quality and access of their education. That was wild to me, to imagine the experiences they went through and had to bear witness to."[4]

Nods of agreement went around the room.

Katie replied, "How about the fact that most of them started out as students in Professor Espinoza's classes? Every year they'd add new members who shared the same passion for education. No initial funds, just a dream and a longing for the world to make sense, that led them to feel like family to one another."

"I couldn't even find anything about educational dignity before they started their handbook!" exclaimed Spencer. "Yet, they were able to create a small bubble of educational dignity when the state still stood behind 'thorough and uniform.'"

Lema spoke: "I read an interview with one member who said they'd been influenced and inspired by enslaved people securing the right to learn in secrecy while harnessing its power to unfit us for servitude.[5] They also mentioned a Du Bois quote, their North Star:

> Of all the civil rights for which the world has struggled and fought for 5,000 years, the right to learn is undoubtedly the most fundamental. If a people has preserved

this right, then no matter how far it goes astray, no matter how many mistakes it makes, in the long run, in the unfolding of generations, it is going to come back to this right.[6]

"They were those folks' dreams, and we are theirs," Soraya observed.

Ms. Padilla-Chavez asked, "What other parts of the amendment do you live out today?"

Arliss joined the discussion: "They defined sanctuary as, 'A sacred space of community to which one belongs, where our humanity is affirmed through the creation of meaningful social interactions.'[7] We live that now! They believed in dignity and sanctuary as concepts that held validity in human rights efforts, and wondered why in education these terms were nonexistent. We gain a sense of our dignity through learning experiences that recognize and cultivate the mind, humanity, and potential. Our inherent and inalienable dignity of a human person is inviolate. Those concepts provided the parameters for spaces we inhabit today. Environments where joy is cultivated through the sacredness of human connection and a validation of self."

"I read," noted Charla, "that they imagined a future where children are seen as capable beings whose curiosities and longings direct their journey and learning. That there would be a shared understanding that insatiable curiosity grows when nourished, and would be plentiful and in many forms. Learning spaces as sanctuary also lead to meaningful participation. Nowadays, we have agency, we can determine the course of our education, we can choose our own paths in life, cocreate our environment, and solve problems to make a difference in the world."

Victor spoke, "Is there not also a link between equity and potential? Dignity requires governmental recognition of and respect for the potential of the human person. Equity is a pragmatic principle that can guide the fulfillment of the moral duty to create the most dynamic environment for all people."[8]

Ms. Padilla-Chavez brought our conversation to a close by reminding us: "You are all far nobler than the prior education clause of our state's constitution. Across the decades, the kind of public education made possible by the clause had shown itself to be inadequate to the imperative of social equality and susceptible to narrow interpretations that aided in the maintenance of caste. The clause was oriented toward the minimum duties of the government and not the existential demands of the human, how education was regarded as governmental service and not an essential activity of human and political life. The only conception of education that can plausibly satisfy the demands of dignity is one that embraces the majesty of life and the splendid potential of the human person."[9]

PRESENTING EDUCATIONAL DIGNITY

Following their class discussion, our narrator Luis reflects on their education while preparing to moderate a presentation about R2L that honors the 50th anniversary of successfully amending the Colorado Constitution.

The wheels of my chair glide against the carpet as I stand and shuffle my papers together, taking the sheets of my carefully crafted speech and sliding them into my folder. I really appreciate Ms. P. for lending me the plant room for the last 2 hours before my speech. I love learning near nature, my mind stimulated by the sheer beauty. Even at school, I still feel connected to the outside world.

I walk past the childcare center and take the long way to my locker, through the atrium where plants line the walls, and small trees adorn the pathways. I let my fingertips graze the green leaves. The lives of these plants represent the generations of students who sprouted from the seeds of life, hopes, and dreams planted by R2L members. Seeds they imagined atom-by-atom, seeds that previously did not exist. We are no longer seeds. We are a generation of strong trees and plants ready to flourish.

School was different before my time. The stories of suffering are, for me, just that—stories. I have never felt a lapse in my abilities, never had severely outdated books, or been told I would never make something of myself. The three interviews I conducted for today's anniversary presentation were long! That was probably the hardest part with this assignment, and this privilege. I am eager to share stories of how profound education is, and what it meant to be denied dignified learning. An oral history of humble dreams, not for themselves, but for my generation and the generations to come.

I wait at the stage and peek at the audience of familiar faces. Principal Rose finally introduces me and the crowd erupts into cheers as I walk out into the spotlight. With each step, I feel magnified in my abilities because of the confidence and reassurance I have always felt at school. The expectation to do well is more of a comfort than a burden because my opinion has always held value with my peers and teachers.

"Thank you! I'm honored to be MCing the 50th anniversary of the amendment passing in our state that uplifted education to a fundamental right, an accomplishment much bigger than us. We've been learning about the Right2Learn Dignity Lab. Their story is one of family, passion, love, sacrifice, and bravery. A noble fight that changed the course of education. Not just for us, but for the generations before us and the generations that will come after us.

"I'd like to take us on a journey through time. This is an oral history from people of different ages and different walks of life. In their stories, a clear resonance of love, care, and trust embrace the senses: memories of teachers and peers who have shaped who we have become because of the spaces and communities that were collaboratively created there. It is our belief that without these qualities, the sanctuaries we envision would not exist nor be sustainable."[10]

I move to the side of the stage. A hologram pixelates from small devices on the floor, projecting the image of an elderly gentleperson sitting in their rocking chair on a porch.

"I'd like to introduce Skye, who described to me their university education before the amendment passed. They were 20 at the time, in 2024, from a generation of learners whose right to education had yet to be defined by meaningful participation. We spoke about a world set up with oppressive systems. With our intersectional identities, experiencing indignities was prevalent. The experience of dignity is contingent. True to this, there lives a yearning for the recognition of our humanness, for safety, and for being seen and accepted. This is what comes through in their story. The promise of the inherent, inalienable, and inviolate recognition and protection of dignity as a chalice of fresh water to those who have walked the desert for generations past.[11] Their story represents power and perseverance. They can help us understand a time when learning pathways were not designed to consider your potential, were not designed to make you feel welcomed in a school."

A FORMER STUDENT REMEMBERS

The projection of an elder with wrinkled hands holding a journal crackles to life onstage. They begin to read.

"My worst nightmare, a class mixed with undergrad and grad students. A perfect potion for my friend anxiety, whose favorite pastime seemed to be eating away at my already fragile self-confidence. His toxic voice filling my ear drums with loud doubts, my willingness to drown the sound out with my positive encouragement dwindling with every step towards my mini group of grad students. Must have been my stupendous luck, my professor volunteered herself to join as our fourth member.

"Sit down. Say Something. Don't make yourself small.

"I couldn't shake the unmistakable feeling of discomfort in university spaces. As if I was a computer and written into my programming was a code making me inherently incompatible with the software for belonging there.

"After a few minutes of silence, I remember offering up an idea, my once dim eyes lit up with wonder. The welcoming smile from my professor and the keen interest of my peers burned forever to memory. I said something about the book we were reading.

"At first nobody said anything. Even though they seemed so welcoming, I immediately began to second guess myself. Wishing I had kept my silly mouth shut.

"Only to realize their pause wasn't one of dismissal, but one of quiet intricate thought and understanding. For the first time I was left baffled in a classroom, people actually heard me . . . saw me . . . considered ME!

"For the first time I felt valued as someone who could offer substance. Not merely the filler person or simple outsider I'd always considered myself. They weren't looking down on me as I'd imagined myself looking up at them. They were looking straight across at me, treating me as an equal.

"As I continued with my university courses, I experienced this same shock over and over again as if the first time never happened. Each time my mind would be blown like a child getting their entire Christmas list from Santa under the tree. Because the feeling was never constant, the comfort was temporary, left for special occasions and specific classes.

"I'm hoping students never experience that shock anymore because all they've ever known was that feeling of belonging."

Luis pauses for a few moments while the audience members' faces turn serious and introspective. Then he addresses the audience.

"Schools were once treated as a means to an end. Students were merely given the basics to get through school and into the workforce. Today, students are treated as seeds of potential. When we walk into a class, the barriers to equitable resources and supplies are gone. The burden of inferior access is lifted from our shoulders. Teachers have pledged a lifelong commitment to address, reflect upon, and heal our schools of bias, racism, and prejudice. No more are students tasked with mustering the courage to face a classroom where they doubt themselves and feel others doubting them as well. Instead, schools and their communities take on a collective challenge to constantly and consciously uphold one another's dignity.

"Our next speaker is Ms. Ari. As a teacher, she wrote a letter to her former students. The letter was written in 2026, two years after the amendment passed. R2L made a wish for everyone—including the educator—to go beyond recognizing. That we must also act and provide so that fundamental rights are given and protected as sacred. Because we are advocates for the protection of students' dignity. R2L knew dignity was a responsibility to be enacted—and argued for—every day. Through her we can see one perspective of a teacher who took this challenge seriously."[12]

A TEACHER'S LETTER

A hologram of a woman with a gypsum complexion appears at the center of the stage. She takes a moment to regard the audience and then begins to read from the paper she holds.

"Dear companions,

"One of you asked recently why I'm a teacher. Actually, one of you asked, 'If we stress you out so much, why are you even here?' I told you all that I needed time to think about my answer. I hope you do not think that I needed time to make something up because what I needed was time to give you a real and honest response. Here's my roundabout answer:

"I started teaching almost 15 years ago now. In my first year, I made great connections with students, and though I felt challenged, I had a strong feeling that I had chosen the perfect career. In my second year, all of my strategies and techniques were challenged by a group of students that I simply was not prepared for. The call-and-response that my previous students loved was met with scoffs, my storytelling received eye rolls, and I often felt defeated because I felt like I was not building strong connections like I had before. More than anything, I tried my hardest not to blame the students. After all, *I* was the adult, and it was *my* responsibility to create a great learning environment. We all soldiered on, and somehow we made it through that tough year. In that same fashion, though with fewer challenges, another five groups of students went by. During my first 7 years, I worked hard. I got along well with students, and felt quite successful. I was even named 'Teacher of the Year' at our school a couple of times. Yet through all of it, I knew something was missing, and felt that my craft as a teacher was not without fault.

"Beginning my 8th year, our principal said we would be using the newly passed amendment to the education clause to plan for a new year with students. The amendment had been passed 2 years prior, and I remember thinking that it was a big victory. I'm not proud to admit this, but the amendment soon started to slip from my mind as I fell back into my routines.

"We were asked that day to get into groups by content, and to brainstorm new and creative ways to meet the new requirements of the education clause. As I joined my group, my principal pulled me aside and said, 'I wouldn't stress this too much, you do a great job already.' What should have been pride actually felt more like guilt. I felt a strange pit in my stomach, thinking, what does that even mean?

"At home that night, I did my own work with the language of the amendment. I read it over and over, and continued to find holes in my practice. The amendment called for meaningful participation, and I thought of all the times I'd brushed off student comments when they said a lesson was boring, insisting that it was not my job to entertain them. Is it not though? Am I not here to make learning enticing and worthwhile?

"I thought of the amendment's promise to 'foster agency' and remembered that I still required students to ask for permission to use the restroom, something that felt so weirdly controlling. So how much of the amendment was I actually following? Not enough, in my opinion. I decided then that I would reach out to like-minded educators and continue to work on my practices. I promised myself, and all future students, that I would not be the teacher who got by with the bare minimum. I started meeting with other educators, and together we came up with new structures that allowed for a safe classroom environment while also putting student dignity at the forefront. We had honest conversations with students about what their experience was like in school, and received invaluable feedback from them.

"So, to answer the initial question, I am here because that principal was partially wrong. Maybe I was doing a great job at teaching before the amendment. But I certainly was not doing a great job with implementing the new education clause. Now, it is my personal wish to leave this profession feeling like I genuinely gave it my best effort. I was frustrated the other day because I am a human, and sometimes I get frustrated. That does not mean, however, that I do not cherish all my time with you all, and that I am not fully invested in bringing to life our education clause to the best of my ability."

Luis returns to the stage.

"Thank you, Ms. Ari, for showing us how the act of questioning opens the gates for dialogue and change. As Professor Manuel Espinoza observed about meaningful participation, 'When you ask a question, especially in the classroom, you have the power to control the future, for at least the next few seconds.'"

The crowd chuckles and some students lovingly raise their hands. Luis gestures appreciatively at them and continues.

"A couple weeks ago I was at parent–teacher conferences when I saw my friend's mother. She's a woman I admire and respect. While walking with her through our school, something compelled me to ask her about her perspective. The amended constitution is an argument for the human fully realized. What does a mother or father do with their understanding of the amendment? Do they walk through the schoolhouse door differently? What do their children demand? What do adolescents insist upon? How have parents allowed themselves to imagine education as an odyssey through which a child acts as a full participant in their own life, education as a means for becoming the person they imagine themself to be?[13]

"Please help me welcome Mrs. Valencia."

A PARENT'S STORY

> As applause fills the room, Mrs. Valencia steps onto the stage, nervous but determined, and starts reading from a piece of paper.

"A few weeks ago, I was participating in my child's parent–teacher conference. It was hard to fathom how much things have changed since I was in grade school. Like most things in life, there are pros and cons. However, I was fixated on systemic challenges I experienced rather than the good;

overcrowded schools, lack of funding, crumbling infrastructure, more innovation in teacher education, even outright disrespect for students and their potential. I recall once when I was in 7th grade. A social studies teacher popped his head in our English as a Second Language classroom and stated—for all of us to hear—that resources were being wasted on us because we wouldn't ever amount to anything and would not attend college.

"What a long way we have come. I am surprised at how the education system has shifted positively for this generation. Parents, like me, are more engaged in our children's education because we feel more welcome and invited to help foster academic success through at-home activities and in-class participation. We feel valued as integral pieces of this learning community.

"My child has never come home with stories of institutional disregard of their human worth. On the contrary, everything in the school building is engineered to let them know that they are at the center and in charge of their educational path. It is clear that teachers are also more financially sustained and given better resources and social and emotional development training. Through these investments, students now have an equal chance for success because anyone that steps into educational spaces does so with the understanding of educational dignity and the utmost regard for every little human life in their hands. What a difference it makes to have schools be supported in recruiting, training, and offering overall support to teachers, educators, and administrators. The switch to a new standard and process for public school education based on the needs of dignity-bearing and rights-holding persons. When education is seen as a fundamental right, our obligations to students are more durable, and the duties of the state more heightened.[14]

"Schools today are places of human growth and potential, sanctuaries built around compassion, community-building spaces that are safe and healthy, and abound with meaningful participation.[15] Since this was not always the case, at times these hallways have felt foreign to me. The contrast is vastly different. Nowadays, students work on a solar greenhouse, graphing plant growth, classifying and comparing plants, and harvesting food and flowers. Applicable stuff. They learn about physics from the structure of the building, and they investigate visual electrical–mechanical systems to learn about input and output similar to the arteries and veins in their bodies. The problems they study in this 'classroom' are real-world efforts, not bits of abstract work. Rather than completing worksheets, students participate in the concrete experiences that underlie mathematics, engineering, science, and social studies.

"The classrooms have been redesigned into a new system that includes several modular interdisciplinary pavilions: a design studio for drawing and painting; a spatial relationship environment for construction, movement, music, drama, and cognitive skill development; a garden; a portable cooking center; a media center with computer and audiovisual instruments; the 'nest,' a soft and flexible environment with subdued color, texture, and sound, for listening and role-playing; a showcase environment for drawing, creative dramatics, and learning about light, color, reflection, and refraction; and a trash management center for developing ecological understanding. Real-life and applicable learning in an environment that is a functional art form, a place of beauty, and a motivational center for learning.[16] The landscape and cultural community are part of the learning environment, too. The structure and spaces where our children go to school matter. Today, our children feel belonging—from the chair where they sit to the way they engage with curricula—that's the embodiment of our state's education clause."

A CURRENT STUDENT SPEAKS

Following these remarks, Luis introduces a current student named Emilia Valentina, the last speaker at the celebratory presentation whose comments conclude the event.

"We are grateful to our speakers who joined us physically, holographically, and through writing. Their experiences not only help us celebrate this occasion, they remind us of the unique beauty of the human experience. We thank them for sharing with us tonight.

"Today, as we celebrate this anniversary, I think it's important to acknowledge how far we've come since the days of our ancestors. When some people ask me about this, I find it hard to describe because so much is a feeling. But, as we've heard, examples help, too. I think of our school's design and how our classes and curriculum are structured. I feel love and care. I see how much thought is put into the different aspects of our education. Consider, were you surprised that we get to choose what time to arrive at school by taking our chronotype into consideration? It's incredible how much our teachers care about so many aspects of our well-being, including how our biological rhythms affect our energy levels and performance.[17] Or how when we first entered this school, we were given the time to get to know one another deeply as individuals to a point where we are encouraged to share our vulnerabilities, daily challenges, and learn the aspects of communicating emotion to strengthen our bonds.[18]

"To us, some of what I mention may be things that we take for granted because it's part of our everyday lives. These things are normal to us, but they were things that our predecessors dreamt could be reality, and as a community we live these dreams into being by virtue of how we consistently uphold and value one another's dignity.

"As we close this evening, we invite you to stay in this space of dignity. Behold one another and the community we have created together, built upon the foundations created by our ancestors. Remember the work that was done before us, and take it with you everywhere you go. Dignity isn't contained within school, nor should it be. It was the dream of R2L that schools would be dignified spaces, yes; but that was only the beginning. Imagine a world where the dignified experiences of school are so commonplace that you expect them everywhere else. What a vision that would be."

CODA

What is preventing us from fighting to secure an education that affirms our human rights? What does dreaming these possibilities provide for our sociological imagination? We, the Right2Learn Dignity Lab, envision the prior vignettes as both plausible and necessary. Our dreams took shape in 2018, when we decided to channel all we had learned from the interdisciplinary study of educational dignity toward amending the Colorado Constitution. In 2020, we drafted the amended clause shared at the beginning of this chapter. In 2021, alongside members of the Student Bill of Rights working group from Denver Public Schools, we testified before the Colorado Legislative Council about our amendment. At present, we are building a grassroots network to collect required signatures from Colorado residents that will place our citizen-initiated proposal on the November 2024 state-wide ballot.

We are not on this journey alone. While imagining and writing about the future can be challenging, we held onto possibilities and broke through our own walls of limitations, whether perceived or real. Together, we each broke down our mind blocks and stepped into the future; within R2L, the feeling of dignity in an academic setting is no longer a dream, it is an embodied reality. As a group, we have participated in various exercises to help us share our dreams of the future. For example, we once asked one another to recall indignities encountered in the educational system. We did this not to easily identify the opposite, for that is not dignity; rather, this helped us think about the most delightful ways that future generations of learners could experience educational dignity. This exercise, like others, and including our writing of this book chapter, allowed us to see ourselves as already triumphant while, day-to-day, we continue an arduous journey to change the law and educational practices as we know it. We have derived comfort and joy knowing that we trust in each other's dreams, that we treasure potential and humanity, and that we are journeying with others in the pursuit of educational dignity.

We invite you to find us online at www.educational-dignity.org, on social media, and to send us mail[19] to learn more about our campaign to amend the Colorado Constitution's education clause and foster dignity in schools. This work is not just for R2L, but for all of us. We would love nothing more than to connect with others about these important topics.

NOTES

1. Founded in 2007, the Right2Learn Dignity Lab (R2L) is part research collective and part political campaign whose complementary scholarly and civic efforts are grounded by cultural–historical perspectives on learning as a dignity-conferring human right. In addition to the authors of this chapter, R2L members include Manuel Luis Espinoza, Frida Silva, Adria Padilla Chavez, Lema Alali, Charla Agnoletti, Soraya Latiff, Katie Ruiz Gonzalez, Spencer Childress, Victor Sanchez, Skye O'Toole, Verinique Moua, Valencia Seidel, Tamara Lhungay, Diego Ulibarri, and Arliss Howard. R2L is thankful for the mentorship, over many years, from Edelina Burciaga, Enrique Lopez, Rene Galindo, Shirin Vossoughi, Walter Kitundu, Rebecca Kantor, and Mike Rose.
2. This chapter was written throughout 2022.
3. Throughout this chapter, we reference R2L's original research and prior writing, referred to in our footnotes as "microessays." We note microessay authors where appropriate. We also reference our scholarly influences using footnotes to preserve the narrative flow of our speculative vignettes.
4. Adapted from a microessay by Charla Agnoletti.
5. See, for example, Patel (2016).
6. Du Bois (1970).
7. Adapted from a microessay by Adria Padilla Chavez and Tania Soto Valenzuela.
8. Adapted from a microessay by Professor Manuel Espinoza.
9. Ibid.
10. Adapted from a microessay by Verinique Moua, Frida Silva, & mandy wong.
11. Adapted from a microessay by Adria Padilla Chavez and Tania Soto Valenzuela.
12. Adapted from a microessay by Katie Ruiz Gonzalez and Soraya Latiff.
13. Adapted from a microessay by Karina Sanchez Velasco and Professor Manuel Espinoza.
14. Adapted from personal communication with Professor Manuel Espinoza.
15. Adapted from a microessay by Professor Manuel Espinoza and Lema Alali.
16. Our interest in the material design of schools as built environments is influenced by Taylor (1993).
17. Pink (2018).
18. Brown (2021).
19. R2L can be contacted at: 1380 Lawrence St., Room 734, Denver, CO 80204.

REFERENCES

Brown, B. (2021). *Atlas of the heart: Mapping meaningful connection and the language of human experience.* Random House.

Childress, S., Espinoza, M., & Padilla-Chavez, A. (in press). *So say we all: Equity and meaningful participation in STEM education.* The National Academies Press.

Du Bois, W. E. B. (1970). The freedom to learn. In P. S. Foner (Ed.), *W.E.B. Du Bois Speaks* (pp. 230–231). Pathfinder.

Dunham, H. H. (1959). Colorado's Constitution of 1876. *Denver Law Review, 36*(2), 121–130.

Engdahl, T. (2013, May 28). High court reverses Lobato ruling. *Chalkbeat Colorado*. https://co.chalkbeat.org/2013/5/28/21102037/high-court-reverses-lobato-ruling

Espinoza, M. L., & Vossoughi, S. (2014). Perceiving learning anew: Social interaction, dignity, and educational rights. *Harvard Educational Review, 84*(3), 285–313. doi:10.17763/haer.84.3.y4011442g71250q2

Espinoza, M. L., Vossoughi, S., Rose, M., & Poza, L. E. (2020). Matters of participation: Notes on the study of dignity and learning. *Mind, Culture, and Activity, 27*(4), 325–347. https://doi.org/10.1080/10749039.2020.1779304

Martinez, A. (2020). *Counterstory: The rhetoric and writing of critical race theory*. National Council of Teachers of English.

Mirra, N., & Garcia, A. (2020). "I hesitate but I do have hope": Youth speculative civic literacies for troubled times. *Harvard Educational Review, 90*(2), 295–321. doi:10.17763/1943-5045-90.2.295

Patel, L. (2016). Pedagogies of resistance and survivance: Learning as marronage. *Equity & Excellence in Education, 49*(4), 397–401. https://doi.org/10.1080/10665684.2016.1227585

Pink, D. (2018). *When: The scientific secrets of perfect timing*. Riverhead Books.

Sanchez, M. (2022). Student success: From an educator perspective. *The Denver Journal of Education & Community, 3*(1). https://djec.org/sample-page/

Taylor, A. (1993). The learning environment as a three-dimensional textbook. *Children's Environments, 10*(2), 170–179. https://www.jstor.org/stable/41514891

Tivaringe, T., & Kirshner, B. (2021). Learning to claim power in a contentious public sphere: A study of youth movement formation in South Africa. *Journal of the Learning Sciences, 30*(1), 125–150. https://doi.org/10.1080/10508406.2020.1844713

Toliver, S. R. (2020). Can I get a witness? Speculative fiction as testimony and counterstory. *Journal of Literacy Research, 52*(4), 507–529. https://doi.org/10.1177/1086296X20966362

UNICEF. (1990). *Convention on the rights of the child*. https://www.unicef.org/child-rights-convention/convention-text

About the Editors and Contributors

Alexandra R. Aguilar is a graduate student in the Department of Curriculum and Instruction at the University of Texas–Austin. Her previous graduate work explored the barriers to undergraduate student access to calculus at San Francisco State. Currently, her research focuses on how the mathematics classrooms' valorization of quantification and number have contributed to structural antifatness and affected what mathematics students can see and imagine.

Alex Alejo is a first-year student at the University of California, Irvine. He is a graduate of the UCLA Community School in Los Angeles and a proud student leader and activist.

Emma P. Bene is a doctoral student in curriculum and teacher education at the Stanford University Graduate School of Education. Inspired by her work with students in Memphis and Atlanta, her research examines how students engage identity and emotion when reading different genres of text about historic acts of racial violence.

Emily Brooke, MA, is a doctoral student of school psychology in the Department of Psychology at the University of Montana. She received her bachelor of science in psychology from Clemson University and is now a member of the Culturally Responsive Evidence-Based Practices in School Psychology (CRESP) Lab under Dr. Anisa Goforth. Her primary research interests examine disproportionality in disability identification and its impact on racially minoritized students.

Matthew W. Coopilton is a former high school language arts and social studies teacher. They research critical digital literacy learning environments, and codesign these with adolescents and adults. They also codesign games that prototype and rehearse liberated and unpoliced futures, including *Kai UnEarthed* (kaiunearthed.com). By the time of this book's publication, they will have completed their doctoral degree in education psychology from the University of Southern California. Their games, curriculum designs, and publications can be found at mcoopilton.com.

Isabel Correa is a designer, doctoral candidate, and research assistant of communication, media, and learning technologies design at Teachers College, Columbia University. She explores creativity in maker education and biodesign as a space for urban youth to respond to the climate emergency by imagining how we might create with nature and within local socioecological communities. Her work can be found at mariaisabelcorrea.com/.

Arturo Cortez is assistant professor of learning sciences and human development at the University of Colorado Boulder and is the founder of the Learning To Transform (LiTT) Video Gaming Lab. Broadly, he explores the possibilities of codesigning for consequential learning in intergenerational and transdisciplinary learning environments. In particular, he is interested in how young people and educators speculate new possible futures, opening up opportunities for building imaginary and real worlds, using cutting-edge technologies like video games.

Edwin Cruz is a senior at the UCLA Community School in the Koreatown/Pico-Union area of Los Angeles. He is passionate about coteaching and supporting his community.

Michael B. Dando is an assistant professor of English and the director of the Communication Arts and Literature Program at St. Cloud State University in St. Cloud, Minnesota. Dando is a former high school Language Arts teacher, and is currently an education researcher exploring the intersections of youth culture (particularly comic books and hip-hop), critical media literacy, and democratic education. His work explores ways youth become creative, critical, future-oriented participants in making social change.

Eduardo Galindo is a first-year student at Columbia University where he is studying computer science. He is a graduate of the UCLA Community School where he was one of the founding members of the Student Advisory Board.

Antero Garcia is an associate professor in the Graduate School of Education at Stanford University. His research explores the possibilities of speculative imagination and healing in educational research. Prior to completing his PhD, Garcia was an English teacher at a public high school in South Central Los Angeles. He has authored or edited more than a dozen books about the possibilities of literacies, play, and civics in transforming schooling in America. Antero currently coedits *La Cuenta*, an online publication centering the voices and perspectives of individuals labeled undocumented in the United States. Antero received his PhD in the Urban Schooling division of the Graduate School of Education and Information Studies at the University of California, Los Angeles.

Leyda W. Garcia is associate director for professional learning at the UCLA Center for Community Schooling. She is now part of California's State Transformational Assistance Center (S-TAC) for community schools throughout the state. She is also part of the educational leadership faculty at California State University–Fullerton. She was the principal of the UCLA Community School in the Koreatown-Pico-Union area of Los Angeles for 10 years, where she worked alongside students, families/caregivers, and other educators to redefine the project of public education through a community schooling approach.

Emma C. Gargroetzi is an assistant professor in the Department of Curriculum & Instruction at the University of Texas–Austin and cofounder of the Transdisciplinary Civic Learning Collaborative. Inspired by 15 years working with young people in New York, California, Texas, and Latin America, her research focuses on identity, power, and educational justice. Current work examines the use of quantitative reasoning in youth civic composing and possibilities for educational dignity in mathematics learning.

Anisa N. Goforth is a professor of psychology at the University of Montana. An Australian and American citizen, she was born in Yemen and raised in Asia and Latin America. Her research focuses on culturally responsive evidence-based practices supporting mental health and learning of minoritized children and families. She has published over 50 peer-reviewed articles and a recent book titled *Culturally Responsive School-Based Practices: Supporting Mental Health and Learning of Diverse Students* (Oxford University Press).

Rubén A. González, proudly from Greenfield, California, is a doctoral candidate in race, inequality, and language in education at Stanford University. Previously, he was a high school English and English language development teacher in Sacramento, California. He completed his bachelor's degree in English at Sacramento State University after transferring from Hartnell College. Rubén's research explores how students and teachers of color develop, sustain, and operationalize a critical sociopolitical disposition in classroom, school, and community settings.

Niki Graham, a member of the Confederated Salish and Kootenai People, holds an undergraduate degree in health enhancement and a master's degree in public health. She has taught in a public school system, directed the Center for Prevention and Wellness at Salish Kootenai College, and had oversight of the American Indian Alaska Native Clinical Translational Research Program. Niki is currently the director of operations for the University of Montana, Montana Public Health Training Center.

Le'kie Hatfield-Whitlock is a 6th-grade student at the UCLA Community School in Los Angeles. He is a student leader.

Walter Hernandez Mejia is a student leader at the UCLA Community School in Los Angeles. He is in 4th grade.

Debbie Hogenson is a retired teacher, having taught on the Flathead Indian Reservation for 25 years. She spent most of her career as a reading resource teacher. She holds a masters degree in multicultural/bilingual education. Through numerous professional development opportunities, she became a teacher leader in limited English proficiency strategies and resources. Debbie is a member of the Montana Chippewa Little Shell Tribe. She values equity and diversity in education and honors the "whole child."

Nathan Holbert is an associate professor of communication, media, and learning technologies design at Teachers College, Columbia University and the founder and director of the Snow Day Learning Lab. His work involves the design and study of playful tools, environments, and activities that allow all children to leverage computational power as they build, test, tinker, and make sense of personally meaningful topics, phenomena, or questions.

Ronda Howlett is Salish and an enrolled member of the Confederate Salish and Kootenai Tribes. A retired elementary school teacher, she lives with her husband Kevin along the Jocko River. Ronda believes homeland is life-giving and provides the grounding to help individuals and communities step into a well-designed future. Ronda enjoys collaborating with others to develop a social–emotional curriculum that is informed by the past, inspired by the future, and grounded in the living culture.

Raquel Isaac is the last daughter of Trinidadian immigrants and grew up in Aurora, Colorado. Raquel has a bachelors degree in public health and ethnic studies from the University of Colorado Denver [per online sources], and has a passion for social equity as it relates to the intersectionality of race, identity, and health. Outside of her amazing Right2Learn Dignity Lab work, Raquel loves to read, write, spend time with family, travel, and exercise.

Kristen Jackson is a doctoral candidate in race, inequality, and language in education at Stanford University. Her research considers how Black educators sustain themselves, their students, and, by extension, Black community through loving practices rooted in historic ontologies. She is from the Detroit area, and taught high school in Philadelphia.

De'Andra Johnson is a research assistant at the Center for Empowered Learning and Development with Technology at the University of Southern California. She received her bachelor's of science in psychology from Tulane University and master's of science in digital social media from the University of Southern California. Her research interests include the impacts of digital and social media on mental health and behavior, among others. She currently works in market research but hopes to conduct research for film and television in the future.

Remi Kalir is associate professor of learning design and technology at the University of Colorado–Denver School of Education and Human Development. Dr. Kalir is a literacy researcher and teacher educator who studies how annotation facilitates social, collaborative, and equitable learning. He began his teaching career as a public school teacher at Middle School 22 in New York City. He earned his doctorate in curriculum and instruction from the University of Wisconsin–Madison.

About the Editors and Contributors

Lauren Leigh Kelly is an associate professor in the Graduate School of Education at Rutgers University and founder of the Hip Hop Youth Research and Activism Conference. Kelly taught high school English for 10 years in New York where she also developed courses in hip-hop literature, spoken word poetry, and theatre arts. Kelly's research focuses on critical literacies, Black feminist theory, hip-hop pedagogy, critical consciousness, and the development of critical, culturally sustaining pedagogies.

Sisilia Kusumaningsih is a doctoral student in the Department of Teaching and Learning at the University of Montana. She has been an Indonesian for Speakers of Other Languages (ISOL) instructor for 7 years and has taught in Indonesia and Thailand. Currently, she teaches Indonesian to the U.S. military personnel at Mansfield Defense Critical Language and Culture Program (DCLCP). Her research interests cover collaborative learning, social–emotional learning, and foreign language teaching.

José Ramón Lizárraga is assistant professor of learning sciences and human development, and affiliate faculty in information science as well as LGBT studies at CU, Boulder. and is the founder of the Speculative Fabulation Lab. Their work examines how digital fabrication (making and tinkering) can be used for speculative and sociopolitical learning with teachers, youth, and communities.

Nareli J. Lopez is a graduate of the UCLA Community School in the Koreatown/Pico-Union area of Los Angeles. She is a young activist and community leader. She is a first-year student at Santa Monica College.

Aliza Manalo is a graduate of the UCLA Community School in Los Angeles. She hopes to leverage her education to support her community. Aliza is a first-year biology student at California State University–Northridge.

Joanne E. Marciano is assistant professor of English education in the Department of Teacher Education at Michigan State University. She spent 13 years as a New York City public high school English teacher. Her research examines opportunities for educators to disrupt inequities by enacting participatory approaches to curriculum, teaching, and research that acknowledge and extend youths' literacy practices as strengths.

Claire Matias is a 4th-grader at the UCLA Community School in the Koreatown/Pico-Union area of Los Angeles. She is a proud student leader who is multilingual.

Nicole Mirra is an associate professor of urban teacher education in the Department of Learning & Teaching at the Rutgers University Graduate School of Education. Her research utilizes participatory design methods in classroom, community, and digital spaces to collaboratively create civic learning environments with youth and educators that disrupt discourses and structures of racial injustice and creatively compose liberatory social futures. She previously taught secondary literacy and debate in Brooklyn, NY, and Los Angeles, CA. Her books include *Educating for Empathy: Literacy Learning and Civic Engagement* (Teachers College Press, 2018), *Doing Youth Participatory Action Research: Transforming Inquiry with Researchers, Educators, and Students* (Routledge, 2015), and *Civics for the World to Come: Committing to Democracy in Every Classroom* (Norton, 2023). Her work appears in peer-reviewed journals including *American Educational Research Journal*, *Harvard Educational Review*, *Review of Research in Education*, *Journal of Teacher Education*, and others.

Lindsey M. Nichols, PhD, LPC (WYO), LCPC (MT), NCC is a counselor educator at the University of Wyoming. She has her doctorate in counselor education and supervision, masters of education in school counseling, and masters degree in history and social studies education. Dr. Nichols has licensure in Montana and Wyoming. A National Certified Counselor, published author, and presenter, her interests are in PK–12 education and the role of school counselors, social–emotional learning, creativity in counseling, and cultural responsiveness.

Olivia Peace is a student, Academy Award–winning director, and visual artist from Detroit, Michigan, living in Los Angeles. Their work is heavily informed by artistic experimentation, dreamspaces, and a deep reverence for the ecosystems that made them.

Lee Melvin M. Peralta is a doctoral candidate in the College of Education and masters student in the Department of Statistics and Probability at Michigan State University. He taught middle school and high school mathematics for 6 years in New York City. His research draws on traditions of speculative and materialist thought to explore critical and creative approaches to teaching and learning about data literacy, data science, and data storytelling by young people and adults.

Jaune Reyez is a senior at the UCLA Community School. He is one of the founding coteachers at the school and his approach to teaching and learning continues to inspire his school community.

Adriana Rios-Cruz is a graduate of the UCLA Community School in Los Angeles. Her goal is to contribute to her community through her leadership and community engagement. She is a first-year student at Santa Monica College.

Maria Karina Sanchez is a daughter of Mexican immigrants and grew up in the small mountain town of Gypsum, Colorado. She attended the University of Colorado–Denver as an undergraduate and is working on a masters. She has taught in Commerce City, Colorado, for 5 years and advocates for biliteracy access. She joined Right2Learn and continues to grow in her dignity studies with the group. She loves to spend time with her husband and dogs.

Tania Soto Valenzuela moved to the United States from Mexico with her family when she was 9 years old. Tania's lived experience of over 20 years as unauthorized immigrant was always closely tied with inequity, lack of opportunity, and exclusion. This led her to work toward dismantling inequalities as a researcher, community organizer, and artist. Tania now guides conversations toward positive community change, using tools to assist people to reimagine and shape collective liberation.

Jingjing Sun is an associate professor of educational psychology at the University of Montana. She studies children's cognitive, social, and emotional development in school. Collaborating with community members and interdisciplinary colleagues in the United States and China, she investigates the impact of broader ecological systems, including culture, land, community, and tribal sovereignty, on children's learning and social–emotional well-being. She also examines how to support teachers' learning and well-being through coaching and sustained professional development.

Duy Tran is originally from Viet Nam but grew up in the southwest Denver, Colorado, neighborhoods. He received a bachelor's in communication, a minor in psychology, and a master's in leadership for educational organizations. Duy's passion has always been working with students and improving the education system. He wants to focus on implementing and looking into new concepts and ideas to help create an education system that provides equity and equality to all students.

Brendesha M. Tynes is Dean's Professor of Educational Equity, professor of education and psychology, and founding director of the Center for Empowered Learning and Development with Technology at the University of Southern California. Her research focuses on the racial landscape adolescents navigate in online settings, online racial discrimination, critical race digital literacy, and the design of digital tools that empower youth of color.

mandy wong is a Chinese-Malay restaurant child born to the Colorado Rocky Mountains. She is a voice actor, poet, crafter, dignity scholar, wanderer, dreamer, and environmental and educational steward based in the heart of Japan. When not behind the mic or tracing the lineage of dignity in education with her Right2Learn familia, she can be found with her nose in a book, traveling on foodie adventures, snail mailing, and fawning over fluffy bees.

Lynne M. Zummo is an assistant professor of learning sciences at the University of Utah. She holds a joint appointment as curator of learning sciences at the Natural History Museum of Utah. Her research examines the interactions of social, cultural, and cognitive factors that influence learning around contentious issues in science, such as global climate change, in a variety of contexts, including museums, classrooms, and the digital space.

Index

The letter *n* after a page number refers to a note.

Abolitionism, 69–70, 81, 140. *See also* Participatory design: *Kai UnEarthed*
Abolitionist Gaming Network, 77
Abolitionist world-building process. *See* Participatory design: *Kai UnEarthed*
Abstract-to-specific link, 41
Adinkra symbols, 19, 26, 27
Adult talk, 98–99
Adult-youth partnerships. *See* Youth-adult partnerships
Aesthetic, 130
Affinity spaces, 164
African diaspora, 13–14
Afrofuturism, 13–14, 17, 23, 28–29. *See also* Participatory design: *Kai UnEarthed*
Afrofuturist development theory, 68–69, 71–72
Agnoletti, C., 171n4
Aguilar, A., 38
Aguilar, G., 143
Aguilar, L. N., 116
Ahmed, S. M., 109
Alali, L., 178n15
Alejo, A., 143
Alexander, K., 131
Alim, H. S., 123
All Negro Comics #1, 23
Altschul, D. B., 107
Amanti, C., 48
American capitalism, 45
Andrasik, M. P., 109
Animorphs series (Applegate), 1–2
Annamma, S., 132n2
Anthony-Stevens, V., 108
Anxiety, 174–175
Apple, M. W., 13
Applegate, K. A., 2–3, 7
Arellano, S., 158

ARTifACTS collective, 70
Art principles, 25, 27
Axia, G., 133
Ayala, J., 163

Bahn, A., 124, 134
Bakhtin, M. M., 36, 37
Baldridge, B. J., 90
Baltodano, M., 19
Bang, M., 60, 69, 78
Barnabe, C., 110
Barron, B., 48
Bartlett, C., 111
Bass, J., 122
Bastian, R., 116
Becker, B., 75
Becker, B.L.C., 36, 38, 48, 51, 52, 53
Bellotto, R., 101
Bene, E., 38
Bennett, A., 30
Berland, M., 12, 14
Bermudez, M. R., 133
Bertrand, M., 141
Biesta, G. J., 134
Bingham, C. W., 125
Bishop, R. S., 48
Black community in America, 13–14
Black Lives Matter movement, 36, 40–41, 42–43, 131
Bloch, Ernst, 130
Blom, M., 133
Bolin, P. E., 113
Boluk, S., 68
Brave Heart, M.Y.H., 107
Brayboy, B.M.J., 106, 107, 108, 109, 111
Brewer, S. K., 110
Bronfenbrenner, U., 112
Brooke, E., 108, 114

brown, a. m., 69
Brown, B., 179n18
Burt, I., 116
Butler, O. E., 124, 131

Camangian, P., 108, 115
Camino, L., 89, 102
Carey, C. M., 110
Cariaga, S., 108, 115
Carrasco-Zylicz, A., 133
Carter Andrews, D., 158
Castagno, A. E., 107, 109
Center for Empowered Learning and Development With Technology (CELDTech), 72, 76
Center for Native American Youth at the Aspen Institute, 107
Center for Research on Civic Learning and Engagement, 35
Centering joy, 160–161, 163
Centers for Disease Control and Prevention, 107
Chase, J., 107
Chavel, A. P., 172n7
Children's literature, 2–3
Childress, S., 169
Chilisa, B., 114
Christopher, K., 107, 108, 109–110, 114
Ciklovan, L (diacritic), 124
Cintorino, M., 30
Clifasefi, S. L., 109
Climate change, 36. *See also* E2020 media project: climate change composition
Coia, L., 158
Cole, M., 53
Collaboration, 30, 64, 73–74, 76–77, 88. *See also* Youth-adult partnerships
Collective action, 159
Collins, S. E., 109
Collura, J., 88, 89
Colorado Constitution, 169–170, 169n2, 169n3, 180
Comics-centric design. *See* Lion Man project: Wakanda 2.0
Commitment level, 46
Community-based participatory research (CBPR), 109. *See also* Project SELA (Social-Emotional Learning in Arlee)
Community connectedness, 88, 95, 105–106
Community core values, 112, 113
Community Day, 105–106
Community school. *See* UCLA Community School

Community well-being, 21–22, 27–28
Complexity and multiplicity, 54, 58–60
Connecting past to present, 42–43
Connect-reflect-project cycle. *See* Past-present-future orientation
Cook-Sather, A., 123, 132
Correa, I., 11, 17
Corroboration. *See* Collaboration
Cortes, K. L., 36, 38, 48, 51, 52, 53, 75
Cortez, A., 36, 38, 48, 51, 52, 53, 78
Cortez, J. M., 158
Cost of tools and materials, 29
Counternarrative, 13, 14
Counterspeculative practices, 135
COVID-19 pandemic, 51, 52, 121–122, 127, 129, 143–144, 145
Crane, L., 110
Creative media use, 47–48
Creswell, J. W., 91
Critical constructionist design (CCD) framework; analysis tapestry, 15–17, 19–23, 26–29; background and affordances, 11–12, 31; data collection and coding, 20, 27–28; design tapestry, 17–19, 25f; documentation and analysis, 15–17; Lion Man project, 23–29; power and legitimacy, 13; Remixing Wakanda project, 17–23; speculative design challenges, 29–31; theory, 12–14
Critical game jam (CGJ), 76–77, 79–80
Critical race theory (CRT), 109
Critical world-building, 77, 82
Crnic, K., 112, 115
Cultural genocide, 107
Cultural humility, 116
Culturally relevant education, 1, 4–5, 113–114, 122–123, viii–ix. *See also* Afrofuturist development theory; Project SELA (Social-Emotional Learning in Arlee)
Cultural multiplicity, 116
Culture and language revitalization, 115
Culture centering, 108
Culture-specific training, 113–114
Current student story, 179–180
Curriculum design, 80
Cutter-Mackenzie, A., 124

Dahlstedt, M., 116
Dando, M. B., 11, 17
Darder, A., 19
Darling-Hammond, L., 122
Davis, N. R., 77

Debaise, D., 124, 128
Decolonizing practices, 109–110
De Freitas, E., 74
Deleuze, G., 125
De los Rios, C., 158
Denver Public Schools, 180
De Roock, R. S., 68
Dery, M., 13
Designed mediators, 17, 22f
Design tapestry, 17–18
Desire, 125, 130
Diaków, D. M., 116
Dialogic approach, 158
DiGiacomo, D. K., 51, 52, 53
Digital technologies and learning design, 52
Dignity, 169–170, 175
Dingus, J. E., 158
Discomfort, 174–175
Dixon, A. D., 158
Dreams, 160–161, 163, 166, 171–172, 180
DuBois, W.E.B., 172n6
Dunham, H. H., 169
Dunne, A., 14, 110
Duong, M. T., 110
Duran, B. M., 109
Durlak, J. A., 108
Dymnicki, A. G., 108

E2020 media project; background, 35–36; Black Lives Matter composition, 40–41, 42–43; climate change composition, 41–42, 44; connecting to one's history, 42–44; limitations of the research, 49; reimagining time and space, 39–42; researcher positionality, 38; rupture and teaching, 46–49; rupture and youth, 37–46, 47; speculative aspect, 36–38, 44–46
Echevarria, R., 77
"Educated hope," 130
Educational dignity, 173–174, 180. See also Right2Learn (R2L) Dignity Lab
Education as fundamental right, 170
Education reset, 122, 135
Educators and social-emotional learning, 113–114
Eglash, R., 30, 31
Ehret, C., 12
Ehret, L., 12
Ejaz, M., 109
Eklund, K. R., 108
Elkins, J., 107
Emdin, C., 141

Engagement level, 110–111
Engdahl, T., 169
Engeström, R., 60
Engeström, Y., 53
Enthusiasm, 5
Equal opportunities for success, 178
Equity research, 5, 172
Escobar, A., 4
Escudé, M., 77
Espinoza, M. L., 36, 38, 48, 51, 52, 53, 75, 169, 172n8, 177n13, 178n15
Evans, Orrin C., 23
Evans-Campbell, T., 107
Everett, A., 78
Everyday-life aspect, 133, 135–136, 141
Expertise centering, 57, 58, 60–61, 63
Eynon, R., 52

Faber, L., 60
Facebook in Real Life, 70
Families, 115, 177–179
Fannie Lou Hamer High School, 142
Feng, X., 133
Ferucci, E. D., 110
Fine, M., 151
Flathead Nation, 105
Flexibility, 30
"Flexing a muscle," 55
Flook, L., 142
Floyd, George, 131
Foster, E., 31
Foster, J., 124
François, A., 140
Freire, P., 37, 90, 123, 157, 159
Fullerton, T. 73, 77, 78–79
Function of texts, 128–129
Furman, G., 141
Future orientation. See Prolepsis; Speculative orientation
Futurism, 4, 124. See also Afrofuturism

Gahman, L., 125
Gaias, L. M., 110
Game interaction types, 57
Gaming, 52, 67, 70, 74–75, 77–78. See also Learning to Transform (LiTT) Video Gaming Lab; Participatory design: *Kai UnEarthed*
Garcia, A., 2, 3, 4, 5, 6, 13, 31, 36, 47, 68, 87, 106, 124, 141–142, 157, 170
Garcia, H. V., 112
García, R., 158
Garcia Coll, C., 112, 115

Index   193

Gargroetzi, E., 38, 47
Gauley, J., 88, 89
Gee, E., 51
Gee, J. P., 37, 52, 74, 77
Gender, 159
Generative power of play, 51
Gerima, M., 101
Gilbert, J. E., 31
Gil-Kashiwabara, E., 109
Giroux, H. A., 13
Global-to-local focus, 41, 44
Goforth, A. N., 107, 108, 109–110, 114, 116
Gonzalez, K. R., 175n12
Gonzalez, N., 48
González, R. A., 159, 163
Goodwin, C., 57
Gordon, A., 125
Gorman, A., 141
Graham, N., 107, 108, 109–110, 114
Grande, S., 157
Grand Theft Auto V, 54, 54n1. *See also* Learning to Transform (LiTT) Video Gaming Lab
Gray, K., 52
Greene, J., 105
Greenidge, A., 125
Guatarri, F., 125
Gurneau, J., 60
Gutiérrez, K. D., 36, 38, 48, 51, 53, 75, 87, 91

Hakkarainen, K., 60
Halbert, M., 110
Hall, R., 51
Halverson, E. R., 17
Hamilton, M., 68, 72, 76, 77, 79
Harkness, S., 133
Harney, S., 158
Hartman, S., 157
Hawes, S. M., 109
Hayes, E. R., 77
He, Y., 158
Healy, B., 110
Hernández, L. E., 142
Heteroglossia, 37, 39–40
Hierarchical relationships, 52–53, 52–59, 89
Higgs, J., 51, 52
Hip-hop workshops and dialogue, 90
Historical actors, 38
Historicity, 60
Hogenson, D., 107, 108, 114
Holbert, N., 11, 12, 14, 17
Holloway, L., 122

Holter, O. G., 116
hooks, b., 51, 101
Hope, 3, 4, 67, 131
Howlett, R., 107, 108, 114
Huffman, T., 109
Huizinga, J., 52
Human-to-animal transformation, 2
Hurd, K., 110

Identity, 42–43, 44, 45, 46, 55, 108, 158
Imagination, 1, 3, 6, 46, 58–60
Imarisha, W., 69
Indigenous culture. *See* Project SELA (Social-Emotional Learning in Arlee)
Individual potential and equity, 172
Interdisciplinary learning, 48, 63, 108
Intergenerational partnerships. *See* Youth-adult partnerships
IRL (in real life) identity, 55
Ito, M., 48

Jackson, A., 77
Jackson, A. Y., 125, 128
Jackson, K., 163
Jagers, R. J., 108, 111, 115
Japanese History and Culture course, 145–146
Jenkins, H., 58
Jenkins, R., 112, 115
Jennings, J., 12
Jennings, S., 30
Johnson, P., 51, 52
Jones, J., 110
Jones, K., 68
Journaling, 72, 74, 113
Juco, J. L., 143
Juel Larson, L., 60
Jurow, A. S., 51, 87

Kafai, Y., 12, 14
Kai UnEarthed. *See* Participatory design: *Kai UnEarthed*
Kampmann Walther, B., 60
Kan, R., 125
Kaufman, C. E., 107
Kelley, R. D. G., 70, 77, 87, 157, 160
Kelly, L. L., 31
Khan, A. M., 109
Kilgus, S. P., 108
Kincheloe, J. L., 13
Kinloch, V., 160
Kirshner, B., 89, 100, 170
Knowledge synthesis, 111

Kohli, R., 158
Kornbluh, M., 88, 89
KQED. *See* E2020
Kratky, Andreas, 73
Krauss, S. E., 88, 89
Kuhfeld, M., 122
Kuhn, T. S., 4
Kus, R., 125
Kusumaningsih, S., 108, 114

Ladson-Billings, G., 4, 51, 109, 124, 134, 135
LaFleur, Ingrid, 36
LaFromboise, T. D., 111
Lamberty, G., 112, 115
Larson, R. W., 89
Laureano Carranza, G., 143
Lawford, H. L., 88, 89, 100, 102
Leap Advisory Board, 109
Learning to Transform (LiTT) Video Gaming Lab; background, 51–52; game play examples, 55–63; implications, 63–64; and leading activity, 52–53; and speculative pedagogies, 54–55
Lee, J. S., 122
Lee, T. S., 106, 107
LeMieux, P., 68
Lemos, M., 53
Leonard, D., 52
Let's Talk About Election 2020. *See* E2020 media project
Lin, C. Y., 110
Lion Man comics, 23–24
Lion Man project: Wakanda 2.0, 23–29
Literary machine, 128–129
LiTT City. *See* Learning to Transform (LiTT) Video Gaming Lab
Livingstone, S., 48
Lizárraga, J. R., 36, 38, 48, 51, 52, 53, 75, 78
Lomawaima, K. T., 106, 107
Lopez, N. J., 143
Love, B. L., 68, 140
Low, B., 12
Low, D. E., 14
Loyola-Sanchez, A., 110

Macdonald, C., 159
Macedo, D., 37, 157, 159
Mahfouz, J., 108
Maker sessions, 17
Makin, D., 125
Malik, S. S., 111
Marciano, J. E., 122, 158

Marginalization, 4, 174–175
Marin, A., 60
Marshall, A., 111
Marshall, M., 111
Martinez, A., 170
Martínez, L., 142
Matias, C. E., 158
Matthews, B., 109
Matthews, S., 109
Mazzei, L., 125, 128
Mbiti, J. S., 29
McAdoo, H. P., 112, 115
McCarty, T. L., 106, 107, 109
McGee, E. O., 124
McKoy, A., 51, 52, 78
Mediation, 53–54
Mendoza, E., 51, 52
Mentor, M., 13
Mentoring, 94
Metagaming, 74–75
Metaphors, 55
Miller, J. L., 123
Miller, K. A., 109
Mirra, N., 3, 4, 5, 6, 13, 31, 36, 87, 106, 124, 141–142, 157, 170
Miss, S., 125
Mitchell, C. M., 107
Mitra, D. L., 89
Moll, L. C., 48
Morrell, E., 6
Moscardino, U., 133
Moten, F., 158
Moua, V., 174n10
Multicultural education. *See* Culturally relevant education
Multiliteracies, 30, 37, 39–40, 48
Multimodal composing, 47–48, 74, 81
Multiple timescales, 48–49
Multiplicity and complexity, 54, 58–60
Muñoz, A., 77
Muñoz, J. E., 54, 125, 130, 133
Murray, M., 165
Music as theme, 129–132, 135

Naomi television series, 100–101
Narratives. *See* Right2Learn (R2L) Dignity Lab; Stories
Neal-Barnett, A., 165
Neff, D., 48
Nelson, A., 14
Nelson, L. A., 109
Networked video game play, 52
New London Group, 30, 87

Index 195

Nicasio, A. V., 109
Nicholas, S. E., 106, 107, 109
Nichols, L. M., 107, 108, 109–110, 114
Nishi, N. W., 158
Nkʷusm School, 107
Noguera, N., 106, 107
Normative expectations, 46

Oberle, E., 108
O'Donnell, C., 30
Office of Minority Health, 107
Olamina, Lauren, 131
Oliva, A., 133
Online meetings, 123
Online workshops, 76
Oppositional imagination, 141–142
Orfaly, V. E., 109
Otieno, E., 157

Paavola, S., 60
Padilla-Chavez, A., 169, 174n11
Palermo, A. S., 109
Pandemic. *See* COVID-19 pandemic
Paper prototyping, 81
Papert, S., 14
Paris, D., 123
Participation level, 110–111
Participatory design: *Kai UnEarthed*; abolitionist teaching, 69–71; Afrofuturist development, 72; background, 67–68; *Kai UnEarthed*, 70–75, 77, 78; outcomes, 81–82; play-centric methods, 72–75; player experience, 80; recommendations for educators, 81; the researchers, 69; theory, 68–69, 72; world-building game design, 79–80
Past-present-future orientation, 14–15, 16f, 18f, 19, 20–22, 27, 124
Patel, L., 7, 171n5
Pathmaps, 132–134, 132n2
Payne, M. R., 165
Penados, F., 125
Pendergast, L. L., 108
Penna, A. N., 13
Penuel, B., 48
Peralta, L. M., 122
Pham, A. V., 116
Physical space of school, 18–19, 177–179
Pink, D., 179n17
Pizarro, M., 158
Play-centric design methods, 72–75
Pondside Houses, 126
Porter, J., 52

Power and legitimacy, 13
Power differentials, 89
Poza, L. E., 169
Practice-based learning, 110
Project SELA (Social-Emotional Learning in Arlee); background and description, 105–108; community engagement, 108–110; cultural training, 113–114; design and implementation, 110–112; educator program, 113–114; family program, 115; and speculative education for Indigenous students, 116; student program, 112–113
Prolepsis, 53, 58–60, 64
Protest movements, 36, 42–43, 131
Public voice platforms, 47
Pullmann, M. D., 110
Pyke, K., 116

Quantitative literacies, 43, 44
Quartz, K. H., 140
Quilombos, 80
Quotidian aspect of imagination, 133, 135–136, 141

R2L (Right to Learn) Dignity Lab. *See* Right2Learn (R2L) Dignity Lab
Raby, F., 14, 110
Racial affinity spaces and dialogue, 161–163
Racism, 13, 42, 107, 109, 116, 159, 161
Ramey, H. L., 88, 89, 100, 102
Ranciere, J., 130
Rash, E., 125
Reader feedback, 2
Reality pedagogy, 140–141
Reciprocity, 112, 113, 115
Recycling program, 148–149
Relationality, 125, 130
Relationship building, 54, 112
Remixing Wakanda workshop, 17–23
Representations of Earth, 41
Representations of time, 41
Reset in education, 122, 135
Responsibility for change, 46
Re-storying, 13, 14
Restructuring relationships, 102
Rhodes, J., 48
Richmond, G., 158
Right2Learn (R2L) Dignity Lab; about the collective, 169n1, 180; amendment proposal, 169–170, 180; Colorado right to education, 169–170, 169n3; current student remarks, 179–180; former student

Right2Learn (R2L) Dignity Lab (*continued*)
 reflections, 174–175; history, 170–172; a parent's reflections, 177–179; speculative celebration, 173–174; speculative class conversation, 171–172; a teacher's reflections, 175–177; Rios-Cruz, A., 143
Rivas-Drake, D., 108, 111, 115
Rivero, E., 36, 38, 48, 51, 52, 53, 75
Rodela, K. C., 141
Rodriguez Espinosa, P., 109
Role-play, 55
Rose, M., 169
Rosemurgy, H., 122
Ross, J., 109, 116, 124, 131
Rousell, D., 124
Rupture, 36, 37–38

Sabzalian, L., 106, 116
Salazar, M., 158
Salen, K., 48
Salley, B. B., 165
Sanchez, M., 169
Sanctuary, 172
Sandoval, A., 105
Sankofa, 14, 27
Sannino, A., 53
San Pedro, T. J., 157, 160
Sarcedo, G. L., 158
Saunders, M., 142
Scaffolding, 80–81
Schellinger, K. B., 108
School-community relationships, 106, 114
School start time, 179
School-university partnership. *See* UCLA Community School
Schor, J., 48
Schuschke, J., 68, 72, 76, 77, 79
Sealey-Ruiz, Y., 13
Sefton-Green, J., 48
Segregation and separations, 59
Self excavation, 13
Self-identity, 26, 29
Settler colonialism, 109
Sexism, 159
"Shadow work," 158–159
Shame, 174–175
Shaviro, S., 124
Shaw, A., 52
Sheridan, K., 17
Shim, J. M., 158
Shindorf, Z. R., 116
Sicstmist, 111
Sidorkin, A. M., 125

Siloing, 49
Silva, F., 174n10
Simon, R. I., 13
Situated approach to teaching, 6
Sleeter, C. E., 158
Smilansky, M., 110
Smith, L. T., 109
Snow, S., 109
Snow Day Learning Lab, 17
Social commentary in literature, 4
Social design–based research, 91–93
Social-emotional learning (SEL). *See* Project SELA
Social Justice Humanitas, 142
Societal reckoning, 35
Solidarity, 45, 46
Solórzano, D. G., 13
Song sharing, 129–130, 131, 133, 134, 135
Soto, C., 60
Souto Manning, M., 158
Space ruptures, 39, 40–42, 46
Speculative complexity, 54, 58–60
Speculative orientation. *See also* Right2Learn (R2L) Dignity Lab; civic literacies, 157; and critical constructionist design, 13; and everyday life, 133; game play, 52, 53, 54–55; multiplicity and complexity, 54, 60; relationality and desire, 57–58, 124, 134–136; re-storying, 13, 14; and social-emotional learning, 106–107, 109–110, 113; teacher education, 157–158, 161–167; transforming schools, 4, 5–6, 141–142, 163–164
Speculative transdisciplinary worldmaking, 54
Spicer, P., 107
Springgay, S., 124
Squire, K., 77
Stadulis, R., 165
Stanton, C. R., 109
Stanton, J., 109
Stasis, 46
STEM ideas and practices, 23, 29–30
Stengers, I., 124, 128
Stewart, A., 68, 72, 76, 77, 79
Stories, 4, 157, 173–175
Storm, S., 68
Stornaiuolo, A., 12
Straits, K.J.E., 109
Strauss, V., 142
Student-adult partnerships. *See* Youth-adult partnerships
Suicides, 107

Index

Sun, J., 107, 108, 109–110, 114
Super, C. M., 133
Syncretic forms of learning, 53

Takeuchi, L., 51
Tate, W. F., 109
Taylor, A., 179n16
Taylor, M., 158
Taylor, R. D., 108
Teacher as expert, 52–53
Teacher preparation; background and introduction, 155–157; landscape of, 158–159; learning in community, 163–164, 166–167; speculative methods, 157–158; voices of teacher candidates, 157–159, 160–161, 164–166
Teaching vocation, 176
Tech-centric design. *See* Remixing Wakanda workshop
Tesfahuney, M., 116
"Thinking with theory," 128–129
This book, 1–7
Thomas, A., 165
Thomas, E. E., 12
Tien, J., 51, 52
Time ruptures, 39, 40–42, 46
Tivaringe, T., 170
Toliver, S. R., 14, 170
Tools and materials, 18, 23, 25, 27, 28, 29–30, 47, 131–132
Topic choice, 47
Torre, M. E., 163
Torres, R. D., 19
Traditional art materials, 25, 27
Transdisciplinary learning, 48, 60–63, 108
Transformative justice, 69–70
TribalCrit (tribal critical race theory), 109
Tribal critical race theory (TribalCrit), 109
Truman, S. E., 74, 124
Trust development, 100
T-shirt design, 149–150
Tuck, E., 124
Turn-on-your-camera campaign, 144–145
Two-Eyed Seeing, 111–112
Tynes, B., 68, 72, 76, 77, 79

UCLA Community School; about, 139–141; acknowledgments, 151–152; green team, 148–151; pandemic response, 143–145; speculative approach, 141–142; stories introduction, 142; students as coteachers, 145–147
Uncertainty, 161, 163

UNICEF, 170
University–school partnership. *See* UCLA Community School
Utopian vision, 133

Vachon, W., 88, 89, 100, 102
Vakil, S., 51, 52
Valenzuela, T. S., 172n7, 174n11
Van Steenis, E., 89
Velasco, K. S., 177n13
Villegas, K., 36, 38, 48, 51, 52, 53, 75
Violante, A. E., 107, 108, 109–110, 114
Visionary fiction, 69–70
Vizenor, G., 107
Von der Embse, N. P., 108
Vossoughi, S., 69, 77, 79, 169
Vygotsky, L. S., 52, 73

Walker, K. C., 89
Wallerstein, N., 109
War stories, 2–3
Wartella, E., 51
Wasik, B. H., 112, 115
Watkins, S. C., 48, 78
Weissberg, R. P., 107
Wellness, 111, 113
Where Once There Were Cages, 70, 71f
White, D. T., 124
Whiteness and education, 158, 159
Whitesell, N. R., 107
White supremacy, 107
Wildfires, 44
Williams, B., 108, 111, 115
Williamson, B., 52
Windchief, S., 157
Winn, M. T., 123
Wolfe, P., 107
Wong, C. P., 165
wong, m., 174n10
World Building Media Lab, 78
Wyman, L., 109

Xuc, F., 125
Xʷcstwexʷ (reciprocity), 112, 113

Yin, P., 36, 38, 48, 51, 52, 53, 75
Yosso, T. J., 13
Young adult literature, 2–3
Young readers, 2–3
Youth–adult partnerships; adult energy, 94–95; adult role, 88, 100; clear guidelines for collaboration, 100; design process and youth centering, 90–91; implications for

Youth–adult partnerships (*continued*) teaching, 101–102; introduction, 87–88, 88n1; nonyouth participants, 93–94; positive aspects, 88–89, 94–97; tensions, 89–90, 97–99; youth participatory action research (YPAR), 122

Youth civic composing. *See* E2020 media project

Youth empowerment, 88

Youth media. *See* E2020 media project

Youth participatory action research (YPAR). *See* Youth Voices Project

Youth perspectives on partnerships with adults., 94–99

Youth Voices Project; background and introduction, 126–128; counterspeculative practices, 135; COVID-19 pandemic, 121–122, 123–125; music as theme, 129–132, 135; participants, 126–127; pathmaps, 132–134; project development, 126; relationality and desire, 130; speculative practice, 134–136; theory basis, 122–123, 128–129; youth participatory action research, 122–123, 132

Zeldin, S., 88, 89
Zummo, L. M., 38
Zylicz, P. O., 133